FAMILIES AND HEALTH

Janet R. Grochowski

College of St. Benedict | St. John's University

Volume III in the Series
Families in the 21st Century

General Editor

Susan J. Ferguson
Grinnell College

Allyn & Bacon

Boston   Columbus   Indianapolis   New York   San Francisco   Upper Saddle River
Amsterdam   Cape Town   Dubai London   Madrid   Milan   Munich   Paris   Montreal   Toronto
Delhi   Mexico City   Sao Paulo   Sydney   Hong Kong   Seoul   Singapore   Taipei   Tokyo

Executive Editor: Jeff Lasser
Associate Editor: Lauren Macey
Executive Marketing Manager: Kelly May
Production Manager: Kathy Sleys
Production Assistant: Maggie Brobeck
Full Service Project Management/Composition: Suganya Karuppasamy/GGS Higher Education Resources, PMG
Printer/Binder and Cover Printer: R.R.Donnelley & Sons, Inc.
Design Director: Jayne Conte
Cover Designer: Bruce Kenselaar
Cover Art: John Henley/Corbis
Back Cover Image Credits: © JupitorImages, © Veer, © Monkey Business Images/Shutterstock, ©Value
RF/Corbis

Many of the designations by manufacturers and sellers to distinguish their products are claimed as trademarks. Where those designations appear in this book, and the publisher was aware of a trademark claim, the designations have been printed in initial caps or all caps.

Library of Congress Cataloging-in-Publication Data
Grochowski, Janet R.
  Families and health / Janet R. Grochowski.
      p. ; cm. — (Families in the 21st century ; v. 3)
  Includes bibliographical references and index.
  ISBN-13: 978-0-205-62720-2
  ISBN-10: 0-205-62720-X
  1. Families—Health and hygiene. 2.   Family medicine.   I. Title. II. Series: Families in the
twenty-first century ; v. 3.
  [DNLM: 1.   Family Health—Case Reports. 2.   Health Behavior—Case Reports.   WA 308 G873f 2010]
RA418.5.F3G76 2010
613—dc22

2009033301

10 9 8 7 6 5 4 3 2 1— DOH— 13 12 11 10 09

**Allyn & Bacon
is an imprint of**

www.pearsonhighered.com

ISBN-10:   0-205-62720-X
ISBN-13: 978-0-205-62720-2

CONTENTS

FAMILIES IN THE TWENTY-FIRST CENTURY

The family is one of the most private and pervasive social institutions in U.S. society. At the same time, public discussions and debates about the institution of the family persist. Some scholars and public figures claim that the family is declining or dying, or that the contemporary family is morally deficient. Other scholars argue that the family is caught in the larger culture wars currently taking place in the United States. Regardless of one's perspective that the family is declining or caught in broader political struggles, family scholars are working to address important questions about the family, such as, what is the future of marriage? Is divorce harmful to individuals, to the institution of the family, or to society? Why are rates of family violence so high? Are we living in a postdating culture? How does poverty and welfare policy affect families? How is child rearing changing now that so many parents work outside the home and children spend time with other caretakers? How are families socially constructed in different societies, cultures, and time periods?

Most sociologists and family scholars agree that the family is a dynamic social institution that is continually changing as individuals and other social structures in society change. The family is also in a social construction with complex and shifting age, gender, race, and social class meanings. As we begin the twenty-first century, many excellent studies are currently investigating the changing structures of the institution of the family and the lived experiences and meanings of families. *Families in the Twenty-First Century* is a series of short texts and research monographs that provides a forum for the best of this burgeoning scholarship. One goal of this series is to recognize the diversity of families that exist in the United States and globally. A second goal is for the series to better inform pedagogy and future family scholarship about this diversity of families. The series also seeks to connect family scholarship to a broader audience beyond the classroom, by informing the public and ensuring that family studies are central to contemporary policy debates and to social action. Each short text contains the most outstanding current scholarship on the family from a variety of disciplines, including sociology, demography, policy studies, social work, human development, and psychology. Moreover, each short text is authored by a leading family scholar or scholars who bring their unique disciplinary perspective to an understanding of contemporary families.

Families in the 21st Century provides the most contemporary scholarship and up-to-date findings on the family. Each volume provides a brief overview of significant scholarship on that family topic, including critical current debates or areas of scholarly disagreement. In addition to providing an assessment of the latest findings related to their family topic, authors also examine the family utilizing an intersectional framework of race, ethnicity, social class, gender, and sexuality. Much of the research is interdisciplinary with a number of theoretical frameworks and methodological approaches presented. A particular strength of the series is that the short texts appeal to undergraduate students as well as to family scholars, but they also are written in a way that makes them accessible to a larger public of well-informed individuals.

About This Volume

Health issues affect families in numerous ways, from caring for individuals with chronic illnesses or loved ones who are aging, to families trying to figure out how to economically meet the high costs of health care in the United States. This volume on *Families and Health* describes the multidimensional nature of health issues and the various ways health issues can affect families and how families can affect the health status of individuals. The author, Janet Grochowski, is a family studies professor who recently became the endowed professor of education and department chair at the College of St. Benedict | St. John's University. After defining a number of determinants of family health and examining some current health issues for families in the United States, Grochowski develops an interdisciplinary model for understanding the complex relationships between health and families. In the sections that follow, Grochowski closely examines a number of variables that affect health, beginning with biological factors such as family health history and genetics. She then turns her attention to family decision-making and behavioral patterns that affect health outcomes. Next, Grochowski examines socioeconomic circumstances, such as poverty, that create family health disparities and inequalities. Grochowski then broadens her lens even further to investigate how the environment both locally and globally is affecting family health. She also discusses the need for changes in public policies and services to ensure that more American families get the health care information and coverage that they need.

Topics covered include health care access and coverage in the United States, health behavior theories and models, family caregiving issues, global family health concerns such as HIV/AIDS and childhood asthma, the State Children's Health Insurance Program (SCHIP), and how some states are trying to reform health care. Grochowski also looks at current health care debates around childhood vaccinations, obesity, abstinence-only sex education, the stress of the workplace, and concerns related to death and dying. In all the chapters, Grochowski includes three to four cases to illustrate the personal side of health care issues and how they affect individuals and families.

Families and Health is appropriate for use in any class concerned with family issues, medical sociology, social inequality, health care, and government policy. This book is a valuable resource to teachers and students in beginning or advanced courses in sociology, psychology, family studies, public health and other health care classes, women's studies, human development, social work, public policy, and many other disciplines. It also finds an audience among those who work in various human service fields, including human development, social work, education, counseling, health services, and the government.

Other Volumes in the Series

Families in Poverty—Karen Secoombe, Portland State University

Global Families—Meg Wilkes Karraker, University of St. Thomas

Susan J. Ferguson, Ph.D.
General Editor
Grinnell College

PREFACE

The *Families in the Twenty-First Century* series, edited by Susan Ferguson, provides a unique set of lens for studying families. *Families in Poverty* by Karen Seccombe is a sobering examination of the scope and consequences for American families living in poverty. While poverty remains a troubling issue, Karen is able to provide some optimism and encouragement in addressing poverty, if we commit to reducing poverty. The second book in the series, *Global Families* by Meg Wilkes Karraker, expands the globalization theory through the use of a multidisciplinary approach. Karraker presents a rich image of the complex and critical impacts of globalization on families and the resulting effects on our increasingly interactive global community.

Families and Health is the third book in the *Twenty-First Century* series. Family scholars often agree that family health is multidimensional in nature, vital to family well-being, and requires community support and resources. What may be absent in discussions regarding family health, however, is active interdisciplinary communication, cooperation, and programs, such as called for in a biopsychosocial approach. I offer a unique approach to studying family health that builds on an interdisciplinary paradigm, Family Health Determinants Model.

Families and Health begins with an introduction to the Family Health Determinants Model and provides an overview of the status of American families' health. This introduction also explains the impacts of the biopsychosocial model, General Systems Theory, and related family health theories on the transition toward a more dynamic family health concept. Using the Family Health Determinants Model as an organizational scheme, Chapters 2 to 6 explore the impacts and issues related to each of the five determinants of family health, including: biology–genetics, behavior patterns, social-cultural circumstances and disparities, environmental exposures on a global scale, and health care reform and redesign, which together weave the fabric of family health. Within each chapter are three or four case studies, based on real families' health experiences, to help illustrate the human condition and a more personal side of the data.

Authors often talk about the adventure they experience while writing. I found authoring *Families and Health* not only a somber journey, but also one that truly encouraged and energized me. I was honored to study and write about families' health experiences in hopes that their collective stories will strike a collaborative chord with family scholars and practitioners. We are at a point when Americans are engaged in discussions and actions that call for support and wise use of medical advances and genomic research; encourage healthful behaviors; eliminate health disparities; engage in leadership to promote healthful (and reduce unhealthy) environmental exposures; and invest in families through affordable, equitable access to higher-quality and efficient health care. Family health is fundamental to being able to perform well in our homes, our workplaces, and our communities and, therefore, is not a privilege, but a right and responsibility for the global community.

ACKNOWLEDGMENTS

As a young child, I witnessed my mother's death to breast cancer, and 10 years later my father's to heart disease. These two events planted the seeds for a lifelong interest and career in health studies and family studies. Books about the interacting determinants of family health that are played out on personal, national, and global stages are needed. I am grateful to have had the opportunity to author such a work. Yet, solo authors are the first to recognize that without support, they often are unable to complete the challenge and opportunity of authorship. I wish to thank Susan Ferguson, General Editor, who provided valuable guidance, suggestions, and endless encouragement. Susan, as well as Jeff Lasser, Executive Editor at Pearson Education, recognized the unique nature of the proposed manuscript that ventured beyond databases by providing an interdisciplinary approach to better understanding family health. I also value the editorial assistance provided by Lauren Macey, the marketing efforts of Kelly May, production guidance of Maggie Brobeck, and the project management/composition of Suganya Karuppasamy.

While I extend my gratitude to all those who helped transform this book from idea to solid form, I take full responsibility for any errors.

My years at the University of St. Thomas provided a wealth of experience and I am thankful for the support I received in terms of research projects and sabbaticals. I particularly value the encouragement of colleague Meg Wilkes Karraker (Professor of Sociology, University of St. Thomas). I extend my gratitude to the countless medical, social, and educational professionals who have broadened my understanding of and interest in family health. I am especially grateful to the women and men who unselfishly shared their family health stories that served as the foundation and very human side to the case studies.

As I age, I increasingly appreciate the gifts of learning and curiosity instilled by my departed parents, Gladys and Edward Kortens, who fostered my desire to explore our interconnected world. My immediate family is my most treasured asset and constant source of support and patience. I wish to thank my lifelong partner, Richard A. Grochowski, who sparks the adventurer in me to expand my understanding of others. Finally, I am grateful to our adult children, Eric A. Grochowski and Emily R. Grochowski whose enthusiasm to make a difference and help others reflects the much needed optimism and hope for our global community.

Janet R. Grochowski

About the Author

Dr. Janet R. Grochowski currently serves as the Marie and Robert Jackson Endowed Professor of Education and Department Chair at the College of St. Benedict | St. John's University in St. Joseph, Minnesota. She is also the professor emerita of health studies and previous director of the Family Studies at the University of St. Thomas in St. Paul, Minnesota. She earned both her doctor of philosophy, specializing in the social and philosophical foundations of learning with an emphasis in family resilience, and her doctor of education, with a dual major in family social science and health studies, at the University of Minnesota. Her bachelor of science was earned at the University of Wisconsin-Madison, specializing in international studies and biology. She taught numerous undergraduate and graduate courses related to personal, family, consumer, environmental, national, and global health and well-being, as well as educational leadership. Dr. Grochowski is the coauthor of *Families with Futures: A Survey of Family Studies for the Twenty-First Century* (with Meg Wilkes Karraker). She is a recent recipient of the University of St. Thomas Multicultural Student Services Ally and Carl Knutson Health Education awards.

Dr. Grochowski's professional interest in family health springs from a long career devoted to interdisciplinary work that seeks to better understand complex communities, such as families, and the interactive impacts of complex health determinants on individuals and their families. She completed international studies (e.g., in Australia, New Zealand) and remains active in organizations that aim to improve family health on local, national, and global levels.

Dr. Grochowski lives in White Bear Lake, Minnesota with her best friend and husband, Richard A. Grochowski, surrounded by friends and fictive kin. Their adult children, Eric A. Grochowski, an international mathematics and economics teacher and Emily R. Grochowski, graduate student are experienced and compassionate global travelers and citizens. In addition to sailing, trekking, running, cooking, and reading, Dr. Grochowski is most content looking out over the South Pacific and drinking in the simple beauty of a sunset.

1

INTRODUCTION: FAMILIES AND THEIR HEALTH

❧

When health is absent, wisdom cannot reveal itself, art cannot manifest, strength cannot fight, wealth becomes useless, and intelligence cannot be applied.

(Herophilus of Chalcedon 335 BC to 280 BC,
in Durant 1966:638)

THIS QUOTE FROM ANTIQUITY IS AS TRUE IN THE TWENTY-FIRST CENTURY as when first scribed, yet understanding the dimensions and determinants of health, particularly family health, has never been more challenging as our understanding of the complexity of illness increases. American families confront a paradox of their country spending more on health care than any other nation on the planet, yet on almost every measure of health status, such as infant mortality and adult longevity, the United States ranks below many developed countries. What can be done to remedy this inconsistency? A first step demands recognition that family health is multidimensional and impacted by the interactions of determinants. This book offers a plausible, pertinent approach to such recognition. The introduction provides working definitions as well as an interactive Family Health Determinants Model, which serves as a framework for the remaining chapters. Included in this chapter is an overview of the status of family health as well as a description of the theoretical foundation in the evolving concept of family health and well-being. Case studies[1] are woven into this and following chapters so as to provide human context to this very dynamic process called family health.

Family Health: Definitions and Determinants

Scholars and practitioners from family and medical sciences, as well as many in the general public, recognize the crucial effect of family health and wellness[2] on overall family well-being and quality of life. Many of these scholars and practitioners agree that family health goes beyond absence of disease and dysfunction, and therefore accept a more multidimensional portrait of being healthy and well.[3] In this book, the terms *health* and *wellness* will be used interchangeably to mean an ability to live life with vitality and meaning regardless of disease and disability.

Applying this multidimensional definition to family health broadens related concepts of family well-being and health-related quality of life. While defining well-being enjoys strong agreement as a "state of being healthy, happy, or prosperous" (Webster's 1984:1310), health-related quality of life is less easily explained or measured. According to the Centers for Disease Control and Prevention (CDC), health-related quality of life is how individuals and or families "perceive physical and mental health over time" (Moriarty, Zack, and Kobau 2003:1). With advances in medical science and technology, the issue of health-related quality of life increasingly challenges patients, their families, health care providers, insurers, educators, along with those in government and business. Families increasingly struggle with questions of not only the availability, accessibility, quality, and cost of health care, but also of health-related quality of life issues of survivors and their families. "Is it worthwhile to keep a comatose person alive on a respirator? ... Traditional indicators like mortality rates and objective clinical parameters are no longer adequate for answering these questions" (Chen, Li, and Kochen 2005:1). Who decides when life is worth living? How to aid families physically, intellectually, emotionally, and socially with such life and death decisions and resulting ramifications? Such are questions increasingly facing families in the twenty-first century. Family health, therefore, is a dynamic process. In response, this book incorporates Perri Bomar's definition of family health as "encompassing a family's quality of life, the health of each member, family

---

[1] Names, locations, and other personal specifics are altered to protect confidentiality.

[2] Wellness expands the concept of health beyond uncontrolled factors (e.g., genes, age) to include health decisions made about how to live life (i.e., perceptions, attitudes, choices, actions).

[3] Dimensions of health and wellness include: a physical, emotional, intellectual, spiritual, social, and interpersonal, plus environmental-planetary components (Insel, Paul M. and Walton T. Roth. 2008. *Core Concepts in Health Brief*. Boston, MA: McGraw-Hill).

interactions, spirituality, nutrition, coping, environment, recreation and routines, sleep, and sexuality" (2004:11).

Along with a multidimensional appreciation for family health, there are five determinants that significantly impact health. These interconnected determinants include biology (genetics), behavioral patterns, social-cultural circumstances, environmental exposures, and health care (policy and services). Figure 1.1 provides a model to aid in understanding the dynamic interactive nature of these determinants and their impacts on family health. This model is based on the *Healthy People 2010* concepts; Michael McGinnis, Pamela Williams-Russo, and James Knickman's (2002) "determinants" of health; the work from the National Research Council and Institute of Medicine (2004); and David Kindig's (2007) Expanded Population Health Model.

The Family Health Determinants Model illustrates some of the complexities involved in family health issues not only due to the interactions among determinants, but also in terms of health equity as revealed in the social-cultural circumstances determinant of Figure 1.1. Health disparities among individuals, families, groups, regions, and nations are glaringly evident in basic local, national, and global health

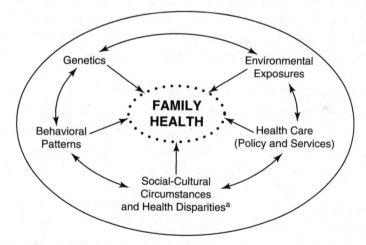

Figure 1.1 Family Health Determinants Model

[a]*Health disparity* is a disproportionate burden or risk of disease, disability, ill health, or death in a particular population or subgroup. *Healthy People 2010*, a national health promotion and disease prevention initiative, placed major concern over health disparities on the basis of gender, race, ethnicity, education, socioeconomic status, disability, geographic location, and/or sexual orientation.

Sources: Compiled from the U.S. Department of Health and Human Services. 2000. "Determinants of Health." *Healthy People 2010 Report*. p. 30. Retrieved May 3, 2008. (www.healthypeople.gov/Document/html/uih/uih_bw/uih_2.htm); and the National Research Council and Institute of Medicine. 2004. Pp. 28–44. *Children's Health, The Nation's Wealth*. Washington, DC: The National Academies Press.

findings (e.g., mortality, morbidity, incidence, or prevalence rates of a disease or illness). Dennis Raphael (2006) argues that such data avoids the causes for such disparities, which he identifies as "health inequalities." Health disparities or health inequalities, therefore, are disproportionate burdens or risks of disease, disability, ill health, and/or death on a particular population or subgroup. *Healthy People 2010*, a national health promotion and disease prevention initiative, placed major concern over health disparities on the basis of gender, age, race, ethnicity, education, socioeconomic status, disability, geographic location, and sexual orientation.

The health of individual members and their families is determined by these determinants "acting not in isolation but by our experience where domains [determinants] interconnect" (McGinnis, et al. 2002:83). Genetic predispositions are influenced by behavioral patterns and/or environmental exposures. Families' behavior patterns and environmental exposures are affected by their social-cultural circumstances and access to quality health care. "Our genetic predispositions affect the health care we need, and our social [cultural] circumstances [environmental exposure and behaviors] affect the health care we receive [or do not receive]" (McGinnis, et al. 2002:83). Families, medical and social scientists, as well as practitioners need to appreciate these dynamic interactions in the family health process. The following story about Tyra and her family provides an opportunity to identify these determinants and the impacts of interactions on this family's health and well-being.

Case 1.1 Tyra: Influences on Family Health

As an energetic, 42-year-old, Tyra thought she was in good health. Well, perhaps she could lose a few pounds, but she was worried more about her husband Gabe's high blood pressure and their twin daughters' asthma than about her own health. She knew she should stop smoking, eat better, and get some exercise, but there never seemed to be enough time. Gabe and she both worked full-time at low paying jobs with neither position providing adequate health care coverage, so regular adult health checkups simply didn't happen. Tyra knew she had high blood pressure and a family history of stroke, but again, like most adults, she thought of heart disease and stroke as male health issues. The air quality of the neighborhood they lived in exasperated their daughters' asthma and caused the girls to stay inside rather than play outdoors. This environmental exposure added to the strain of the girls' chronic illness, plus fears over losing the children's Medicaid coverage heightened Tyra's stress level to where she often couldn't sleep through the night. The stress on both Gabe and Tyra also wounded their marriage and intimacy as they fought more and communicated less. Tyra, nor anyone else in her family, thought she might have a serious health condition, so when the event happened it was sudden and without warning. Tyra returned from work just as Gabe was leaving for his job. She felt dizzy and a terrible headache pounded as she climbed the stairs to their drab apartment. Fumbling with her keys, panic gripped her as she realized her left side was numb. Falling like a rag doll, she hit the dirty floor dropping a bag of groceries and breaking a jar of spaghetti sauce she had picked up for dinner. Hearing breaking glass, Gabe raced into the hallway and found Tyra crumpled on the floor, unable to speak or move her left side. The next door neighbor peeked out into hallway and called 911 as Gabe carried Tyra into their apartment. Unfortunately for Tyra and her family, the hospital she was taken to did not have a primary stroke center so while they were able to save Tyra's life, they could not minimize the extent of damage caused by the stroke. After treatment in the intensive care unit, Tyra stayed in the hospital a few days before being discharged. Tyra was fortunate to have survived since each year twice as many women die from stroke than breast cancer. Yet, African Americans aged 20 to 44 years are 2.4 times as likely to have a stroke and twice as likely to die from a stroke than non-Hispanic whites (National Stroke Association 2008:1). Tyra lived, but suffered from severe stroke-related disabilities that forced her to quit her job and begin physical therapy in hopes of regaining her speech and improve movement of her left side. Her inadequate health insurance only covered a fraction of the cost of the needed physical therapy and provided no coverage for mental health needs. Family health, however, is more encompassing than physical illness and disability. While the physical trauma subsided, the psychological and social issues intensified as Tyra and her family struggled with the anxiety over the loss of income, adjustments to shifting household and parenting roles, Tyra's growing depression over her disability, plus trying to deal with the increasing stress of staggering medical bills.

All five determinants (see Figure 1.1) significantly impacted Tyra's family health and well-being. Consider Tyra's genetic predisposition to stroke and how that may have been impacted by her behavior patterns. Their daughters' asthma may have been influenced by inside (e.g., poor ventilation, secondhand smoke) and outside (e.g., air pollution) environmental exposures. Considering Tyra's and Gabe's family health histories of high blood pressure and stroke, they both should have had access to regular preventative health care, yet several social-cultural determinants (e.g., socioeconomic status, geographic location) served as barriers to the health care they needed. While this family had strengths, such as a loving relationship and some health coverage, the challenges posed by interactions among the five determinants negatively swayed the quality of this family's health and well-being. Chapters 2 to 6 will examine each of these five determinants with Chapter 4 focusing on the impacts of health disparities. Serving as a foundation for these later chapters, the following sections offer a glimpse at the status of family health in the United States as well as a brief review of the theoretical foundation of this multidimensional, interactive process called family health. One of the first steps in understanding this dynamic process is measuring the health status of American families.

The Status of American Families' Health

Life expectancy and infant mortality are fundamental measures of health. In 2008, it was estimated that Americans experienced their highest life expectancy measure at 78.1 years. Yet, this increase lacked equity as sex and race disparity gaps grew with white females living over a decade longer than black males: white females (81 years), black females (76.9 years), white males (76 years), and black males (70 years) (National Center for Health Statistics 2008a:1). On a global scale, this increase in overall life expectancy (78.1 years) was still meager when compared with other developed nations. When compared with 30 most developed nations that comprise the Organization for Economic Co-operation and Development (OECD), American families fell near the bottom with 23 nations ranking higher in longer life expectancy at birth while 26 nations ranked lower in infant mortality rates (OECD 2007:3). The U.S. Census Bureau (2008) reports that even when compared to the larger world community of over 220 countries, 43 countries have a higher life expectancy and 41 countries have lower infant mortality rates than the United States. Table 1.1 presents data on infant mortality and life expectancy for 28 nations.

Specific causes of death and levels of chronic illness are additional measures of health. When compared with seven developed nations (i.e., Canada, France, Japan, Germany, Spain, Greece, and the United Kingdom), Americans had the highest morality rates for ischemic heart disease;[4] trachea, bronchitis, and lung cancer; and diabetes mellitus; as well as ranking higher than six of these seven nations in unintentional injuries, intentional injuries, and neuropsychiatric conditions[5] (World Health Organization 2007). In the area of chronic disease, American families' health ratings likewise fell short when compared to 10 European countries. Americans experienced higher rates of heart disease, high blood pressure, high cholesterol, stroke, diabetes, chronic lung disease, arthritis, and cancer with the prevalence of obesity twice that seen in these European nations (Thorpe, Howard, and

---

[4] Ischemia heart condition is when blood flow (i.e., oxygen) to the heart is restricted, also known as coronary heart disease [American Heart Association. 2008a. "Silent Ischemia and Ischemic Heart Disease." Retrieved March 9, 2008. (www.americanheart.org/presenter.jhtml?identifier=4720)].

[5] Neuropsychiatry involves neurology and psychiatry and is commonly called *behavioral neurology*. A medical discipline focusing on dementia, epilepsy, head injury, attention deficit disorder, and so on. (Silver, Jonathan M. 2006. "Behavioral Neurology and Neuropsychiatry Is a Subspecialty." *Journal of Neuropsychiatry and Clinical Neurosciences* 18:146–148).

Table 1.1 Infant Mortality Rate and Life Expectancy for 28 Nations, 2009

Country	Infant Mortality Rate (Deaths per 1,000 Live Births)	Life Expectancy at Birth (Years)
Japan	3	82
Singapore	2	82
Hong Kong S.A.R.	3	82
France	3	81
Switzerland	4	81
Israel	4	81
Australia	5	82
Canada	5	81
Sweden	3	81
Iceland	3	81
New Zealand	5	80
Italy	6	80
Netherlands	5	79
Spain	4	80
Norway	4	80
Greece	5	80
Austria	4	79
Belgium	4	79
Germany	4	79
Finland	4	79
United Kingdom	5	79
South Korea	4	79
Ireland	5	78
United States	6	78
Mexico	18	76
Poland	7	76
China	20	73
Russia	11	66

Source: Adapted from the U.S. Census Bureau. 2009. "U.S. Census Bureau International Data Base (IDB)." Retrieved July 11, 2009. (www.census.gov/ipc/www/idb/informationGateway.php).

Galactionova 2007). When faced with such statistics, American families may become complacent rationalizing that the United States is more heterogeneous than countries such as Japan, Switzerland, or Iceland. Stark disparities in health status among American families certainly exist across gender, geographic, racial-ethnic, and socioeconomic status demographics (see Chapters 4 and 5). Yet, when the health status of only white Americans is compared with peers in other developed nations the results again find the health of American families falling short (Schroeder 2007). While some gains exist, for example, lower infant morality rates, the nagging reality is that Americans spend more on health and health care than any other developed nation, yet experience lower measures of wellness. For example, the 2006 health care cost per capita in the United States was $6,714 or more than twice the average ($2,694) for the remaining 30 OECD nations (OECD 2008a:1). Alarmingly, American health spending is estimated to rise from approximately $2.2 trillion in 2006 to over $4 trillion by 2016 (Schoen et al. 2007a:ix). Ellen Nolte and Martin McKee (2008) raised additional alarm as the United States dropped further behind peer OECD nations in overall health care system performance. When compared with 17 countries (14 western European nations plus Canada, Australia, New Zealand, and Japan), on causes of deaths that occurred before 75 years of age that are considered "amenable"[6] to health care, the United States' ranking was unacceptably low. Between 1997 to1998 and 2002 to 2003, a decrease in amenable mortality averaged 17 percent in all countries except the United States which had only a 4 percent reduction (Nolte and McKee 2008:59). Their findings suggest that if the American health care system had reduced its amenable death rate as the three top-performing nations, 101,000 fewer deaths would have occurred over this five-year period (2008:59).

These international comparisons reveal a gap between how much Americans spend and what they receive for their health care dollars that frustrates providers and consumers alike. Yet, American families have experienced some health improvements as reported by the United Health Foundation in their 18th annual report on the nation. These successes include reductions of infant mortality, infectious diseases (with the exception of sexually transmitted diseases among adolescents, see Chapter 4), prevalence of smoking, cardiovascular deaths, violent crime, children in poverty and occupational fatalities, plus increases in immunization coverage and prenatal care. These findings are welcome news. This same report includes other measures, however, that reflect a less positive side of American

---

[6] Amenable deaths are those that systematic health care should have prevented, for example, "bacterial infections, treatable cancers, diabetes, cardiovascular and cerebrovascular diseases, and complications of surgical procedures." (Nolte, Ellen and C. Martin McKee. 2008. "Measuring the Health of Nations: Updating an Earlier Analysis." *Health Affairs* 27(1):58–71).

family health including a rapid increase in the prevalence of obesity, escalating rate of uninsured, increasing number of reported missed days of work due to poor mental or physical health (United Health Foundation 2007:1). The first two, increases in rates of obesity and uninsured (i.e., limited access to health care) emerge as highly detrimental to family health. Both issues are discussed more fully in Chapters 3, 4, and 6, but a brief review follows.

Overweight and Obese

In 2003 to 2004, approximately 67 percent of American adults (20 to 74 years of age) were overweight or obese[7] with 32 to 34 percent overweight and another 34 to 33 percent obese (National Center for Health Statistics 2007:40). The prevalence of obesity also varies by sex, age, race, and ethnicity. For example, in 2001 to 2004 one-half of non-Hispanic black women were obese as compared to nearly one-third of non-Hispanic white women, while the prevalence of obesity in men, remained similar by race and ethnicity (2007:40). More alarming, however, are increasing rates of being overweight and obese among children (6 to 11 years of age) and adolescents (12 to 19 years of age). In 2001 to 2004, 17.5 percent of children (6 to 11 years of age) and 17.0 percent of adolescents (12 to 19 years of age) were overweight (2007:292). The condition of being overweight is common even among preschool children (two to five years of age) with a rate of 14 percent, double than what it was in 1988 to 1994 (2007:292). Table 1.2 offers a view of overweight among American children and adolescents by age, sex, race, ethnicity, and poverty level.

It is tempting to focus on one determinant domain, for example, behavioral patterns, when studying complex issues such as obesity of family members. To do so, however, skews our understanding of how best to intervene and work toward prevention since complex conditions involve many determinants with underlying disparities and inequalities. The incidence of obesity in families is shaped by the interconnections and interactions of all five determinants. For example, obesity, as most health conditions, often has a genetic predisposition that interacts with social determinants (e.g., education, socioeconomics) as well as environmental exposures, such as available food sources and physical activity options. These three determinants interact with behavioral patterns that family members engage in

---

[7] Overweight and obese are determined by the measure of body mass index (BMI). For adults (20 to 74 years of age) overweight ≥ 25 but < 30, obese ≥ 30. For children, overweight is defined as BMI at or above the sex- and age-specific ninety-fifth percentile BMI cut points from the 2000 CDC growth charts [National Center for Health Statistics. 2008b. "Prevalence of Overweight among Children and Adolescents: United States, 1999–2002." p. 41. Retrieved May 3, 2008. (www.cdc.gov/nchs/products/pubs/pubd/hestats/overwght99.htm)].

Table 1.2   Overweight Children and Adolescents by Age, Sex, Race, Ethnicity, and Poverty Level: United States, 1976–1980 to 2001–2004

Age, Sex, Race and Hispanic Origin, and Poverty Level	1976–1980	1988–1994	2001–2004
6–11 years of age	Percentage of Population		
Both sexes	6.5	11.3	17.5
Boys	6.6	11.6	18.7
Non-Hispanic or Latino:			
Black or African American	6.8	12.3	17.2
White	6.1	10.7	16.9
Hispanic origin	13.3	17.51	25.6
Girls	6.4	11.0	16.4
Non-Hispanic or Latino:			
Black or African American	11.2	17.0	24.8
White	5.2	9.8	15.6
Hispanic origin	9.8	15.3	16.6
Percentage of poverty level[a]			
Below 100%		11.4	20.0
100%–less than 200%		11.1	18.4
200% or more		11.1	15.4
12–19 years of age			
Both sexes	5.0	10.5	17.0
Boys	4.8	11.3	17.9
Non-Hispanic or Latino:			
Black or African American	6.1	10.7	17.7
White	3.8	11.6	17.9
Hispanic origin	7.7	14.1	20.0

Table 1.2 (*continued*)

Age, Sex, Race and Hispanic Origin, and Poverty Level	1976–1980	1988–1994	2001–2004
Girls	5.3	9.7	16.0
Non-Hispanic or Latino:			
Black or African American	10.7	16.3	23.8
White	4.6	8.9	14.6
Hispanic origin	8.8	13.4	17.1
Percentage of poverty level[a]			
Below 100%		15.8	18.2
100%–less than 200%		11.2	17.0
200% or more		7.9	16.3

Source: Adapted from the U.S. Department of Health and Human Services. 2007. "Health, United States, 2007, Table 75." p. 292. Retrieved March 13, 2008. (www.cdc.gov/nchs/data/hus/hus07.pdf).

[a]2008 Poverty guidelines: Income per year for a family of one person = $10,400, two persons = $14,000, three persons = $17,600, four persons = $21,200 (higher levels in Alaska and Hawaii) as defined by the U.S. Department of Health and Human Services. 2008a. "The 2008 HHS Poverty Guidelines." Retrieved August 3, 2008. (http://aspe.hhs.gov/poverty/08Poverty.shtml).

(e.g., choosing healthier foods) and do not engage in (e.g., daily physical activity). Finally, the political determinant of health care (policy and services) determines whether or not preventive measures are provided, and/or needed medical intervention and follow-up treatment occur.

Overweight and obesity, therefore, are not "just about eating too much," but rather represent a complex condition that threatens health and health-related quality of life. Family members who are overweight or obese experience elevated risks of heart disease, diabetes, and some cancers, as well as conditions such as hypertension, arthritis, and other musculoskeletal problems. These diseases and conditions account for excess medical expenditures estimated at $92.6 billion in 2002 dollars, plus even higher lifetime costs that go underreported (Finkelstein, Fiebelkorn, and Wang 2003:1). Chapters 2 through 5 explore possible family roles in addressing acute and chronic health concerns. The political determinant of access to equitable and quality health care is the other measure where the United States lags, which will be discussed in Chapter 6.

Access to Health Care

Schoen and her colleagues (2007b) surveyed approximately 12,000 adults in Australia, Canada, Germany, the Netherlands, New Zealand, the United Kingdom, and the United States about their health care systems. When compared to the other six countries, American adults had the highest incidence of foregoing needed medical care, as well as skipping required medications, because of cost. Such concerns over the affordability of health care might have spurred 34 percent of American respondents to state that their country's health care system required significant rebuilding, the highest percentage among the seven countries surveyed (Schoen et al. 2007b:1–2). Concerns fueling this call for improving delivery of American health care include issues of being uninsured and underinsured.

Uninsured and Underinsured

Increasingly, Americans are losing health care coverage in the workplace (that is "group health insurance") and often are forced to go without insurance due to high cost of "non-group health insurance" coverage. The percentage of Americans under 65 years of age without health insurance increased from 15.3 percent (44.8 million) in 2005 to 15.8 percent in 2006, increasing the ranks of the uninsured to 47 million (U.S. Census Bureau 2007a:1). In mid-2008, the U.S. Census Bureau reported that 45.7 million Americans were uninsured, a decrease from the 47 million estimate. This new statistic reflected the 1.3 million children who were added to Medicaid and State Children's Health Insurance Program (SCHIP) coverage due to the efforts at the state level. Cathy Schoen and her colleagues argued that this 45.7 million statistic failed to capture the dramatic spike in unemployment and the subsequent loss of health care coverage, and according to their data approximately 42 percent or 75 million Americans were uninsured or underinsured in 2007 (Schoen et al. 2008a:w298).

The continued growth in the number of uninsured has reshaped the image of "what is important" in a job for families. In late 2007, when 1,200 fully employed American adults over 18 years of age were asked what is most vital in a job they listed the following (Center for State and Local Government Excellence 2007:3):

- Health insurance coverage was first at 84 percent
- Job security was next at 82 percent
- Retirement and pension were tied for third at 76 percent
- Flexible, family-friendly workplace was fifth at 71 percent
- Pay was 10th at 65 percent

Finding health insurance and job security ranked at the top of job desires is not surprising with a decreasing percentage of families covered by employment-based, group health insurance, as well as the escalating out-of-pocket health costs even for those with group health insurance. In 2006, the percentage of families covered by group health insurance dropped to 59.7 percent, and the percentage of family members covered by government health programs decreased to 27.0 percent (DeNavas-Walt, Proctor, and Smith 2007:58). For those without group health insurance or government programs (e.g., Medicare and Medicaid) the only alternatives are "non-group" (individual) coverage or no coverage. Paul Jacobs and Gary Claxton (2008) argue that their analysis of non-group policies reveals two significant problems.

- Non-group policies may be unreliable in their payments for routine, necessary medical care and services.
- Non-group policies tend toward higher costs in monthly premiums, deductibles, and co-pays plus are under less regulation than group plans.

In fact, Jacobs and Claxton (2008:1) reported that cost for non-group policies vary significantly: "for example, over the 2006–2007 period, annual premiums for single coverage varied by age from $1,163 to $5,090, and between $2,325 to $9,201 for family coverage depending on the age and number of family members covered."[8] While affordability was a major factor in the decision to or not to purchase non-group health insurance, especially among lower income families, even among those at higher income levels most of those families eligible for non-group coverage did not purchase it (2008:7). Choosing not to purchase health insurance is a serious decision, yet the rationale for this action often is complex. In addition to high cost, other factors impact the decision not to purchase coverage, such as lower levels of financial literacy (e.g., confusion with insurance products, such as co-payments, deductibles, coverage limitations), as well as dissatisfaction with coverage adequacy. Insurers in many states may raise premiums or limit eligibility due to current health status or family health history (Jacobs and Claxton 2008:8). The issue of family health history and genetics information privacy and confidentiality are discussed in Chapter 2.

Mirroring this decreasing trust in health care coverage, in 2007, Gallup's annual Health and Healthcare poll revealed that 73 percent of Americans thought that the health care system is "in a state of crisis" or "has major problems" with 72 percent describing health care as "only fair" or "poor" (Gallup 2007:1). Families are increasingly concerned not only if they have health coverage, but how adequate their policies are in terms of what is and is not covered and the cost of out-of-pocket health expenses.

---

[8] America's Health Insurance Plans. 2007. "Individual Health Insurance 2006–2007: A Comprehensive Survey of Premiums Availability, and Benefits." Center for Policy and Research, December 2007. Retrieved January 3, 2008. (www.ahipresearch.org/pdfs/Individual_Market_Survey_December_2007.pdf).

Concerns over health care coverage negatively impact families' health-related quality of life and overall well-being. The Kaiser Health Security Watch monitors Americans' concerns related to their ability to access and pay for health care. In 2008, 43 percent of American families responded that they were "very worried" about their incomes not keeping up with rising health care costs, 56 percent were "very" or "somewhat" worried about the quality of health care getting worse and not being able to afford needed health care (55 percent) and prescription drugs (50 percent) (Brodie et al. 2008:1). More families felt the strain of health care costs both directly (e.g., out-of-pocket purchases of monthly premiums, medications, co-pays) and indirectly on family well-being. For example, an indirect strain is when higher health care costs result in lower increases in annual paychecks as employees pick up more of their health insurance coverage leaving less for other family needs as revealed with Tyra's family in Case 1.1. Between 2001 and 2007, employee's health insurance premiums rose 78 percent (Jacobs 2008:1). There also are health-related quality of life costs due to increased stress and stain related to families' concerns over whether they can afford needed medical services and rising out-of-pocket health expenses.

Historically, such health care worries are greater "for different demographic groups, with members of racial and ethnic minority groups, people with lower incomes, the uninsured, and women . . ." (Brodie et al. 2008:1), but as the gap between the haves and the have-nots continues to grow, so do family worries and emotional strains over health care. Poverty plays a crucial role in this trend, and while U.S. Census figures note that the overall poverty rate declined slightly (from 12.6 to 12.3 percent) between 2005 and 2006; this decline was largely concentrated among those over 65 years of age who are covered by the Medicare health plan. Growing frustration over health expenditures is spilling over into more middle-income families who are barring an unfair burden of health costs that threaten to lower their standard of living. Eighty percent of the uninsured are native or natural-ized U.S. citizens and 70 percent are from families with at least one full-time worker (National Coalition on Health Care 2007:1). Thus lower- and middle-income families are not only failing to share in economic gains enjoyed by higher-income groups, they are also struggling under the weight of health insurance coverage disparities, which are discussed more fully in Chapters 4 and 6. Karen Seccombe (2007) explains that poor and low-income families not only suffer greater risks of serious medical problems, but often delay or forgo needed treatment. Hispanic families were more likely than non-Hispanic white, non-Hispanic black, or non-Hispanic Asian families to be uninsured for at least part of a year. The percentage of uninsured Hispanics increased to 34.1 percent or 15.3 million in 2006, while the percentage of uninsured African Americans increased to 20.5 percent or 7.6 million

(DeNavas-Walt, Proctor, and Smith 2007:21). These rates did not improve in 2007 when over 30 percent of Hispanic and 15 percent of non-Hispanic black Americans were without health insurance coverage (Cohen, Martinez, and Free 2008:10).

The demographic of age also emerges in health insurance coverage disparity. The number of children under 18 years of age without health insurance increased to over nine million in 2007 (Children's Defense Fund 2008:1). The Medicare, Medicaid, and SCHIP Extension Act of 2007, passed in December 2007, extended federal funding for those already enrolled in SCHIP, but failed to meet the growing need for health care among poor children and neglected to improve enrollment policy for the six million children who were eligible for SCHIP, but not enrolled (2008:1).

A far less recognized health care access factor is the significantly high percentage of young adults between 18 and 34 years of age who are uninsured. Findings from the 2006 and 2007 National Health Interview Surveys reveal that the percentages of young adults who were uninsured at the time of the surveys were over 25 percent, with males more frequently being without health insurance coverage than females, see Table 1.3.

These findings also indicate "a total of 54.5 million (18.4 percent) individuals of all ages were uninsured for at least part of the year prior to the interview" with 31.1 million (11.9 percent) of people under 65 years of age being uninsured for over one year (Cohen, Martinez, and Free 2008:3–4). What this means for families is that access to affordable quality health care coverage remains a major concern, especially for young working adults. What these data do not explain as completely, however, is about the millions of family members who are inadequate or "underinsured" in terms of health care, see Chapter 6. In 2007, a study of 2,905 Americans between 18 and 64 years of age found that 29 percent of those with health insurance were underinsured since they had to postpone required medical care due to out-of-pocket costs not covered by their health plans. Forty-three percent of the insured stated that they were "completely" to "somewhat" unprepared to cope with a costly medical emergency (Consumer Reports 2007:1). Young adults aged 19 to 29 years represent one of the fastest growing and largest segments of uninsured and underinsured Americans (Kriss et al. 2008:1). Consider Trent's situation in Case 1.2.

Case 1.2 Trent: Uninsured Young Adults

When Trent graduated from college, he worried about his college debt, but ignored the warning from the college about losing his health insurance coverage after graduation. Typically, young adults lose their health care coverage as dependents under their parent or guardian on their 19th birthday, if they are not enrolled in a post-secondary school. Full-time students, such as Trent, are considered dependents and

Table 1.3 Percentage of Uninsured Individuals under 65 Years of Age, by Age and Sex, January–September, 2007

Age and Sex	Percentage Uninsured Jan.–Sept., 2007
Under 18 years	
Total	9.2
Female	9.2
Male	9.1
18–24 years	
Total	28.1
Female	25.1
Male	31.1
25–34 years	
Total	26.2
Female	21.5
Male	30.8
35–44 years	
Total	19.2
Female	17.1
Male	21.2
45–64 years	
Total	13.3
Female	12.4
Male	14.3

Source: Cohen, Robin A., Michael E. Martinez, and Heather L. Free. 2008. Adapted from the National Center for Health Statistics, "Health Insurance Coverage: Early Release of Estimates from the National Interview Survey, January–September 2007." National Center for Health Statistics (Figure 4, p. 13). Retrieved March 10, 2008.
(http://www.cdc.gov/nchs/data/nhis/earlyrelease/insur200803.htm).

continue to be covered until soon after graduation or age 23 when all coverage ends. Trent's first entry-level job did not provide group health insurance coverage and he could not afford an adequate health insurance plan without a high deductible of $2,500[9] plus a $300 per month premium, which was a fourth of his monthly take-home pay. Trent, therefore, found himself in a situation experienced by many American young adults being forced to forgo health insurance coverage, simply hoping that he did not need medical care or hospitalization. Unfortunately, illness fails to impact only the insured. On his way home from work, Trent fell on icy stairs and suffered a compound fracture of his wrist. Without insurance he ended up in an emergency room as an 'uninsured' patient. A few weeks after the accident, the hospital bill arrived with the amount of $2,775 for the emergency room, X-rays, and cast with future fees for follow up medical visits. Trent's parents dipped into their own savings to help him pay this bill. "Trent, you simply have to have health insurance. Let's look into buying a non-group, individual policy," they coaxed. The high cost of quality non-group health insurance, particularly plans with regular preventative care, included staggeringly high-deductibles[10] along with monthly premiums that proved cost prohibitive. Sixty-three percent of non-group plans restrict benefits and have additional cost sharing that may prohibit families from accessing needed health services (Kaiser Family Foundation 2002:1). Trent was in the process of looking into purchasing health insurance when he noticed that his left testis was slightly swollen and lumpy. He thought that perhaps he had some kind of an infection or maybe a sexually transmitted disease, so he stopped in at a neighborhood sexual health clinic for what he thought would be a routine test. The physician examined Trent and told him he needed to see a specialist immediately. "Why, can't you just give me some antibiotic or something?" asked Trent. "Mr. Smith, this is not a sexually transmitted disease, you need to see an oncologist," said Dr. Isha. "Are you saying you think I have cancer?" Trent said as he bolted out of his chair. Dr. Isha stood and calmly told Trent, "We won't know until we run some tests, but your symptoms do warrant immediate treatment." "But I don't have health insurance. How am I going to pay for this?" Trent whispered as he dropped into the chair. "Look, the important thing is that you get treatment. Let's call your parents and get you to a specialist," the doctor added as he reached for the phone. Trent was fortunate that the oncologist was able to save his life, but Trent had to quit his job while focusing on treatment and recovery. The strain and

---

[9] All costs are estimated based on actual insurance costs.

[10] High-deductible health plans, also known as consumer-driven health plans, work if you stay healthy. They generally have annual deductibles of $1,000 or more and monthly premiums that can be $100 or more [*Medical News* Today. 2007. "Los Angeles Times Examines High-Deductible Health Plans." Retrieved January 3, 2008. (www.medicalnewstoday.com/articles/73091.php)].

worry only added to concerns over mounting medical bills that became a burden not only for Trent, but for his near-retirement-aged parents who were now financially responsible for their adult child.

Some may argue that it was Trent's responsibility to have health insurance. To some extent that is true, yet when Americans cannot afford health care coverage, the nation as a whole also bears significant responsibility. The other lesson of Case 1.2 is that even the "healthy" need to have coverage for illness because disease can and does strike without regard if one is or is not insured. While testicular cancer is rare, it is the most common form of cancer in young men between 15 and 34 years of age, who are most often uninsured.

While over 47 million uninsured hit numerous headlines in 2008, this number failed to reveal the full extent of health care coverage problem for families. Those who are underinsured have insurance and are not counted among the uninsured, but being underinsured hardly covers the real costs of health care. The federal government's inadequate response to the health insurance coverage needs of under and uninsured young adults, such as Trent in Case 1.2, in the first few years of the twenty-first century, spurred state legislatures[11] to take action. In the past few years, 17 states passed laws allowing young adults to stay on the family group policy longer. For example, Delaware, Indiana, and South Dakota requiring health plans cover young adults on their parents' or guardians' insurance until age 24, while in Colorado, Idaho, Maine, Maryland, Massachusetts, Minnesota, New Mexico, Rhode Island, Texas, Washington, and West Virginia the age was set at 25 years, and in New Hampshire and Utah young adults are covered by their parent's policies until age 26. New Jersey set the coverage until their 30th birthday as long as they do not have dependents of their own. These state laws cover all young adults except in Idaho, Rhode Island, and South Dakota, where the laws apply only to full-time students (Commonwealth Fund Commission 2007:8). See Chapter 6 for further discussion of international, national, and state health care issues.

Family health has emerged as a fundamental issue in the early twenty-first century. Prior to the 1980s, traditional family social scientists hardly addressed the multidimensional nature of families in terms of their health and well-being. The following section offers an overview on the evolution of the dynamic concept of family health and well-being, and the role twenty-first century social scientists played in its development.

---

[11] For a complete listing of state legislative actions, see National Conference for State Legislatures. 2008. "Covering Young Adults through Their Parents' or Guardian's Health Policy." Retrieved February 20, 2008. (www.ncsl.org/programs/health/dependentstatus.htm).

Family Health Concept: From Insularism to Interdisciplinary

Family social scientists and practitioners in the twenty-first century not only need an understanding of global families (Karraker 2008), but also of "healthy families." Prior to the 1980s, family social sciences appeared to ignore the biological dimension of families. Likewise, medical sciences only began to recognize the impact of outside determinants, such as family relationships, on individuals' health in the later decades of the twentieth century. The early beginnings of a multidimensional, interactive view of family health emerged in the medical community.

Reconnecting Mind–Body–Spirit in Health Care

In Western culture, the impetus for introducing a multidimensional understanding of health began as early as the 1920s and 1930s with biomedical research on the interconnections of emotions and the neuroendocrine and immune systems.[12] While Eastern traditions always embraced mind–body–spirit connections in terms of health and well-being, Western science and philosophy forwarded the seventeenth century doctrine of universal mechanism.[13] Whether out of fear of punishment from the Catholic Church[14] or solely based on his personal beliefs, an influential seventeenth century philosopher, René Descartes, advanced the concept of separating the mind from the body in which the mind (e.g., thought and emotion) remained in the domain of the Church and the body (e.g., biology and physics) in that of science (Wozniak 1992). One significant result of this artificial severing was the current "biomedical model." In the biomedical model,[15] disease and illness are explained in biological terms eliminating psychological and social dimensions. Under this model, health was defined as the absence of disease. For conventional medicine, the biomedical model remains highly effective in diagnosing and treating disease, especially with the powerful determinant of genetics on health. Yet, the biomedical model is incomplete in studying chronic illness (e.g., cancer, heart conditions, diabetes, asthma) and

---

[12] For a historical review of emotions and disease interconnections see Brown, Theodore M. 2005. "Emotions and Disease in Historical Perspective." Retrieved May 4, 2008. (www.nlm.nih.gov/hmd/emotions/historical.html).

[13] The universal mechanical model reflected the view that nature could be defined and understood in terms of matter and motion (Cohen, Bernard I. 1985. *Revolution in Science*. Cambridge, MA: Harvard University Press). Hence, sciences such as biology and physics were to ignore intangibles including human emotion or thought or social context. This model is no longer accepted.

[14] The Catholic Church burned the philosopher Giordano Bruno at the stake and forced Galileo to recant his theories simply for challenging Church dogma and power (Rowland, Ingrid D. 2008. *Giordano Bruno: Philosopher/Heretic*. Rome: Farrar, Straus and Giroux).

[15] Traditionally, the biomedical model focused on physical processes (e.g., biochemistry, physiology, pathology) of diseases, while ignoring social, and/or psychological dimensions, such as social disparities, emotional embodiment, or health care with limited access, uneven quality, and inefficiency [Williams, Simon, Ellen Annandale, and Jonathan Tritter. 1998. "The Sociology of Health and Illness at the Turn of the Century: Back to the Future?" *Sociological Research Online* 3(4). Retrieved June 3, 2008. (www.socresonline.org.uk/3/4/1.html)].

the impacts of behaviors, social circumstances, and/or environmental exposures since it ignores psychological and sociological aspects of illness, health, and healing. A new model was needed and took form in the "biopsychosocial model."

The Biopsychosocial Model and Beyond

Challenges to the biomedical model approach to health care continued into the twentieth century when scholars and health practitioners, such as Robert Ader and Nicholas Cohen (1975), George Engel (1977; 1980) and Aaron Antonovsky (1979), offered more inclusive approaches to health care. Ader and Cohen (1975) were among the earliest scientists to argue that emotions impact health and healing. They coined the term *psychoneuroimmunology* (i.e., the interactive relationship among an individual's psychology, neurology, and immunology) to explain that a state of the mind (e.g., depression, anxiety) affects the immune system and thus predisposing an individual to risk factors. For example, while depression does not cause one to "catch a cold," untreated depression can negatively affect the immune system thus increasing the risk of contracting a virus. This indirect impact of emotions on physical health also influences noninfectious, chronic illnesses, for example, cardiovascular disease, cancers, type 2 diabetes (Ader 2000). More recently, molecular neuroscientists support this "bi-directional communication" between our emotions and immune systems and have coined the term *neuroimmunomodulation*[16] (i.e., communication between one's nervous and immune systems) in support of the psychoneuroimmunology concept.

Engel (1977) boldly expressed a "need for a new medical model" that would include the impacts of psychological and sociological factors related to health and well-being. He proposed the "biopsychosocial model" that, as the name implies, recognizes that biological, psychological, and social factors interact and influence individuals' health and resulting health care as illustrated in Figure 1.2.

The biopsychosocial model embraces the concept of health-related quality of life, and thus includes issues such as perceptions, socioeconomic factors, culture, and family relations. These issues directly influence health-promoting behaviors and treatments such as diet, exercise, medication taking, counseling, and so forth. For example, the biopsychosocial model not only requires gathering more information from patients and their families, but brings together integrated teams of professionals including physicians, nurses, psychiatrists, family therapists, family

---

[16] For more information on neuroimmunomodulation, see International Society for NeuroImmuno-Modulation. 2008. "What is the International Society for NeuroImmunoModulation (ISNIM)?" Retrieved July 2, 2007. (www.isnim.org); and Greer, Steven. 2000. "What's in a Name: Neuroimmunomodulation or Psychoneuroimmunology?" *Annals of the New York Academy of Sciences* 917:568–574.

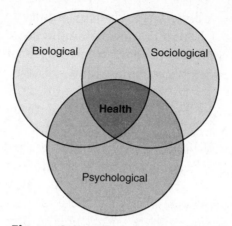

Figure 1.2 Biopsychosocial Model

sociologists, social workers, family educators, and other health-related disciplines. Psychosocial factors play especially pivotal roles in illnesses and disorders that involve behavioral choices and treatments. When treating a young adult with type 2 diabetes, for example, it is beneficial to include the individual's family in discussions regarding treatment, health behaviors, attitudes, family communication and support, nutritional knowledge, and regular physical activity, in addition to treating the biological needs related to hypertension and high blood sugar. Doing so helps to educate the family about the condition as well as clarifies how best to support the ill family member and encourage creation of a healthful environment in terms of diet, activity, and adhering to medical appointments and medication regimens.

Antonovsky (1979) also contributed to the biopsychosocial approach by encouraging the medical field to shift its focus from the typical pathogenic orientation (i.e., focus on causes of disease) toward a salutogenic approach (i.e., focus on causes of health). At the core of this philosophical approach is what Antonovsky (1994) termed a "sense of coherence," an approach to living that embodies three interrelated components of (1) comprehensibility—a cognitive ability to understand and keep events in perspective thus giving a sense of control; (2) manageability—a belief that the individual and or family has the resources (e.g., health insurance) to cope successfully; and (3) meaningfulness—an ability to find meaning from situations and the demands they create plus learn from the experiences, such as reinterpreting problems as challenges (Grochowski 2006a:65–66). This approach to living helps foster an emphasis on prevention by encouraging individuals and their families to engage in healthful behaviors as discussed in Chapter 3, such as reducing consumption of soft drinks, cessation of smoking, exercising more, using positive communication styles, obtaining recommended vaccinations, and seeking professional help for emotional concerns.

Along with a more inclusive multidimensional definition of health, the biopsychosocial model presented a new "whole person" approach to health care and helped foster the emergence of "integrative medicine," which combines high-quality evidence-based conventional and complementary[17] medicines (Grochowski 2006b; Kam 2007). Francesc Borrell-Carrió and her colleagues argue that this interdisciplinary nature of the biopsychosocial model, therefore, demands collaboration among patients, their families, family science scholars, practitioners, and health care providers (2004:582):

> [The] biopsychosocial model was a call to change our way of understanding the patient and to expand the domain of medical knowledge to address the needs of each patient. It is perhaps the transformation of the way illness, suffering, and healing are viewed that may be Engel's most durable contribution.

In conjunction with this transformation in patient–medical care "partnerships" and collaborative relationships between physical and social sciences, is a keen emphasis on the vital roles and influences of families on the health and well-being of their members, which emerges as a paramount area for family scientists. Kathleen Ell and Helen Northen (1990) argued that the theoretical underpinning of the biopsychosocial model, which sparked family-focused medical care and health promotion efforts, reflects a general systems paradigm.

General Systems and Related Family Health Theories

The general systems theory was originally proposed by biologist Ludwig von Bertalanffy (1968) who noted the nonlinearity of the interactions of a system's components. Springing from this early work, "systems theory" was adapted throughout biological and social sciences. This paradigm resulted in shifts away from mechanistic to holographic views, from direct cause–effect to mutual causality, from hierarchically ordered to interactive influences, and toward seeing problems as complex, diverse challenges. Within the systems paradigm exists an

---

[17] Complementary or alternative care approaches include acupressure, acupuncture, massage, chiropractic, herbal therapies, homeopathy, yoga, meditation, and so forth.

ecological approach that recognizes the importance of a multidimensional environmental context in which individuals and their families adapt to changes (stressors). According to Janet Grochowski (1997; 2000), families appear to have significant resilience potential when responding to stressors as "strategic living communities©," that is families positively adapting to change from a strength-centered perspective bolstered by encouragement and support from outside communities. The social-ecological approach found in population (public) health is an example in which complex conditions, such as chronic diseases, are approached from a context of multiple determinants (e.g., Family Health Determinants Model, Figure 1.1). Likewise, the influence of systems theory and thinking on family theory is evident.

During the 1980s and early 1990s the field of family social science bloomed. This period witnessed the beginning of medical science inviting family science professions into clinic settings as well as the start of the National Council of Family Relations in 1984 and the *Family Relations: Interdisciplinary Journal of Applied Family Studies*, with a special issue "The Family and Health Care" (Doherty and McCubbin 1985). "Family systems theory" played a major role during this early period. In family systems theory, families are viewed as entities or systems with subsystems (family members) who are seeking to find and/or to maintain balance or harmony. Studying how families strive to find balance serves as a helpful tool in understanding the complexity of family health. For example, family therapy expanded the use of family systems theory as a means to better understand patterns and boundaries of family life.

Knowledge is built on the foundation laid by the efforts of earlier scholars and practitioners. The pioneering work of social scientists, such as Rubin Hill's (1949) research on families under stress (i.e., ABCX model), M. Sussman's (1976) studies on the family lives of elders, T. J. Litman's (1974) landmark article naming the family unit as crucial in medical care plus his research revealing the economics of family health (1976), and Lois Pratt's (1976) engaging work on family health factors that "energize" families, led the field to focus on the interactive impacts of families and health.

"Family stress and coping theory" examines how families respond to stressors (changes) and factors that enhance and hinder healthful coping. How families perceive the stressors is vital to determining their response and coping strategies that impact how a family adjusts, adapts, or goes into a family crisis (McCubbin and Patterson 1983; Boss 1988). Family stress response, therefore, impacts the overall family's health promotion and health maintenance efforts (i.e., "health work" as discussed in Chapter 3).

The following parsimonious multidisciplinary listing offers foundational efforts in the field:

- William Doherty and Macaran Baird's (1987) focus on a need for family-centered medical care;
- William Doherty and Thomas Campbell's (1988) work on families during illness;
- Norman Garmezy (1981) and Joseph Matarazzo's (1982) examination of the psychosocial impacts of stress on adolescence;
- Göran Dahlgren and Margaret Whitehead's (1991) proposal for greater emphasis on health equity;
- Michael Rutter's (1987) focus on psychosocial resilience in families;
- Marilyn McCubbin's (1989) and John Rolland's (2003; 2004; 2005) works on families with chronically ill children;
- John Rolland and Janet Williams's (2005) incorporation of a biopsychosocial approach in the advanced medical world of genetics; and
- The efforts of Catherine Gilliss (1989), Perri Bomar (1996; 2004), Marion Broome, et al. (1998), and Bonnie Benard (1991) to engage families in healthful behaviors and enhance family resilience.

While family theories, such as family systems, are valuable in studying and understanding various family health concerns, there remains an underlying reality that theories are tools, not absolutes. Kerry Daly argues that there is "a significant disjunction between the way families live their lives and the way we theorize about families" (2003:771). It is important to remember that while the everyday realities of families (i.e., emotions, attitudes, perceptions, myths, spirituality) are crucial in studying family health and current family theory, these realities alone do not provide for complete understanding of the complexity of family health.

During the early twenty-first century, interest in families and their health expanded rapidly among practitioners and researchers from numerous disciplines and professions. This growth began with increasing recognition of family health as a dynamic process composed of multiple dimensions and impacted by five determinant domains that interact and change over time. Understanding the interactions of these five determinants demands strong collaboration among social and biological sciences. For example, completion of the human genome opened a new era in understanding, treating, and in time, preventing some negative health conditions. Yet, these biological discoveries cry out for social and psychological contributions as families and medical communities learn how to best use this genetic information, see Chapter 2. The complexity of family health demands interdisciplinary approaches, therefore, scholars and clinicians from physical and social sciences need to work collaboratively with families for all health issues whether at local (see Chapters 2, 3, and 4), national (see Chapter 6) or global (see Chapter 5) levels. The process of family health weaves our biological, behavioral, social, environmental, and political determinants into a dynamic reality that demands collaboration, caring, and commitment from all of us.

Conclusion and Book Organization

Families and Health offers a unique approach that may prove valuable to family health scholars and practitioners in their efforts to better understand and assist twenty-first-century families. Family health is not a static state merely measured by the health status of its individual members, but rather a complex process that includes multiple dimensions responding to the dynamic determinants of biology (genetics), behavioral patterns, social-cultural circumstances, environmental exposures, and health care policies and services. *Families and Health* does not purport to review all the literature on family health care,[18] nor exhaust the theories related to promoting health in families.[19] What *Families and Health* provides, however, is an innovative model that adds depth and functionality to the study of families and their health and well-being.

Families, as well as scholars and clinicians, not only need to understand the impacts of these interacting determinants, but become responsive and proactive in the enhancement, maintenance, and promotion of family health. The concept of "family health promotion" adds an inclusive dimension to the field of family health. Perri Bomar explains that "[f]amily health promotion is the process of achieving family well-being in the biological, emotional, physical, and spiritual realms for individual members and the family unit" (1996:11). Prevention and reducing the risk of disease and illness go hand in hand with promoting healthful living. Families need to engage in "health work" a term coined by Moyra Allen (Allen and Warner 2002) to label the process families use in maintaining or attaining family health and well-being. Emphasizing family health promotion and assisting families in learning their unique health work required to enhance and maintain desired levels of family health are indeed focal points in the twenty-first century for medical and social science professionals. The Family Health Determinants Model

---

[18] See medical resources, for example, American Medical Association. 2004. *American Medical Association Family Medical Guide*. New York: Random House; Harvard Medical School. 2004. *Harvard Medical School Family Health Guide*. New York: Free Press; Johns Hopkins. 1999. *Johns Hopkins Family Health Book*. New York: HarperCollins; and Mayo Clinic. 2003. *Mayo Clinic Family Health Book*. New York: William Morrow; plus Web sites, for example, Mayo Clinic. (www.mayoclinic.com); National Institute of Health. (www.nlm.nih.gov); and Harvard Medical School. (www.health.harvard.edu).

[19] See Bomar, Perri J. 2004. *Promoting Health in Families: Applying Family Research and Theory to Nursing Practice*. Philadelphia, PA: Saunders.

presented in *Families and Health* reflects this proactive approach to family health, plus the model also serves as an organizational tool for the remaining five chapters. While each chapter focuses on a specific determinant domain, the vital element of interaction among determinants remains the primary focus throughout the body of each chapter.

Chapter 2, *Biology and Family Health: Beyond Genomics*, explores the powerful determinant of genes on health and the vital nature of family health histories. Issues of confidentiality and protection from misuse of genetic data also surface as critical issues for families. The chapter discusses the impact of chronic illnesses, such as breast cancer and Alzheimer's Disease, on families and how members cope with caring for loved ones with declining health. Family health includes life transitions from birth to death. This chapter concludes with a section on hospice and palliative care in aiding families as they live with those who are dying.

Chapter 3, *Behavior Patterns: Families' Health Choices*, explores the multifaceted aspects of families' health behavior patterns. Chronic illnesses (e.g., cardiovascular disease, cancer, diabetes) not only drive up the cost of health care, but also lower the quality of life for patients and their families. A significant percentage of chronic disease can be reduced or prevented through engaging in healthful behavior patterns. While many families understand it is important to engage in healthful behaviors, such as getting vaccinated, stop smoking, healthier eating, and regular physical activity, they often do not choose such behaviors. This chapter includes discussion on behavior and family systems theories in order to aid in understanding more effective intervention and prevention strategies to engage families in healthful behavior patterns. Accessing, evaluating, and using health information and support through online strategies holds great promise and challenge as the budding science of "consumer health informatics" aims to enhance patient–physician partnerships in treatment and prevention of illnesses. Three timely family health concerns, nonimmunization of children, women's cardiovascular risks, and higher overweight and obesity rates in youths, serve as examples of the significant impact of families' health behaviors. A primary theme of this chapter is family "health work" as it applies to the choices and actions that families need to engage in and the support they may need in order to pursue more healthful behavior patterns.

Chapter 4, *Social Determinants and Family Health*, presents the complex determinant of social-cultural circumstances. This chapter discusses the often graded relationship between social position and health status that impacts all families within a social hierarchy with some segments of the population experiencing health disparities in terms of higher prevalence of diseases that result in greater health care needs (Thomas 2003). Health disparities are disproportionate risks or burdens of disease, illness, disability, and death that befall specific groups of a population along racial-ethnic, gender, socioeconomic status, education, geographic location, disability, and/or sexual orientation demographics. Examples of health conditions where health disparities in prevalence and severity exist include infant mortality, cardiovascular disease, diabetes, cancer, HIV infection/AIDS, undervaccination, and mental illness (e.g., anxiety and depression). Chapter 4 also discusses the troubling discrimination and stigmatization of certain health conditions, such as HIV/AIDS and mental illness. Mental health is indispensable to the individual well-being, interpersonal relationships (e.g., family and friends), and full participation in one's community. The passage of the Paul Wellstone and Pete Domenici Mental Health Parity and Addiction Equity Act of 2008 was a major step in working toward parity of mental illness in terms of respect, treatment, and support. Case studies presented in this chapter examine health disparities in one community, underscore the pivotal roles families play in fostering mental health and securing treatment for mental illness, and explore the need for accurate health information and education for all aspects of family health (e.g., sexuality education). Comprehensive and culturally sensitive health education along with effective communication strategies aid families in achieving their role as "partners" with the medical community in a quest for better family health.

Chapter 5, *Environmental Exposures and Global Family Health*, offers a more global view of family health. Human actions (e.g., war, genocide, violence, stigmatization and discrimination, waste, pollution, destruction of natural resources, overuse of pediatric antibiotics, stressful work atmospheres) and inactions (e.g., inadequate allocation of resources, limited access to health care, and ineffective responses to epidemics and pandemics, or ignoring work–family conflicts) result in devastating global health conditions. Such negative actions or inactions foster an array of unhealthy environmental exposures including family displacement, urban crowding, poverty, rapid spread of infectious diseases, climate change (e.g., increased frequency of draughts, floods, storms), rise in the prevalence of asthma, and/or unhealthy psychosocial worksites that tear at the fabric of families and threaten families' collective health and well-being. This chapter, therefore, discusses how unhealthy environmental exposures not only play a role in increased risks of acute diseases (e.g., malaria, HIV/AIDS), but also directly and indirectly influence the prevalence and severity of chronic illnesses (e.g., cardiovascular disease, asthma). The safety, equity, and psychosocial environment of worksites are included in this chapter since work–family and family–work conflicts greatly impact the health of families throughout the world.

Chapter 6, *Health Care and Families*, examines concerns over the access, equity, quality, and efficiency of American health care as compared to that in other developed nations. The health care in the United States is ailing not only in terms of high costs resulting in increasing numbers of uninsured, underinsured, and those families seeking medical treatment abroad (i.e., medical tourism), but also in terms of inadequate quality and efficiency in delivery of health services. This chapter argues for health care reform and redesign that focuses on primary care and creating "patient-centered medical homes" that promise more effective care through universal use of health information technology (e.g., electronic medical records), better coordination, higher levels of safety, focus on patient–provider collaborations and interdisciplinary cooperation (e.g., integrative medicine), plus greater availability of care when needed, that is, timeliness. The field of "biomedical and health informatics" also plays a crucial role in the redesign and delivery of health care. Health care is a vital determinant of family health. Several health care reform proposals, for example, "Massachusetts Health Insurance," "Building Blocks," and the "President Obama" administration plans, are discussed, as the promise of authentic health care reform ignites American families. Meaningful improvement of health care in the United States, therefore, requires that health care is affordable and equitable for all citizens, is delivered with high quality and efficiency, has increased accountability and leadership among providers, and focuses on enhancing meaningful responsible partnerships between providers, patients, and their families.

Critical Thinking Questions

1. Choose a health condition that you are most interested in. Explain how each of the five health determinants, as outlined in the Family Health Determinants Model (Figure 1.1), can positively and negatively impact this condition and family health.

2. Assume you are charged with contacting university seniors about health insurance coverage after graduation. How would you prepare for this assignment? Outline four or five talking points of what you would convey to these seniors to be most convincing. Try this out on a small group of friends and record their responses to this presentation.

3. Explain the concept of *interdisciplinary* to your classmates. For example, outline or draw what an interdisciplinary approach to studying cancer, diabetes, or heart disease might look like.

2

BIOLOGY AND FAMILY HEALTH: BEYOND GENOMICS

❧

GLORIA WORRIES THAT SHE MAY DEVELOP THE FORM OF EMPHYSEMA that runs in her family. She fears that having the DNA test for inheritable emphysema[1] may affect her ability to get health insurance or even a job if this genetic predisposition is recorded in her medical records. Even with passage of the Genetic Information Nondiscrimination Act (GINA) in 2008, she remains leery over possible genetic discrimination when she applies for future jobs or health insurance. Gloria ponders if it would be safer to use an independent "genetic underground" testing program, so as to avoid scrutiny. Even if she completes this genetic test, should she share the findings with her physician, other family members, or her partner?

Families are increasingly struggling with questions related to their genetic health histories as they face the challenges of why, where, when, and how to access genetic information and then what to do with the information once they have it. Gloria reflects a growing segment of the population who fear how to obtain, use, and share personal genetic information. While advances in genetic research promise increased personalized health care, these innovations also raise issues of health information access, treatment availability, and issues related to ethical and financial decisions.

---

[1] Inherited emphysema, Alpha-1 antitrypsin deficiency, can cause lung disease in adults and liver disease in adults and children. It occurs worldwide, but varies by population with higher rates among whites than Asian and black populations [U.S. National Library of Medicine. 2008a. "Alpha-1 Antitrypsin Deficiency." Retrieved April 20, 2008. (http://ghr.nlm.nih.gov/condition=alpha1antitrypsindeficiency)].

Arguments over which is more important in family health, biology or environment, are less relevant as our understanding of the crucial importance of interactions among genetic variations, behavioral patterns, social-cultural circumstances, environmental exposures, and health care. David Mechanic (2006:40) suggests that too often medical and social scientists have "talked past each other" and failed to authentically recognize the interplay among health influences as noted in Figure 1.1, Family Health Determinants Model. Our biology remains a key determinant as it directs the unfolding of physiological processes and responses of organ systems to external demands. These "biological response patterns, including responses to stress, novel situations, and primary relationships [family], can directly and indirectly influence other biological, cognitive (learning), and behavioral processes" (National Research Council and Institute of Medicine 2004:47). There is a "biological embedding" in that just as biology changes the ways an individual interacts with social and external environments, the behavioral patterns, social circumstances, environmental exposures, and health care also influence and shape biology (Hertzman 1999). This biological embedding as it relates to family health demands interdisciplinary approaches from medical and social scientists, which in turn requires a sharing of professional language and concepts. The following is a brief overview of important concepts and terminology related to this biological embedding.

Genome-Based Research and Family Health

Genetics is the study of inheritance by genes, which are specific sequences of DNA that provide instructions or codes for proteins that determine one's unique anatomy and physiology. Genes serve as units of heredity that provide a blueprint that is transferred from biological parent to child. In complex organisms, such as humans, mutations or disruptions occur in genes before, during, or after conception that can produce disorders. These mutations can be caused by internal factors (e.g., a genetic disorder passed on by the parent) or by exposure to external conditions or substances that disrupt genes during gestation or after birth. Geneticists group genetic disorders into three categories (National Human Genome Research Institute 2008):

- *Single gene disorders*: For example, sickle cell anemia is the most common inherited blood disorder in the United States affecting approximately 70,000 to 80,000 Americans. This disorder results in distorted sickle shaped red blood cells that break down too quickly causing anemia that leads to reduced oxygen supply to cells. Severity of symptoms varies, but one serious complication of sickle cell disease is high blood pressure in the circulatory system of the lungs causing pulmonary hypertension and increased risk of heart failure (U.S. National Library of Medicine 2008b:1). Sickle cell disease is most common among families with a racial and ethnic ancestry of African, Mediterranean (i.e., Greece, Turkey, and Italy), Arabian Peninsula, Asian, Indian, and of Spanish-speaking areas of South America, Central America, and parts of the Caribbean (National Human Genome Research Institute 2008:1).

- *Chromosome disorders*: Down syndrome occurs in one out of every 800 births in the United States each year (National Institute of Health 2008a:1). This disorder results from an extra copy of chromosome 21 and is the most common cause of mild to moderate mental disability (National Human Genome Research Institute 2008:1).
- *Multifactorial inheritance disorders*: These are conditions caused by a combination of small variations in a number of genes, often accompanied by environmental factors.

Multifactorial Inheritance Disorders

Many of the common health conditions (e.g., heart disease, many cancers, diabetes, asthma, hypertension, epilepsy, along with behavioral disorders, such as alcoholism, obesity, mental illness, and Alzheimer 's disease [AD]) run in families, but do not follow the single gene inheritance pattern, such as sickle cell anemia (National Human Genome Research Institute 2008). These complex diseases are polygenic (involve many genes) and often include environmental factors. While these multifactorial conditions tend to run in families, the pattern of inheritance is not as predictable as with single gene disorders. For example, only 2 to 5 percent of close relatives of diabetics also endure diabetes, since diabetes involves several genes as well as additional behavioral (diet, activity) and environmental (social, physical) factors (Twyman 2003:1). While all diseases have genetic components, not all are hereditary. For example, infectious diseases, such as severe acute respiratory syndrome (SARS), are not inherited, but an individual's immune responses to these diseases are genetically influenced. Again, most diseases and illnesses are multifactorial reflecting interactions among biological, behavioral, social-cultural, environmental, and political (health care) influences.

Genes not only direct the building of specific proteins, but also interact with other biological pathways that can enhance, degrade, or not impact health. When a mutation in a gene is associated with a particular disease, understanding this biological pathway and interactions can aid in effective treatment and perhaps prevention strategies. Once the Human Genome Project (HGP) completed mapping and sequencing the human genome in 2003, the field of genomics (genome-based) research opened a new era of personalized preventative care, and with it new concerns regarding the accessing, usage, and storing of genetic information. With genomics (the study of genes) as a foundation, the field of proteomics[2] (the study of proteins) emerged as arguably more medically beneficial, since it focuses on the structure and function of proteins. Other fields and research tools, such as metabolomics,[3] pharmocogenomics,[4] and nutrigenomics,[5] also contribute significantly to improving treatments (e.g., medication selection in cancer chemotherapy) and prevention strategies (e.g., food choices). Bioinformatics evolved as a field that collects, stores, marshals, and makes accessible the huge amount of data produced by these "omics" fields. Genome-based research also includes studying plants and microbes for the purpose of maintaining healthy body function and understanding disease processes. While the promise of HGP and advancements in molecular biology soar, concerns about unintended impacts of genome-based research on medicine and public health simmer. One of the areas of concern focuses on the issue of race, ethnicity, and genetics in health and health care disparities.

Race, Ethnicity, and Genetics in Health Disparities

Divisions within and between medical and public health scholars remain over the relationships between race, ethnicity, and genes "in determining the susceptibility, prevalence, and outcomes of human disease" (Fine, et al. 2005:2125). Many scientists support a position that population genetics, that is studying genetic patterns over populations identified by race and ethnicity, will aid in tailoring therapies and even preventive measures (Citrin and Modell 2004). Scientists using a biological definition of race and ethnicity note that genetic variations by race, such as in sickle cell anemia, exist and that population genetics research benefits in identifying those families and communities where intervention strategies are most needed. Others, including many in social sciences, health services, and public health, express concern that using race and ethnicity as biological factors overshadows the complex interactions among race, ethnicity, health, and health care in health-related disparities. For this second group the term "race [is] a social and cultural construct, not a biological construct" (Fine, Ibrahim, and Thomas, 2005:2125). The caution raised by health disparities researchers, therefore, hinges on a more

---

[2] The study of proteome (the complete set of proteins produced by a species) focuses on the protein structure and function (Webster's. 2003. *Webster's New World Medical Dictionary*. NY: John Wiley & Sons).

[3] Study to identify, measure, and interpret the complex time-related concentration, activity, and flux of molecules during metabolism [National Institutes of Health. 2008. "Theme: New Pathways to Discovery." Retrieved March 4, 2008. (http://nihroadmap .nih.gov/initiatives.asp)].

[4] Pharmacogenomics is the tailoring of drugs for patients to reduce side effects and improve prognosis as seen in chemotherapy for those with cancer (Webster's. 2003. *Webster's New World Medical Dictionary*. NY: John Wiley & Sons).

[5] The use of genomics to investigate diet and gene interactions involved in health or disease (Webster's. 2003. *Webster's New World Medical Dictionary*. NY: John Wiley & Sons).

complex interactive view of family health and support an eclectic three-step approach to addressing health disparities.

- First Generation Research—Detection of disparities in health or health care
- Second Generation Research—Understanding the causes for observed disparities
- Third Generation Research—Developing interventions to reduce or eliminate disparities (2005:2126).

Chapter 4 returns to these intersections of race, ethnicity, gender, socioeconomic status, sexual orientation, and other social factors that often exacerbate family health care disparities and inequalities. The remainder of this chapter, however, focuses on shifts beyond "protecting" families from potential negative ethical, social, and psychological impacts of genomic research toward a more proactive framework that is interdisciplinary and engages families in wisely using genetic information and genetic counseling. Wise use of genetic information is especially needed when families are confronted with chronic diseases such as AD and end-of-life events.

Family Health Histories

The era of genome-based research promises impressive advances and challenges for families. Knowing the family's health history, that is, identifying the diseases, illnesses, and health behaviors experienced by parents, grandparents, great grandparents, and other biological relatives, is a vital first step in family health. This information raises awareness levels and may spur more preventive health behaviors. Experts[6] suggest that family health histories may serve as interdisciplinary bridges, since they include not just genetic links, but social, behavioral, and environmental contexts as well. "Even with all the high-tech tests, medicines and procedures available in today's modern health-care setting, family health history remains the cornerstone of our efforts to prevent disease and promote personal [family] health. It's clear that knowing your family [health] history can save your life" (U.S. Food and Drug Administration 2006:1). The Centers for Disease Control and Prevention through the National Office of Public Health Genomics established the Family History Public Health Initiative. The purpose of this initiative is to increase awareness within families of the important role family history plays in not only chronic conditions, such as heart disease, diabetes, stroke, and

---

[6] See the Genome-based Research and Population Health. 2005. Report of an Expert Workshop Held at the Rockefeller Foundation Study and Conference Center, Bellagio, Italy, April 14–20, 2005. Retrieved March 10, 2008. (http://dceg.cancer.gov/files/genomicscourse/bellagio-011807.pdf).

cancer, but also infectious, environmental, and occupational diseases. Families need to understand that while family history provides vital clues, a family history of a particular illness alone does not guarantee that individuals will acquire to the affliction. A rare form of familial breast cancer, however, does reveal a powerful family history link to significantly increased risk of developing breast cancer. Asian American, Pacific Islander and Native Hawaiian women traditionally have had a lower risk of breast cancer than non-Hispanic white or African American woman, but greater risk than women of Hispanic, American Indian, or Alaskan Native descent. This trend is shifting as some Asian American women (e.g., Japanese) are experiencing breast cancer with rates that approach those of non-Hispanic white women (American Cancer Society 2002; Office of Minority Health and Health Disparities 2007a:1). Asian women throughout the world have the lowest rates of breast cancer except for those living in Western cultures, such as the United States. The reasons for these variations reflect the powerful interactions of genetics, behavioral (e.g., diet, inactivity), social-cultural (e.g., fewer children), and environmental (e.g., endocrine disruptors[7]) determinants (Deapen et al. 2002).

Mutations in two genes (BRCA1 and BRCA2) are responsible for some instances of familial breast cancer. Few diseases are caused by single gene mutations, such as this rare form of breast cancer, which only makes up 5 to 10 percent of all breast cancer cases. Women who carry BRCA1/2 mutations, however, have a 55 to 85 percent lifetime risk of developing breast cancer or 15 to 60 percent risk of ovarian cancer (Halbert, Kessler, and Mitchell 2005:285). It is important to remember, however, that the majority of breast cancers are not hereditary and research into the complex interactions of behavior, social, and environmental factors continues. Likewise, note that many women considered at high risk for breast cancer do not contract it, while others with no major risk factors do. The following case illustrates these interactions for two young women with similar socioeconomic status and breast cancer family history, but they differ on how they respond to the risk of a family history of breast cancer.

Case 2.1 Victoria and Hope: Breast Cancer in the Family

When Victoria was 15 years of age, her mother died of breast cancer. Twenty-six years later, Victoria's older sister was diagnosed with breast cancer. Victoria is divorced with two teenage daughters. She is concerned about possible familial

---

[7] "Endocrine disruptors are human-made synthetic chemicals and natural phytoestrogens that act on the endocrine systems of humans and animals by mimicking, blocking, and/or interfering in some manner with the natural instructions of hormones to cells" (Goettlich, Paul. 2006. "What Are Endocrine Disruptors?" p. 1. Retrieved May 3, 2008. (www.mindfully.org/Pesticide/EDs-PWG-16jun01.htm)].

breast cancer. She talks openly with friends at work who encourage her to talk with her doctor about possible genetic testing. Three months later Victoria, with support from her doctor and genetic testing counselor, completed genetic testing for BRCA1/2 genetic mutations. She and her family were relieved with the negative results and found the genetic testing counseling they experienced before and after the testing to be beneficial not only in encouraging Victoria to have the test, but also in reducing their cancer anxiety as well as reminding them of the importance of behavioral, social, and environmental risk-reducing strategies for Victoria and her daughters.

Hope is an African American and similar to Victoria in her socioeconomic status, cancer risk perception and concerns, family history of a mother and older sister with breast cancer, and primary care physician discussions of BRCA1/2 testing. Hope is married with three children, two teenage sons and younger daughter. Hope did not discuss the BRCA1/2 testing option with colleagues at work or with her family. She distrusts the health care industry and remains concerned how such genetic information could be used perhaps in employment or health insurance discrimination regardless of the GINA (Corbie-Smith, Thomas, and St. George 2002; Rose et al. 2005). Hope knows that if she does get breast cancer, her risk of dying from it is higher than that of her white colleagues at work. When her doctor asked her to consider the BRCA1/2 test and arranged for her to meet with a genetic testing counselor, Hope declined. While her doctor continues to remind her to get her yearly mammogram, the high co-pay and concerns about the misuse of this medical information caused Hope to skip mammogram testing for the past four years.

These cases reveal that families not only need to be aware of their family health histories, but also confident that their genetic information will not be misused. Likewise, families need to understand the importance of healthful behaviors and screening and not be forced to forgo such behaviors due to financial restrictions. Lastly, "[t]he complex and highly charged relationship between race, ethnicity, and genetics presents a substantial challenge to the translation of advances in human genetics into improvements in health" (Armstrong et al. 2005:1735). Availability, access, and utilization of innovative medical strategies hinges on numerous factors and influences. Even though Victoria and Hope enjoy similar socioeconomic status and geographic location, Hope's reluctance to engage in genetic testing and screening reflect social-cultural issues. While cultural beliefs, attitudes, and values influence most individuals' decisions regarding genetic counseling and testing, little is known about participation, or lack of participation, specific to African American families (2005).

Ethical, Legal, and Social Implications (ELSI)

Genetic information is valuable not only to individuals and their families, but also to the larger community in terms of developments and discoveries. Learning about genetic make-up and susceptibility to certain diseases offers families choices and options to engage in preventative behaviors and perhaps even reconsider reproductive plans and choices. However, as seen with Hope in Case 2.1, concerns and fears over the misuse of genetic information remain serious issues on local, national, and global levels (World Health Organization 2002). While some argue against genetic exceptionalism, that is, treating genetic data as unique from other medical information, families still consider genetic testing and genetic information highly private (Burke et al. 2006). Fears about misuse of genetic information stem from several areas including:

- Within families when a family member is blamed for a mutated gene.
- Predictive possibilities that for some are helpful but for others sources of worry.
- Self image issues: Knowledge of having a mutation may create anxiety and reduced self image.
- Past misuses of genetics (i.e., eugenics): Judging good versus inferior qualities in people.
- "New eugenics" fear that genetic information is used to stigmatize and discriminate (Zallen 2000). Families fear that genetic information may be misused to discriminate against them in health insurance or employment, which is a form of new eugenics.

In 2000, a CNN (Cable News Network) poll noted that 75 percent of those surveyed would not want their health insurance company to have their genetic information out of fear of losing coverage (*USA Today* 2001:1). Even after eight years these fears remain, as another survey noted that many families and individuals fear genetic tests will result in loss of health insurance or job (Harmon 2008). While such discrimination appears infrequent and passage of the GINA in 2008 makes such discrimination illegal, many families still do not want the risk or other financial penalties, such as increases in health insurance premiums, if genetic testing occurs.

As noted with Gloria at the beginning of this chapter, some families who refuse to get genetic tests through their medical care providers, increasingly enter into a genetic underground, where they spend hundreds to thousands of dollars for genetic tests (tests their insurers would normally cover), so as to avoid sharing this information not only with their insurance company but with their physicians as well. "It is pretty clear that the public is afraid of taking advantages of genetic testing,.... If that continues, the future of medicine that we would all like to see happen stands the chance of being dead on arrival" (Harmon 2008:1). The popularizing of independent genetic testing raises concerns in the medical community that such direct-to-consumer gene profiles do not adequately address issues of analytical validity or clinical validity, "the ability to detect or predict the associated disorder" of highly complex chronic diseases such as diabetes, cancer, and heart disease. Another caution involves a question of clinical utility, that is, will knowing about susceptibility lead to other interventions? While genetic testing for some chronic conditions, such as diabetes, may motivate family members to engage in healthful behaviors, would a genetic test result that does not indicate a health risk lead to false confidence and ignoring of preventive strategies (Hunter, Khoury, and Drazen 2008)? The use of family health histories and increasingly more genetic testing for chronic diseases, illnesses, and behaviors demand that families become proactive in enhancing and maintaining their health. These changes also mean that families need to learn how to adapt to chronic conditions that resist treatment and/or prevention.

Families' Adaptations to Chronic Illnesses

One of the most fruitful results of genome-based research in family health may be identifying members who would benefit from medical, behavioral, social, and/or environment interventions based on their risk. While those familiar with the *Crime Scene Investigation* (*CSI*) series recognize this as a reason for genetic testing, there are several others. According to the National Institutes of Health, there are six major medical purposes for genetic testing including:

- *Carrier screening*—testing unaffected individuals who carry one gene for a disease they might pass on to their children, such as with cystic fibrosis
- *Embryo screening*—preimplantation genetic screening for disease
- *Prenatal diagnostic testing*—such as screening for Down syndrome
- *Newborn screening*—such as testing for sickle cell anemia
- *Testing for genetic diseases in presymptomatic adults*
- *Confirmational diagnosis of symptomatic adults* (MedlinePlus 2008a:1)

While some DNA tests and genetic counseling allow families to make more informed reproductive decisions, others aid in early intervention, treatment, and even prevention of disease as seen in newborn and BRAC1/2 screenings. Genetic tests also aid families in early identification so the family can prepare for a chronic condition, such as AD, that currently has limited treatment or preventive measures available.

Family Health and Alzheimer's Disease (AD)

In 2008, it was estimated that approximately 5 million people in the United States had AD, including 50 percent of those older than 85 years of age. "The number of those affected is expected to triple over the next 50 years" (*Science Daily* 2008a:1). According to a national survey conducted by the MetLife Foundation, AD is the second most feared disease in America after cancer, but more than heart disease, stroke, or diabetes. For those over 55 years of age, however, AD is feared as much as cancer (MetLife Foundation 2006:13–16). Three out of five American adults also worry that they will have to care for someone with AD, while one out of three already has a friend or family member with AD. Surprisingly, while 81 percent of adults believe it is important to plan for AD, only 12 percent have actually done so (2006:22–27). This trend is worrisome in light of the aging of the national and global populations. For example, in 2005 there were 36.8 million (12 percent of the total population) people 65 years and older in the United States with this number projected to reach 86.7 million or 21 percent of the total population in 2050 (U.S. Census Bureau 2007b:1). Population aging is indeed a global concern with the current world population of those 65 years and older at 495 million estimated to hit 997 million by 2030 (2007b:1). James Knickman and Emily Snell remind Americans that by 2030 it is estimated there will be 61 million "young old," aged 66 to 84 years, and over 9 million "oldest old," born prior to 1946 (2002:1). This issue of accelerated population aging is reflected in a collaborative report by the National Institute on Aging and National Institutes of Health stating that by 2020 a historic shift will occur in that it will be the first time that people over 65 years will outnumber those under five years of age (2007:8). The social, economic, and health repercussions on families, nations, and the global community will dominate health and health care discussions and focus. While such increases in life expectancy are a tribute to public health, medical advancement, and economic development over injury and disease; an aging world population also brings challenges, such as escalating rates of chronic illnesses (e.g., cancer, heart disease, diabetes, AD), see Chapters 3 and 4. The global community needs to determine how to mobilize and allocate resources to meet this challenge of chronic illness (see Chapter 6) as they continue to struggle with high prevalence of infectious diseases, such as malaria, antibiotic resistant tuberculosis, and HIV/AIDS (see Chapter 5).

Aging and dementia, particularly AD, has captured the attention of medical and social scientists on a global scale. According to the National Institute on Aging,

AD, the most common form of dementia, accounts for 50 to 70 percent of all cases (2007:1). AD is a brain disorder that degrades memory, language, cognitive abilities, behavior, and daily activities to a level where the individual requires complete care. While the definitive diagnosis of AD remains through autopsy, specialists are able to detect "probable" or "possible" AD with 90 percent accuracy by enlisting a combination of tools including (2007:1):

- Questions about patient's general health, medical history, and abilities to carry out daily activities
- Performance tests to measure memory, problem solving, attention, counting, and language
- Medical tests—blood, urine, or spinal fluid.
- Brain scans

As accuracy in identifying chronic illness, such as AD, improves families, the health care community and health coverage providers will be challenged with how to effectively and ethically use such information and resulting diagnosis.

While 75 percent of AD cases are "sporadic" meaning they occur in individuals with no family history of AD, scientists believe that genetics play a role (Bird 2007:1). The remaining 25 percent of AD cases are "familial," that is, when two or more family members have AD. Familial AD has two classifications with "late-onset" (occurring after age 65) accounting for 95 percent of familial AD cases and the remaining 5 percent identified as "early-onset" or occurring before age 65 (2007:1). According to Suman Jayadev and colleagues (2008:373), the risk of developing AD in adult children of couples with AD is over 20 percent and increases to 31 percent of those older than 60 years and to 41.8 percent for those over 70 years. These researchers caution that the majority of the adult children in their study had not yet reached the ages with the highest risk of AD thus "the prevalence of AD in this study group will be even higher once more offspring have lived beyond age 70 years" (2008:376). The importance of family health history, therefore, surfaces as vital to families so as to adequately prepare for this health risk. While a genetic test (such as Apolipoprotein E [APOE])[8] for late-onset AD exists, testing positive means that the individual only has an increased risk of developing AD, not the disease itself. Cathleen Zick and colleagues (2005:483) argue a perfect storm is brewing, as increasing numbers of asymptomatic adults choose to have independent APOE testing and, if the results are positive, they were 5.76 times more likely to alter their long-term care insurance even though such results do not confirm they

---

[8] Testing for variations in the APOE e4 gene increases the risk of developing Alzheimer's disease [Genetics Home Reference. 2006. "Alzheimer's Disease." Retrieved April 20, 2008. (www.ghr.nlm.nih.gov/condition=alzheimerdisease)].

will have AD. Insurers argue that they should have access to such data as well because "genetic testing has the potential to create adverse selection in an insurance market," that is, insurers want to be sure to charge more to those with higher risk (2005:484). This issue raises serious concerns for families who end up being the primary caregivers and supporters for AD members. While the issue of health care coverage is addressed specifically in Chapter 6, here is a clear example of how the impact of access and availability of effective genetic testing and health care interact with the other family health influences, as noted in Figure 1.1.

The global impacts of chronic family health conditions, such as AD, raise alarms among medical and social scientists alike. With projections of AD to quadruple in 2050 to approximately 16 million in the United States and 106 million worldwide, experts warn of "… a looming global epidemic of Alzheimer's disease …" (Johns Hopkins 2007:1). As the worldwide baby boom generation ages, the financial, social, and emotional tolls of this illness alone could be crippling on familial, national, and global levels. These data reveal potential for an overwhelming economic demand as well as challenges to the current health care industry. What these statistics fail to take into account, however, are the tens of millions of caregivers and families also directly impacted when dementia strikes one or more of their loved ones.

Case 2.2 Hank and Lily: A Time of Loss and Love

Hank began to notice Lily's lapses in memory soon after her 77th birthday. "It's just a 'senior moment,' " they would kid each other. Yet, over the next year, Lily's memory worsened and her personality began to shift to being more curt, impatient, and even rude to Hank and their three adult children and five grandchildren. Hank scolded his children when they complained that "Mom isn't herself," maintaining that nothing was wrong with Lily and more patience was required from all of them. He began to cover for her when the children called by telling them Lily was too busy to come to the phone or make the short drive over to see the grandkids. His concern mounted, however, as he recalled how difficult it was for his cousin when their aunt Bessie suffered dementia. "But Bessie was in her 90s, surely Lily was too young for that type of chronic condition," he told himself. Lily's symptoms became more noticeable as she and Hank stopped attending their regular social functions and even skipped religious services more frequently. Nala, their oldest child, questioned Hank about Lily and encouraged him to have Lily examined. "Perhaps it is something physical, like a nutritional imbalance," she pleaded. When Nala voiced her concerns with her twin siblings, Nick and Noel, they expressed their discomfort with the topic of possible dementia and basically told Nala to stay out of dad and mom's affairs. Nala was hurt, but she persisted as Lily's short-term memory slipped further and further. The family's resistance gave away a few months late, however, when Lily was stopped by the police for driving on the wrong side of the road, without identification or recollection of where she lived.

Hank and Nala took Lily to her physician who was relieved that the family was finally addressing Lily's mental health concerns and referred them to a memory specialist for a thorough diagnosis. While the only definite way to diagnose AD is by autopsy, the specialist was able to determine that Lily had "possible" or "probable" AD with 90 percent accuracy. Fighting off feelings of fear and being overwhelmed, Nala and Hank called a family meeting to discuss the next steps in Lily's care. The doctor had provided them with resources that explained the concerns and demands related to dementia patient care. Hank, a retired naval captain, was confident that he could be the "best darn caregiver," and dismissed any discussion of formal or residential memory-center care.

Hank charged into his new role with the determination that reminded his children of when their father was still in active duty. While Lily's specialist strongly recommended that Hank join a support group or use respite care so he could get some time for himself, he refused. Weeks turned into months and by the end of the second year, Hank was showing the strains of a dementia caregiver. Lily's behaviors shifted from periodic rudeness to downright hostility toward Hank, accusing him of "sleeping around," even if he simply took out the trash. Hank started to complain to Nala that he felt trapped in his role of caregiver; he was frustrated with Lily's repetitive annoying behaviors and deeply saddened by the reality that "Lily isn't Lily anymore, I lost my love, my best friend." Hank and Lily's intimacy waned and then disappeared as she slipped further and further into AD. His physical health also declined. Hank took pride in staying fit, but these past two years left him exhausted, irritable, and frequently suffering respiratory illnesses.

To add to the strain, as Lily's memory faded, so did her recollection of her children and grandchildren. Nala, Nick, and Noel and their respective mates grieved at the loss of, "their fun-loving mom, who seemed to keep everyone on their toes." The grandchildren began to resist going to see grandma saying, "She doesn't even know my name." Family gatherings waned and there always were reasons why seeing Lily just didn't fit into their busy lives. Nick and Noel rationalized that their mom didn't recognize them, and seeing her like that made them and their families upset. Nala played the dutiful daughter, but the conflicts with her siblings and then with Hank over Lily wore her down. Her husband of 28 years was supportive, but he too voiced concerns that "If Lily doesn't know who you are, Nala, why all the fuss and being there every weekend? Don't your own children deserve more of your time?"

Lily was an energetic, healthy woman most of her adult life, so when her physical health began to decline as her dementia deepened, Hank struggled with the idea that perhaps it was time for formal, residential care. Questions turned in his mind including, "Could they afford it? Would such a place take good care of his Lily? What would his role be now, without her?"

Yet, as Hank pondered this next step, he realized that aside from the stressful, negative experiences of caregiving, there also were positive ones. He believed that he had become a better person, more patient and kind, plus he felt that his sense of competence in helping Lily had grown as well. His children may not agree, but taking care of Lily for as long as he could was his way of loving who she was. At a family meeting, however, Hank agreed that it was time to move Lily to a memory-center facility. While he grieved the thought of Lily leaving, he believed it was the best for her, his family, and maybe even for him.

The next several months of transitions brought more challenges for Hank and the family. Holidays and family rituals were altered and some were celebrated without Lily present. Hank also had to deal with Lily's new "boyfriend," another patient at the memory-center. Rather than being angry or jealous, however, Hank (working with a family counselor) realized that he could be happy for Lily who was now content and peaceful. Hank, and in time his children, learned to let go of anger, fear, and guilt so as to accept this new chapter in their lives, a life without the Lily they knew.

Family Caregivers

The case of Hank and Lily reveals some common themes found with dementia caregivers and AD patients. Caregivers' negative (e.g., frustration, fear, anger, isolation, exhaustion) as well as positive (e.g., sense of competence, personal growth) experiences are documented and discussed in the literature (Burrack-Weiss 2006; Roberto and Jarrott 2008; Robertson et al. 2007; Scharlach, Li, and Dalvi 2006; Silverberg Koerner and Baete Kenyon 2007). Martin Pinquart and Silvia Sörensen emphasize, however, that the impacts of depression and lowered feelings of self-efficacy among family caregivers are just as important as the physical demands. They also note that those caring for dementia patients suffer more negative effects than those looking after physically frail elders (2005). An issue in Case 2.2 hints at the impact of family conflict on Hank, the caregiver. In this case, the siblings' disagreements and Hank's resistance during the early stages of Lily's illness reflect a crucial aspect for families struggling with AD of a loved one. Caregiver strain is directly influenced by the disagreements, conflicts, and hardships experienced by the caregiver's family. Families need family-centered interventions and effective communications as they deal with decisions related to members with AD (Scharlach, et al. 2006). Even when Lily moved to a formal memory-center facility, the family needed guidance and emotional support in their new roles in Lily's care. Janice Keefe and Pamela Fancey (2000) suggest that families need more education on health care issues (e.g., use and abuse of antipsychotic drugs) and how to be effective resources for loved ones who no longer recognize them.

Hank and Lily's story reflects common stressors and strains dementia caregivers endure. While there may be variations among caregivers' responses, scholars state that the most difficult demands of caring for a loved one with AD fall into the following areas (Frank 2008:1):

- Patient's difficult behavior and the need for hands-on care
- Shortfalls in community and financial support
- Difficulties in communicating with the patient, other relatives, and medical professionals
- Caregiver's loss of personal time and freedom
- Personal grief and loss

The last aspect reflects concerns over "anticipatory grief" along with "ambiguous loss," and intimacy. According to Jacquelyn Frank, the emotional loss of a partner's love, friendship, and companionship takes a greater toll than the physical drain of caregiving. Frank's research reveals that "[t]he fundamental barrier experienced by Alzheimer's caregivers appears to be a combination of anticipatory grief and ambiguous loss, rather than hands-on care issues" (2008:1). Anticipatory grief is the loss of a loved one before he or she has actually died and anticipatory loss is "interacting with a patient who is physically alive but no longer seems present socially or psychologically" (2008:1). Pauline Boss's (1999; 2006) work on ambiguous loss is revisited in the following, but it is novel that this concept is raised, expanded, and included along with anticipatory grief in family dementia caregivers.

Frank (2008) calls on family scholars to consider the concepts of anticipatory grief and ambiguous loss in designing interventions for dementia caregivers. This book, *Families and Health*, also suggests the inclusion of "redirected intimacy" in family interventions, since the issue of intimacy between spouses and partners during dementia causes much confusion and pain on the part of family caregivers and families. In late 2007, former Supreme Court Judge Sandra Day O'Connor shared her story of how she responded to her husband's (John who had AD) romance with another woman, a patient at the same care facility. Judge O'Connor was thrilled that her husband of over 55 years was happy and content (Zernike 2007). This reflects Mary Pipher's (2000) work in which she explains that wanting to be happy is what young love is all about, while wanting someone else to be happy is a sign of mature love.

Chronic illness, such as AD, impacts the entire family community and thus family education, intervention, and support need to be family-focused, not illness or individual-focused. The Alzheimer's Association (2008:1) offers support for dementia caregivers that includes the following guide that families need to recognize and support:

- Educate yourself and family on what to expect and watch for in terms of care and caregiver strain.
- Know what resources are available—adult day care, in-home assistance, and so forth.
- Become an educated caregiver—be informed about AD and caregiver needs.
- Get help—seek support of family, friends, community resources, and support groups.
- Take care of yourself—wise diet, exercise, rest and sleep, and time for yourself.
- Manage your stress level—use relaxation strategies and consult your doctor.
- Accept changes as they occur—AD patients may need more help than you can provide, accept this and seek help.
- Do legal and financial planning—consult attorney, get legal, financial, and care issues resolved. Do this sooner than later.
- Be realistic—you cannot control an AD patient's behaviors, grieve your loss and focus on positives.
- Give yourself credit, not guilt—you are doing the best you can.

Included in family-focused health care for those living with chronic illness, such as AD, are issues that are often tip-toed around, such as grief, loss, dying, and death. The next section raises these aspects as a viable area within the biological influence on family health.

Loss, Dying, and Death—Part of Family Health

While advances in genome-related research promise to relieve suffering, and in some cases, prevent disease and disability, the cycle of living still includes loss, dying, and death. Aiding families through these final stages of life are increasingly recognized as vital aspects of family health.

As noted earlier, ambiguous loss and anticipatory grief remain issues that may be neglected in aiding families as they experience the loss, dying, and death of a loved one due to terminal illnesses, such as AD or an inoperable brain tumor. Yet, ambiguous loss is not limited to families with elders with dementia. The uncertainty and ambiguity of situations often are more stressful on families than negative news (Hirsh and Inzlicht 2008). Such loss and grief also surface within families whose younger members may be absent or missing. For example, Angela Huebner and colleagues (2007) explain that youth (aged 12 to 18 years) experienced significant ambiguity and uncertainty when parents are deployed during times of war, such as in Afghanistan and Iraq. Pauline Boss explains that there are two types of ambiguous loss "goodbye without leaving" and "leaving without saying goodbye" (2007:105). Hank and Lily's story in Case 2.2 reflects the first type of ambiguous loss and grief. The story of Noah and Maria and their family captures the essence of the second type in which a family member is gone, but was unable to say goodbye or add closure.

Case 2.3 Noah and Maria: Gone Without Goodbye

Maria couldn't sleep, so she checked on the children (Micky age 10, Nina age 8, and little Juan age 5) and began to pace in the length of the living room, a habit she started since she first heard that Noah was missing. How could this be? How could Noah be gone? The nightmare began in late 2007, when the private contractor company Noah worked for reported him missing after an ambush in Yusifiya, Iraq. The company's president called Maria trying to calm her, but the fear and anger only grew for Maria. Where was Noah, why couldn't they find him? For almost 12 months, he was "missing in action" and Maria lived with the constant emotional pain of not knowing if he was alive or dead. She did her best to help the children negotiate the unknown regarding their father's fate, yet for Maria the storm of ambiguous loss drained her of her emotional strength and left her immobilized. Time seemed to stand still as Maria and the children struggled to hold on to their hopes and routines, but this ambiguous limbo did not bring peace or growth, but only pain and inaction. Maria slowly realized that in order for her to "live," she had to learn to live with this uncertainty and try to regain some control over her life, if not for her sake, at least for their children. The frustration and confusion stemmed from the ambiguity and not from what Maria did or did not do. Coming to this realization helped Maria and her family move away from the pit of helplessness toward learning how to cope and seek aid in redefining their relationship with Noah.

Both Hank (Case 2.2) and Maria (Case 2.3) along with their respective families experienced ambiguous loss. Boss (1999) explains that ambiguous loss halts the grieving process thus interfering with coping and decision making. Due to the ambiguity, there is no clear closure. "Without information to clarify their loss, family members have no choice but to live with the paradox of absence and presence" (Boss 2007:105). Patient care is expanding to family care and thus issues of loss (ambiguous and other), grief, dying, and death have moved to more prominent positions on the stage of family health. The next case examines this final stage of life and the impacts of loss and grief on families as they learn to live with the dying and death of a loved one.

Case 2.4 Josh: Dying Well

Josh led a charmed life at least that was what his family and friends would say. Josh enjoyed his success as an economics professor and the life a university city offered. He just completed his third book and was well on his way to being the next department chair, quite a feat for a young professor at a major university. Josh and his partner, Matt, worked hard at their careers and were active members of the community donating time and talents in helping others. Due to the long hours, Josh didn't think that his recurring headaches were anything to be concerned about. Headaches were just a nuisance due to the stress, according to him. Matt agreed as he too was busy with his law practice. But Matt's concern grew as Josh's headaches became more severe and frequently accompanied with vomiting. Josh's personality also seemed to be shifting over the last several months as he was less alert and coordinated. Josh too began to worry and agreed to seek medical attention. The specialist entered the examination room and with a heavy heart shared that the battery of tests revealed a primary invasive brain tumor located deep within Josh's brain.

While the causes of adult brain tumors are complex, some inherited conditions may have increased Josh's risk. Josh was aware of the rapidly advancing field of genome-based research, but he also knew that possible breakthroughs were beyond his now limited life span. His options were minimal since surgical removal of the tumor was not possible. The best the medical specialists could offer was palliative care to make Josh more comfortable during his final six months. This palliative care was tailored to meet Josh's needs in terms of reducing symptoms, such as pain, nausea, and difficulty in sleeping, so that he could regain some control over his remaining days.

Denial, anger, fear, guilt, and grief flared in both Josh and Matt as they and their families struggled with the reality that Josh was dying. The loss and grief especially consumed Josh and Matt. In order to assist them and their families in these final stages of life, the palliative care staff recommended that Josh also seek hospice care. It was here in hospice care that Josh, Matt, and their families found "the gifts that grief can bring" (Gibbs 2008:56). These gifts include creating an environment that reduces fear and anger related to the impending death. Hospice care specialists, therefore, provide compassion and hope to dying family members and their families and friends; not hope for a cure, but hope to resolve issues, make peace, and amend. Hospice care also supports family members and friends in their emotional healing and readjustment throughout their bereavement during and after the death of a loved one.

The story of Josh and Matt (Case 2.4) sheds some light on an area of family health that many fear to discuss or even think about, that is the loss of those close to us. While ambiguous loss clouds the grieving process, once the ambiguity is removed, those who have lost a loved one (mentally or physically) can begin to grief that loss. "Hospice is a philosophy of care ... that accepts death as the final stage of life" (American Cancer Society 2008:1). Hospice care offers palliative, bereavement, respite, spiritual care, as well as counseling for families. Who pays for hospice care? As with much of health care in the United States, cost is a major consideration. In the case of hospice care, Medicare, Medicaid, the Department of Veterans Affairs, most private health insurers, and Health Maintenance Organizations (HMOs) provide for this care. For those without health insurance the cost issue becomes murky. If a foundation is not available to cover the costs, some hospice care organizations will charge according to the family's ability to pay (American Cancer Society 2008). As advances in medical technology continue to expand the quantity and quality of life, issues related not only to accessibility and availability of family health and health care, but also to our very attitudes and beliefs require examination and understanding of dying, death, and grief.

How a culture views dying and death significantly impacts families' responses to and acceptance of the end of life. Anthropologists note that cultures exhibit death accepting, denying, or even defying tendencies. Western culture often leans toward death-defying, while other cultures that embrace a Buddhist or Hindu philosophy often view death as a transition to another level of being and not something to be feared. Those in the West often see afterlife as personal, while other cultures perceive it as one being part of a larger universe. Elizabeth Kubler-Ross's seminal work (1969) on the stages of dying helped focus attention on a topic often avoided in American society. Several decades later, as the medical community, insurance providers, and families increasingly recognize and support the important roles of palliative and hospice care, "dying well is emerging as 'part of,' not 'a failure of,' the medical community's mission" (Grochowski 2006b:148). Aiding families during this final transition of life, by reducing ambiguous loss (both saying goodbye without leaving and leaving without saying goodbye) as well as helping them live through their loss and grief, challenges medicine and the social sciences. Hospice care and other services aid individuals and their families in dying well.

Hospice organizations reflect a philosophy that, once fear and regret are removed, the dying process can be one of peace, for death then is accepted as part of life and part of the complex process called family health. Family health means learning to live well and learning to die well, both are vital lifelong lessons for families.

Conclusion

What significance does genome-based research have on family health? This chapter raises several points in response to this question. Genes and the proteins they produce direct a multitude of bodily functions. Enhancing our understanding of genomics is vital to family health, but biology alone is not the only influence on health. While advances in genome-based research promise earlier detection, more effective interventions, and even some preventions, most diseases and illnesses are multifactorial. Genes, therefore, perform vital roles, but are not the only players on the stage of family health as revealed in the following chapters.

Along with a need for greater understanding of the role of genetics in family health, however, is the caution on how this highly personal information is used and shared. How to access personal genetic information along with what to do with the information are areas begging for greater study and guidance. Even with the passage of the GINA in 2008, concerns over the use of genetic data lingers among families, particularly among those with family health histories for certain illnesses, such as familial breast cancer. A primary need surfacing with such concerns is family health education that explains the potentials, uses, limitations, and abuses related to genetics and health. The areas of ELSI regarding genetic information are ripe for study and family health-based education.

Calls for clearer understandings of the impacts of biological (genetic) influence on family health emerge as medicine, the social sciences, health care coverage providers, government, and families adapt to living and dying with chronic illness. Understanding genetic risk factors of inheritable disease is just one aspect of these multifaceted conditions. This chapter discussed a family's responses to a member with AD raising issues of genetic testing, family adjustment, and struggles with "ambiguous loss," "anticipatory grief," and "redirected intimacy" issues. Families need to learn how to accept that the one they once knew is psychologically gone even though he or she remains physically present. This issue is a timely topic in light of the middle-aged baby boomer generation as they near the "young old" and "oldest old" stages of life.

The final segment of this chapter ventures into the often neglected aspects of family health, that is, loss, grief, dying, and death. While many focus on genome-based research as a means to try to avoid or defy death, increasingly those in the medical and social science fields recognize the need to better prepare families about the inevitability of death within the life cycle. Gordon-Kolb, a palliative physician, states "[s]omewhere along the line, we lost the human side of medicine with our searches for cures" (Marcotty 2008:A18). While few would wish to halt the achievements of genome-based research, more are realizing that aiding patients and their families with the final stages of life through palliative and hospice care are vital to total family health care.

One of the major changes emerging from the genome-based research is a call for collaboration among medicine, population (public) health, social sciences, and education, as all of these focus on health promotion and enhanced family health. Contributions from genome-based research and therapy demand greater collaboration among disciplines. The international expert workshop in Bellagio, Italy[9] emphasized the crucial need for knowledge integration within and across disciplines establishing the Genome-based Research and Population Health International Network (i.e., international, interdisciplinary, and integrated) to promote knowledge and technologies for the benefit of population health (Burke et al. 2006).

Such a multidisciplinary and interdisciplinary approach means learning each other's language (e.g., jargon), sharing their findings, and collaborating on common health concerns, such as health disparities as discussed in Chapter 4. The effectiveness of such collaboration demands that families are better educated on the realities and cautions surrounding the genome-related fields, as well as having families become proactive partners in their health. Naturally, such grand hopes will take time and commitment, but without an engaged population on family, community, national, and global levels, these hopes for effective use of genome-based research may not reach their full potential. Our biology and its interactions with other influences shape and define our individual and family health. As discussed in these first two chapters, family health is a complex interactive process in which biology, behavioral patterns, social circumstances, environmental exposures, and health care policy and services intertwine. Chapter 3 explores the powerful influence of behavior patterns on family health.

Critical Thinking Questions

1. Using some examples, explain the meaning of "multifactorial inheritance disorders." Why is it important for families to understand the complex nature of disorders and illnesses?

---

[9] Genome-Based Research and Population Health. 2005. Report of an expert workshop held at the Rockefeller Foundation Study and Conference Center, Bellagio, Italy, April 14–20, 2005. Retrieved March 10, 2008. (http://dceg.cancer.gov/files/genomicscourse/bellagio-011807.pdf).

2. Outline four talking points you would provide to Victoria, Hope, and their families related to the acquiring and use of genetic testing information and their family health histories.

3. If you were working with Hank and Lily's adult children, what suggestions would you give to them about dealing with "ambiguous loss," "anticipatory grief," and "redirected intimacy" so as to aid them in dealing with their mother's illness?

4. If your sibling's partner or spouse was dying as Josh, what three or four points do you believe are important for families to consider regarding the role of palliative and hospice care? Why did you select these points?

3

BEHAVIOR
PATTERNS: FAMILIES'
HEALTH CHOICES

❦

Interactive Nature of Family Health Behaviors

Case 3.1 Alicia: No Vaccinations for My Kids

Alicia huddled in an emergency room chair as the doctor approached. She was frustrated with the ever increasing out-of-pocket health care costs, so she stopped taking her children to the doctor after the birth of her last child and sadly, her children did not qualify for Medicaid under the 2007 guidelines. She simply hoped no one would get sick, and if they did, they would use the emergency room. "Ms. Turner, your one-year old son, Harry, is in a serious condition. He has developed complications from the measles resulting in acute encephalitis, that is, a swelling of the brain, a severe case of pneumonia, an infection of the lungs, and an inner ear infection that may result in permanent hearing loss. He requires extended treatment, and you will need to bring in your other children to be checked," Doctor Meeks said calmly. Alicia sank deeper into her chair. When all three of her children contracted measles several weeks ago, she didn't think much of it. Her beliefs and attitudes about vaccinations reflected those of her mother, siblings, and peers. They simply allowed their children to contract childhood diseases without interference from vaccinations, since their shared attitude was that they were not going to sacrifice their kids for the greater good. "It is just a natural illness," she whispered, "how can things be so serious for Harry?" "Measles[1] is a highly contagious disease with

---

[1] For more information on cause, symptoms, treatment, and prevention of measles, see U.S. National Library of Medicine. 2008c. "Measles." Retrieved March 3, 2008. (www.nlm.nih.gov/medlineplus/ency/article/001569.htm).

damaging effects on young children and pregnant women," sighed the doctor. Already guessing Alicia's response, she asked, "Did your other children receive the two-dose Measles, Mumps, Rubella (MMR) vaccination?" Alicia slowly shook her head no. Without looking up, she responded, "I didn't want to risk them getting autism or some other condition that vaccinations can cause. Besides, with other kids in school being vaccinated, I thought this disease didn't exist anymore."

Alicia (Case 3.1) represents a small but increasing number of vaccine skeptics who object to vaccinating their children and use personal beliefs as reasons for their behaviors to exempt from vaccination requirements and recommendations. While no vaccine is 100 percent effective or free of side effects, a higher standard for safety is applied to preventive vaccines than to drugs (National Network for Immunization Information 2008). Misunderstandings regarding the presence and spread of infectious diseases along with faulty beliefs related to vaccination safety help promote these non-vaccination behaviors. Consider that in 1963 there were 3 to 4 million cases of measles in the United States incurring approximately 400 to 500 measles-related deaths. In reaction to this measles epidemic and resulting amendable deaths, MMR vaccination became a requirement for public school children, which resulted to dramatic declines in incidents of measles, mumps, and rubella. The program was so successful that " . . . measles transmission was declared eliminated in the United States in 2000" (Morbidity and Mortality Weekly Report 2008:1). "The very success of immunization has turned out to be an Achilles' heel. . . . Most of [today's] parents have never seen measles, and don't realize it could be a bad disease so they turn their concerns to unfounded risks. They do not perceive risk of disease but perceive risk of the vaccine" (2008:1). Alicia's belief that the MMR vaccination increases risks of autism, asthma, and/or other neurological disorders is an example of how faulty and misguided beliefs and attitudes can be harmful and even deadly. The data refuting such claims are substantial (Pichichero et al. 2008; Schechter and Grether 2008; Smeeth et al. 2008; Thompson et al. 2007; Wilson et al. 2003). Yet, some families still cling to unproven positions, refusing to have their children immunized.

This behavior pattern of rejecting vaccination produces poor health results as seen with the outbreaks of mumps in 2006 and measles in 2008 in the United States. Other developed nations that allowed for exemptions or laxness in MMR vaccinations also experienced measles and mumps outbreaks and epidemics. Japan's 2007 measles epidemic caused college campuses to empty and classes to halt (Norrie 2007). In 2002, there were 594 hospitalizations and four measles-associated deaths during Italy's measles epidemic, also spurred by inadequate vaccination coverage (Morbidity and Mortality Weekly Report 2003:1). Germany, where vaccinations were not compulsory, likewise experienced a major measles outbreak in 2006. In less-developed countries, the results of such epidemics are exceedingly more deadly, such as in Nigeria, between January and March 2008, there were over 10,000 reported cases of measles and cerebrospinal meningitis out of which no fewer than 410 infants died (All Africa 2008:1). Vaccine-preventable diseases have not disappeared and only require a supply of unprotected victims and uninhibited access in order for outbreaks to become epidemics and pandemics. This issue of infectious disease is revisited in Chapter 5.

Vaccinations have saved millions of lives. On a global scale, deaths from measles decreased 68 percent from 2000 to 2006 due in large part to MMR vaccinations (Steinhauer 2008:1). The medical community warns, however, that outbreaks, such as the one that occurred in the United States during the first four months in 2008, illustrate an increasing risk of epidemics, especially as global mobility increases and vaccination rates decline threatening the health for the unvaccinated and those they come in contact with (Morbidity and Mortality Weekly Report 2008). Why then do parents and guardians refuse to comply, or ignore this health behavior of vaccination? The answer is more complicated than one might expect. The National Immunization Study (Smith, Chu, and Barker 2004) found differences between families whose children were "undervaccinated" (i.e., did not receive the full recommended doses) and those who were "unvaccinated." The families of the former tended to be black with younger, less educated, and often unmarried mothers. Somewhat surprisingly, the unvaccinated were primarily from non-Hispanic white families with a mother who was older, married, and college educated. Families in the unvaccinated group also tended to question the safety of immunizations and resisted the medical community's vaccination recommendations more frequently than those undervaccinated families (2004). Unvaccinated children pose health risks not only to themselves in terms of contracting avoidable illnesses, but also once infected, they become carriers of the disease spreading it to others who may be more vulnerable to the serious nature of infections. Encouraging families to engage in healthful behaviors, therefore, requires medical and social science professionals to not only provide accurate health information, but also to aid in the skills of healthful decision making, that is families' "health work."

Family Health Promotion—"Health Work"

Health behaviors may be intentional (e.g., eating more vegetables) or impulsive, reflexive (e.g., social smoking with peers), health promoting (e.g., going for a daily brisk walk), or health impairing (e.g., neglecting necessary vaccinations). Family members' behaviors that threaten their health or that of other individuals also raise concerns for the entire family and outside communities. Changing health behaviors, however, is not easy nor linear. Simply telling someone to quit smoking, get more exercise, improve their diet, get more sleep, learn to be calm, practice safer sex, get health checkups, use seat belts, have their children immunized, and so forth rarely invokes significant, enduring behavior change. Such a simplistic approach often reveals ignorance about or disregard for how health behavior change occurs. Families need to be active participants in their "health work," that is choosing behaviors that enhance family health based on accurate information and wise behavior choices (Allen and Warner 2002). Health education plays a vital role in providing families with accurate, accessible, and understandable health information. Families increasingly access the Internet in seeking health-related data, information, and support about health promotion, disease prevention, treatment, and management of specific conditions and chronic illnesses. Thomas Ferguson (2000) notes that support provided by these "online patient-helpers" can serve as a valued resource not only to patients and their families, but also in strengthening patient–physician relationships. Becoming proactive "health information consumers" often empowers and encourages families to become more active participants in their family health. Of course, families need to be wise consumers of health information and learn how to recognize reputable health information resources. The science of "consumer health informatics"[2] has become a valued part of the medical field in determining what health information is needed and how best to present it so as to positively impact healthful behavior patterns (Lewis et al. 2005). Engaging families in health work, therefore, requires a clear understanding of why health behaviors are made and what interventions reinforce healthful behaviors and reduce unhealthful behaviors. In order to understand health behavior patterns and assist families in promoting healthful and reducing unhealthful behaviors, a firm appreciation of health promotion and behavior change concepts is needed.

An Ecological Approach

An ecological approach emphasizes interaction and interdependence of factors impacting health behaviors. As revealed in Figure 1.1 (Family Health Determinants Model), multiple influences interact in the process of family health. A similar set of interactive factors are involved in individual family members' behaviors. Two

---

2 "Consumer health informatics is the branch of medical informatics that analyses consumers' needs for information; studies and implements methods of making [health] information accessible to consumer; and models and integrates consumers' preferences into medical information systems" (Eysenbach, Gunther 2000. "Consumer Health Informatics." *British Medical Journal* 320:1713–16).

concepts prevail in understanding health behavior change: (1) Behavior both affects and is affected by several factors, and (2) Behavior impacts and is impacted by the social and physical environments.

As defined by the National Cancer Institute's (2005) seminal work on health promotion, the first concept focuses on three interactive levels:

- *intrapersonal*—individual beliefs, attitudes, knowledge, and personality traits
- *interpersonal*—social network with family, friends, work colleagues, and peers which provides role and social identity plus social support
- *community*—standards along with formal and informal rules, regulations, and policies that promote or restrain behaviors

For example, consider Alicia's refusal of the MMR vaccination for her children. At the intrapersonal level, her inaction was in part due to ignorance related to infectious disease as well as to unfounded fears of MMR causing autism. On an interpersonal level, her social network of family and peers fostered and supported a negative position related to MMR vaccinations. Their social norm reflects a striving for less governmental interference and for reducing the power of schools and agencies to set rules, regulations, and polices. At the community level, incomplete health care coverage made access to vaccinations more difficult, and led to reduced regular medical checkups, health education, and wellness guidance. Likewise, the public policy of nonmedical, personal belief exemptions in Alicia's state prevented the schools from requiring her older children to be vaccinated in order to attend school. Researchers at Johns Hopkins University note that 21 states[3] allow personal belief exemption from vaccination requirements (Institute for Vaccine Safety 2007). If policies regarding requiring children to be vaccinated before they are allowed to attend schools are relaxed, then compliance wanes. While undervaccination remains a concern, the growing numbers of unvaccinated children is equally disconcerting. How to reach these "exempters," who often "are well educated and financially stable, and hold a host of like-minded child-rearing beliefs," challenges medicine and the social sciences on local, state, national, and global levels (Steinhauer and Harris 2008:1). Families need to understand that infectious diseases, such as measles, have not disappeared. Globally, over 20 million measles cases occur each year resulting in vaccine-preventable deaths, such as the 311,000 children under the age of five years who died from measles in 2005 (Centers for Disease Control and Prevention 2008a:1).

---

[3] Arkansas, Arizona, California, Colorado, Idaho, Louisiana, Maine, Michigan, Minnesota, New Hampshire, New Mexico, North Dakota, Ohio, Oklahoma, Oregon, Pennsylvania, Texas, Utah, Vermont, Washington, and Wisconsin.

The second concept considers the reality that individuals' behaviors not only influence others, but are influenced by those they come in contact with. Consider the repercussions of Alicia's behavior. Her unvaccinated children not only were unnecessarily susceptible to measles, mumps, and rubella, but also posed a danger to those who were vaccinated—MMR is only 95 percent effective—and to those who were unvaccinated as their brother, Harry, or others too young or unable to be vaccinated. Making vaccinations a family affair in which parents and guardians are educated and aware of the facts related to infectious disease and the importance of immunization has become a primary focus for some communities (Pupillo 2008). Some epidemics and pandemics, as discussed in Chapter 5, can be contained and even prevented when individuals make healthful behavior choices. It is vital, however, to recognize that health behavior choices reflect an interactive web of factors at individual, interpersonal, and community levels. Theories provide tools for understanding these interactions. The following sections explore health behavior theories and models related to each of the three levels using several family health issues.

Health Behavior Theories and Models

Christopher Armitage and Mark Conner (2000) argue that while socioeconomic factors, as discussed in Chapter 4, are crucial to understanding health disparities, social-cognitive variables can account for the individual differences in health behaviors. For example, when an entire family is exposed to the same socioeconomic dynamics and health information, why do some family members choose to engage or not to engage in certain health behaviors (e.g., exercise, not smoking)? Health behavior theories guide scholars and practitioners in investigating the why, what, and how of health behavior choices.

Experts in family health promotion (National Cancer Institute 2005) state that there are two theory bases at work in health behavior. *Explanatory theories* explain contributing factors and why the health behavior exists. This explanation aids in identifying modifiable factors that contribute to the health concern (e.g., insufficient knowledge, low self-efficacy, lack of resources, inadequate social support). *Change theories* focus on identifying and implementing interventions that enhance or reduce health behaviors while remaining sensitive to families' social-cultural contexts. Within each of these two theoretical bases are couched various health behavior models. As in other challenging family areas, no single theory holds center stage in health behavior patterns due to the complexity of health conditions, individuals, behaviors, and social-cultural contexts. When theoretical models are combined, however, they are valuable tools in enhancing, understanding, and intervening various health behavior models. The following three sections discuss examples of theory-driven models and case applications relevant to the intrapersonal, interpersonal, and community levels.

Intrapersonal Models

Two examples of contemporary models that explore why people choose the health behaviors are the Health Belief Model (HBM) (revised) and the Theory of Planned Behavior (TPB). The core assumptions of the HBM focus on the individual's *motivation* to act. HBM includes one's beliefs and attitudes concerning:

- perceived threats (susceptibility and severity) of a health condition;
- perceived benefits of taking action to reduce the risk or seriousness;
- perceived barriers to taking action;
- readiness to take action, that is, knowledge and awareness of how to act;
- self-efficacy or confidence in ability to take action.

Individuals will engage in healthful behavior if they: (1) feel that the threat of the health condition can be avoided; (2) have positive expectations that the healthy behavior will help them avoid a negative health condition; and (3) believe that they have the skills to carry out the healthy behavior, that is, self-efficacy (National Cancer Institute 2005).

While HBM serves as a valued model, adaptations led to additional health behavior theories and models. The TPB and the related Theory of Reasoned Action (TRA) went beyond consideration of motivations to examine the beliefs and the attitude of *intention* surrounding behavior choices. The concept of "behavioral intention" appears to be vital in determining health behaviors, since it examines the likelihood of engaging in the behavior (National Cancer Institute 2005:xxiii). Determining behavioral intention involves identifying our attitudes toward the behavior, the subjective norm (i.e., the acceptability of the behavior in the social network), and how much control one feels he or she has in terms of presence or lack of things that impact the performance of the behavior. For example, one's intention to be active or exercise regularly often is determined by the attitudes held about exercise, that is, influences of past exercise experiences as being more positive or negative. The intention is also influenced by how an individual's social network views and encourages (or discourages) being active. Likewise, the individual's intention to exercise also hinges on the presence of opportunity, location, and equipment. Living in an environment that not only encourages being active, but also provides opportunity (e.g., extended lunch breaks to those who exercise, safe and clean activity environments, discounted gym memberships, and so forth), the

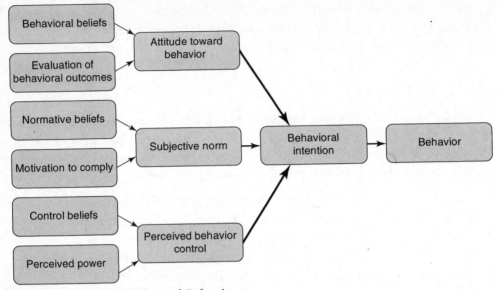

Figure 3.1   **Theory of Planned Behavior**

Source: Adapted with permission from the National Cancer Institute. National Cancer Institute. 2005. *Theory at a Glance: A Guide for Health Promotion Practice*, Figure 3, p. xxv. Washington, DC: National Institutes of Health. Retrieved January 6, 2008. (www .cancer.gov/PDF/481f5d53-63df-41bc-bfaf-5aa48ee1da4d/TAAG3.pdf).

intention to exercise is more positive and sustained. As seen in Figure 3.1, behavioral motivations and intentions drive or hinder health behaviors.

Figure 3.1 provides a visual to a nonlinear process. The purpose of this figure is to help clarify the interactive nature of personal and societal beliefs along with one's perceived ideas of control as related to engaging or not engaging in a behavior. A family member's behavioral intention, therefore, is a product of individual and social influences. Consider this image of behavioral intention in the following case related to "heart healthy behavior choices."

Case 3.2 Simone: Sex and the Heart

Simone is 62 years of age and believes she is healthy enough for someone of her age. She has tried to cut back on calories, but still remains 25 pounds overweight. Her only physical activity, other than work, is taking care of the house. "When I get home from work, the only thing I want to do is relax and not work up a sweat" is her comment to her adult children who urged both her and her mate to exercise. Like many women of her age, she rarely thought about the health of her heart.

"Good grief, men are the ones who die from heart attacks," she argued. Besides, at her last physical exam the doctor said that aside from needing to "drop a few pounds," she was fine. Yet, several times during the past week she experienced shortness of breath and dizziness episodes at work. She told herself, "I have too much on my mind, that's all it is. I'll be fine once I get home and sit for a bit." Driving home after one of those episodes demanded more energy than usual, and when she finally pulled into the driveway, her fatigue turned to exhaustion accompanied by abdominal and back pain. "Maybe I'm getting the flu," she thought. All she wanted to do was curl up and sleep. When Grace, her daughter, visited her that evening, she noticed Simone was not only tired, but seemed confused and in pain. "Mom, do you feel any pressure anywhere else, like in your chest?" Grace inquired. "Yes, but it can't be my heart. Heart disease is what men get. I am concerned about cancer, Grace, not a heart attack!" Simone lectured. "These symptoms are serious, Mom. I'm driving you to the hospital."

Fortunately for Simone, her daughter followed her suspicions. Simone had suffered a mild heart attack. Her doctor explained that women often are underdiagnosed, since the symptoms they experience vary from the classic ones identified in studies that underrepresented women. This knowledge gap helps to explain why cardiovascular health in women was not improving as rapidly as that in men. What was known, however, was that Simone had to make changes in her health behaviors.

The disparity between women and men in terms of awareness, symptoms, and treatment related to cardiovascular disease (CVD) remains a glaring problem as revealed in a 2008 international study (Dey et al. 2008). CVD is the leading cause of death in women claiming over a quarter million annually in the United States, which is more than the death toll for breast cancer, accidents, and diabetes combined, yet most women fail to see the connection between their personal risk factors (e.g., high blood pressure) and developing heart disease (National Heart, Lung, and Blood Institute 2008). While genetic predisposition exists in CVD, over 90 percent of all heart attacks for both women and men across all racial-ethnic and geographic contexts involve modifiable risks including smoking, high blood lipid levels, hypertension, diabetes, obesity, low daily intake of fruits and vegetables, and lack of physical activity (American Heart Association 2008b). A first step in assisting family members in changing health behaviors begins with understanding their behavioral motivations and intentions.

Let's return to Simone (Case 3.2). Part of her "healthy heart" health care emphasized beginning a daily walking program. The health benefits from regular physical activity would not only improve her cardiovascular health, but would aid in relaxation, coping, emotional health, and reducing body fat. Simone may not follow the prescribed activity plan, however, unless she believes her health is indeed in danger and that the benefits of daily exercise will make a difference. According to the HBM, she may need encouragement and a "workout buddy" to help her in learning how to set up and stick with a program. The longer she can stay with the program the greater her confidence and self-efficacy that she can stick with the activity program. As outlined in the TPB, her behavioral intention is impacted not only by her beliefs and attitudes toward the walking program, but also by how this exercise behavior fits into her beliefs about social standards and motivation to comply, in other words, is it an acceptable behavior and does she really want to engage in it? Equally important in forming her behavioral intention is her perceived behavioral control, that is, the presence or lack of things that make it easier or harder to complete the walking program. These "causal chain of beliefs, attitudes, and intentions drives [her] behavior [change]" (National Cancer Institute 2005:xxv). Along with these intrapersonal factors are interpersonal impacts on health behavior.

Interpersonal Approaches

Family systems theory, according to J. LeBron McBride, is a primary theory used in family medicine. McBride explains that instead of linear causality where A impacts B causing C, family systems theory incorporates a "more circular causality" in which interactions and feedback loops exist. "Family systems theory is based on the premise that individuals should be viewed in the context of interactions, transitions, and relationships inherent in the family rather than in isolation" (2006:3–5). This complex approach reflects the biopsychosocial concept as discussed in Chapter 1. Family members' health, therefore, is not only impacted by the biological (i.e., genetic predispositions, family histories) noted in Chapter 2, but also the psychological and sociological contexts (i.e., family and outside communities) in which they live. Consider recent findings regarding the impacts of social relationships on the addictive behavior of cigarette smoking.

Cigarette Smoking Is Addictive, But Stopping Can Be Contagious

Tobacco use is a major contributor to deaths from chronic diseases, such as CVD and cancers, on a global scale.[4] Within the United States, it is estimated that 20.8 percent (45.3 million) adults 18 years and older smoke cigarettes. (Rock et al. 2007:1157). According to Nora Volkow (2007:1), the majority of American adults

---

[4] The Global Youth Tobacco Survey (GYTS) suggests that the worldwide rate of deaths related to smoking will double (from 5 million to 10 million) by 2020. [Warren, Charles, Nathan R. Jones, Armando Peruga, James Chauvin, Jean-Pierre Baptiste, Vera Costa de Silva, Fatimah el Awa, Agis Tsouros, Khalil Rahman, Berke Fishburn, Douglas W. Bettcher, and Samira Asma. 2008. "Global Youth Tobacco Surveillance, 2000–2007." Morbidity and Mortality Weekly Report 57(SS01):1–21. Retrieved May 8, 2008. (www.cdc.gov/mmwr/preview/mmwrhtml/ss5701a1.htm)].

who smoke cigarettes want to quit, but they struggle to do so. While researchers (National Institute of Drug Abuse and Addiction 2008:1) "have identified a genetic variant that not only makes smokers more susceptible to nicotine addiction but also increases their risk of developing two smoking-related diseases, lung cancer and peripheral arterial disease . . . ," a family member's social experiences and surrounding environments are also crucial not only in if that individual will begin smoking, but how difficult it will be to quit the behavior. Nicholas Christakis and James Fowler (2008) examined the impact of relationships (e.g., family, friends, and coworkers) on smoking behavior for over 12,000 participants. According to their findings, a person is 67 percent less likely to smoke, if a spouse quits, 36 percent less likely, if a friend quits, 34 percent less likely to smoke, if a coworker stops smoking, and 25 percent less likely to light up, if a sibling quits smoking (2008:2249). The influence of these "social circles," however, was stronger for casual smokers than for heavy smokers (i.e., those with greater nicotine addiction). Therefore, while genetics significantly impacts nicotine addiction and intrapersonal factors (e.g., perceived threats, benefits, barriers, and readiness to quit) hone behavior patterns, the influence of interpersonal social dynamics of family and friends can help carve health behavior patterns. Along with the need for families to know and share their family health histories so as to identify potential genetic concerns (as discussed in Chapter 2), there is also a need to recognize that social networks remain crucial to family health and health behaviors, as discussed further in Chapter 4. Theories of health behavior, therefore, recognize that people's health behaviors are impacted by the social-cultural circumstances. For example, Mozhdeh Bruss and her colleagues' study of ethnicity and diet of 1,225 children in the Commonwealth of the Northern Mariana Islands revealed a strong correlation between ethnicity and food selection (2007).

While many theories focus on this interpersonal level, Social Cognitive Theory (SCT) is one of the most dynamic and is often used in health behavior studies. In addition to exploring the interactions of individuals and their environments, SCT also addresses psychosocial aspects of health behavior. According to SCT, three primary issues affect the potential for health behavior change: (1) self-efficacy, (2) goals, and (3) outcome expectations (National Cancer Institute 2005:xxvii). For example, a family health issue that demands multilevel approaches, with special attention to interpersonal impacts, is the escalating rates of youth overweight and obesity.

Case 3.3 Julio: Childhood Obesity—Beyond Family Concern

Julio's family did not think that their son's weight was a health concern. "Everyone in our family is big. Besides he is young so what is the problem with a few extra pounds?" his mother contended. That was three years ago, now at age eleven Julio was extremely overweight. His high blood pressure and elevated blood lipid level meant an increased risk of heart disease. "Your son also has type 2 diabetes," the clinician explained. "Julio is sick and needs immediate intervention or his health will get much worse. In order to improve his health, he needs to reduce his body weight." Julio's mother and father stared at each other and asked, "How can someone so young have such health issues? How on earth are we supposed to help him?"

Data from two National Health and Nutrition Examination Surveys (NHANES)[5] reveal alarmingly increasing overweight rates among youth. Based on comparisons between the two surveys, the increased rates for being overweight by age group from 1976 to 1980 to 2003 to 2004 were:

- two to five years of age from 5.0 percent to 13.9 percent;
- six to eleven years of age from 6.5 percent to 18.8 percent;
- twelve to nineteen years of age from 5.0 percent to 17.4 percent (Centers for Disease Control and Prevention 2008b:1).

Being overweight and obese are complex health concerns that involve biological, behavioral, social-cultural, environmental, and political influences. As with most epidemics, the causes are complex and not solely a matter of genetics. As overweight and obese are chronic health conditions, an overweight and obese youth requires biopsychosocial awareness and interpersonal interventions. Reversing this epidemic demands more than substituting apples for chips and unplugging the television. Intrapersonal behavior change is only one aspect of this puzzle. "If you don't have the healthy options and the policies being implemented around you, it's hard to execute a healthy behavior" (Friedrich 2007:2728). Health behaviors are significantly impacted by interpersonal and community factors. While increased rates of overweight and obese youth touch all socioeconomic and racial-ethnic groups, youth from lower-income families regardless of race and ethnicity experience a greater prevalence of overweight and obesity than those from higher-income families. Jihong Lie and his colleagues (2007) note that minority youth were more likely to be overweight than either urban or rural non-Hispanic whites and that, as family income declines, the rate of youth overweight increases. Notice in Table 3.1 that the highest rates of overweight youth occurred among Mexican American boys and non-Hispanic black girls at both younger (6 to 11 years) and older (12 to 19 years) ages. Since data show even higher rates of overweight and obesity among

---

[5] For more information on NHANES, see National Center for Health Statistics. 2008c. "Prevalence of Overweight among Children and Adolescents: United States, 2003–2004." Retrieved April 8, 2008. (www.cdc.gov/nchs/products/pubs/pubd/hestats/overweight/overwght_child_03.htm).

Table 3.1 Prevalence of Overweight Youth by Age, Sex, Race, and Ethnicity—2004

Race and Ethnicity	Ages 6–11 Years		Ages 12–Years	
	Boys (Percentage)	Girls (Percentage)	Boys (Percentage)	Girls (Percentage)
Non-Hispanic whites	16.9	15.6	17.9	14.6
Non-Hispanic blacks	17.2	24.8	17.7	23.8
Mexican American	25.6	16.6	20.0	17.1

Source: Compiled from the American Heart Association. 2008b. "Overweight in Children." Retrieved May 2, 2008. (www.americanheart.org/presenter.jhtml?identifier=4670).

adults, the medical community warns that the risk of overweight teens becoming overweight adults is 70 percent and that risk rises to 80 percent, if both of their parents are overweight (Surgeon General 2008:1).

Geographic trends in overweight and obese youth also emerge. Children and teens living in the rural South had the highest rate of overweight and obese youth at 33.1 percent compared to the Midwest at 30.2 percent, the Northeast at 29.5 percent, and the West at 28.1 percent (Lie et al. 2007:i–ii). The social-cultural environment in which overweight and obese youth live appears to have significant impact on this intrapersonal behavior. Consider that in 2008, 40 percent of children in Washington, DC and 39 percent of children in Kentucky were overweight compared to 22 percent in Colorado and 21 percent in Utah (Walsh 2008:74). Geography or location affects not only accessibility of recreational options (e.g., walking and bike trails), but social cultural circumstances (e.g., poverty) that limits the availability of affordable healthful food options, which appears to be a major factor in why the poor suffer higher rates of being overweight and obese. Amy Burdette and Terrence Hill (2008) also explain that there is a link between chronic neighborhood disorder (e.g., violence) and increased rates of obesity in the same location. Therefore, where families live and how the neighborhood environment impacts these families in terms of food choices, activity levels, and distress over neighborhood disorder, all need to be factored into addressing the overweight and obese youth epidemic. The perceptions by and support (or lack of support) from peers and adults regarding girls' physical activity enjoyment levels appear to play significant roles in the actual activity levels of female adolescents. Mira Grieser and her colleagues (2008) studied differences among 1,466 non-Hispanic African American, Hispanic, and white adolescent girls at 36 middle schools across the United States. The findings reveal that non-Hispanic African Americans and Hispanic girls perceived significantly lower physical activity enjoyment and received less support in being active than their white female peers and boys. These lowered perceptions and support contributed to reduced physical activity levels of these diverse young females. Issues of creating healthful neighborhoods, therefore, are part of the battle to alter the "obesogenic" (i.e., obesity supporting) environment in which supersized fast foods and inactivity must be fought on personal, familial, and community fronts (Walsh 2008:74).

While many concede that being overweight or obese are multifaceted conditions, researchers caution that genetics cannot be ignored (Wardle et al. 2008). The advances in genome-based research, as discussed in Chapter 2, promise effective strategies in identifying individuals with a genetic predisposition, such as those predisposed to overweight and obesity. For more immediate and long-term success, however, medical and social scientists also contend that interventions need to be multileveled, culturally sensitive, and community-based. These multileveled approaches are reflected in J. Jiang and his colleagues' study on family and school interventions for Chinese schoolchildren in Beijing (2007). The "intervention schools" in this study engaged children and their parents in nutrition education and physical activity programs that were not offered in the control schools. Findings from this three-year study revealed that the prevalence of overweight and obese youth were lower in the intervention schools as compared to their peers in the control schools, that is, overweight: 9.8 percent versus 14.4 percent, and obesity: 7.9 percent versus 13.3 percent (Jiang et al. 2007:641). Similar findings also emerged from a Canadian study in which students who participated in "school-based healthy eating" programs that included family input, exhibited lower rates of youth overweight and obesity (Veugelers and Fitzgerald 2005). It appears, therefore, that interventions that bring home and school environments together in addressing escalating rates of overweight and obese youth promise successful outcomes.

Applying an interpersonal, culturally sensitive approach to Julio and his family entails several criteria as pointed out by Leslie Kaufman and Adam Karpati (2007). Their research identified several implications for programs targeting low-income Latino families that can be applied to Julio's case. Since the family is in close contact with extended family and friends, it is vital to extend the program beyond Julio and his immediate family. The social influences (social networks, social support, and social norms) play a major role in determining Julio's and his families' practices regarding food selection and preparation plus physical activity. In addition to including these social influences, recognition of shared sociocultural values, norms, histories, and economic resources related to diet and exercise is also necessary. According to Kaufman and Karpati, "[f]amilies' resources and choices about how to use them are filtered through cultural notions of parental identity and well-being, as well as meanings of food and gratification that are deeply tied to histories of food insecurity, poverty, and personal experiences" (2007:2186). Julio's social network and social norms dramatically shape his health behavior. Understanding these perceptions, beliefs, attitudes, and social norms is fundamental to successful behavioral and medical intervention programs. As the health problems associated with being overweight or obese (e.g., type 2 diabetes, CVD, hypertension, and high blood lipid levels) continue to increase among younger patients, the medical community echo calls for a biopsychosocial response. Erinn Rhodes and David Ludwig note that "Childhood obesity has become a clear example of this new type of challenge, requiring that the full biopsychosocial context of a disease be considered in daily care of the patient" (2007:1695).

Julio and his social network of family, extended family, and friends need to explore their perceptions related to overweight and obesity in a nonthreatening environment. Along with understanding their perceptions, they will need accurate, culturally appropriate information on how to improve diet and exercise practices within their social network. While combining intrapersonal and interpersonal levels of intervention are vital to health behavior change or enhancement, often health issues require community level involvement. The following section introduces the concept of community-based approaches as applied to family health behaviors. Adding community to the intrapersonal and interpersonal aspects of intervention is critical to effective family health promotion and health behavior patterns.

Community-Based Approaches

Geography is often used to define communities, yet communities usually reflect other criteria. For example, communities can be defined by shared interests, such as schools, or a collective identity as found in Hmong immigrant communities. Understanding the community's social and cultural characteristics is crucial in community-based programs. Rather than theories, interventions at the community level employ conceptual frameworks that emphasize participatory models such as the community organizing model. This model is community-driven in assessing and solving health behavior concerns. While community-based approaches may focus on building consensus, problem solving, or enhancing community capacity to achieve change or solve health concerns, they all reflect six central concepts (National Cancer Institute 2005:xxxi):

- *empowerment*—process in which individuals gain mastery over lives and in their community
- *community capacity*—ability to identify, mobilize around, and address problems
- *participation*—engaging community members as capable equals
- *relevance*—community sets agenda, shares power, and understands available resources
- *issue selection*—identifying specific, realistic foci for change so as to build unity
- *critical consciousness*—recognition of social, political, and economic influences that impact the health problem

For example, effective interventions to reduce and prevent overweight and obese conditions in youth require community support and involvement. Julio's community needs to believe that they can master this health problem (i.e., empowerment), which includes their willingness to recognize that this is a serious health issue requiring the full mobilization and engagement of the community (e.g., parents, youth, schools, restaurants, grocery stores, park and recreation services, businesses, and local and state governments). Such community-based programs often begin with seeing the relevance of how addressing this health concern will aid the community followed by identifying a realistic focus, such as organizing a "switch-off the TV and let's get active" after-school youth programs. Fundamental to this community-based approach is attitude and recognition that this health issue requires personal, social, economic, and political involvement. Blaming parents or schools, however, misses the fact that the important point for solving health concerns is active community participation.

The primary purpose of community-based approaches, therefore, is to engage community members so as to enhance their power and to encourage the development of their capacities to take control of their lives. Community-based models are to be driven by the community's self-interest that they are working to reduce and prevent overweight and obese youth for the good of their community and to improve their personal lives. Changing family members' health behaviors, therefore, demands changing the social environment and pursuing community-based approaches. International public health experts working to reduce rates of type 2 diabetes in developed nations (Garcia 2004) or malnutrition in Africa (Chaiken, Deconinck, and Degefie 2006) purport community-based programs that engage individuals, families, schools, businesses, and government services enjoy greater success than programs that fail to engage the community.

Youth overweight and obesity are global issues that threaten a serious future public health crisis for communities. It is evident that individual behavioral change is only one aspect of this multifaceted health problem. While the family and social networks remain crucial players in health behaviors, it is increasingly apparent that truly effective interventions and prevention programs must include the larger community beyond the family. In the case of overweight and obese youth, foods provided by schools play a significant role not only in the actual nutrition, but in teaching youth about wise diet choices. Contrary to popular belief that "[youth] overweight comes mainly from nonschool sources," Paul von Hippel and his colleagues (2007:702) argue that schools need to serve as models for healthful eating behaviors. Kimberley Procter and her colleagues (2008) concur that schools play an important role, yet vary in how effectively they address overweight and obese youth health issues. Junk foods (i.e., overly processed, high calorie, low nutrient) cannot be part of a nutritionally sound school meal program. When schools are forced to offer such fast-food options due to financial restraints or other issues, the community at local, state, and federal levels need to recognize their responsibility, and offer genuine and substantial support for improved school menus (i.e., breakfast, lunch, snacks). The communities beyond the family and school, therefore, need to participate in programs to curb and prevent this debilitating health condition of overweight and obese youth. Three examples of community-based programs that appear to be making positive impacts on reducing the prevalence of overweight and obese youth are the Australian "Be Active, Eat Well," and the American "Shape Up Somerville," and "CHANGE" programs.

"Be Active, Eat Well" is a three-year community-based program started in Victoria, Australia, which focused on reducing overweight and obesity among children aged 6 to 12 years of age (McConnell 2002). The aim of this program was to increase capacity within the communities to do the interventions themselves. The results offered support to community-based intervention on this health issue. Findings from another community-based project, "Shape Up Somerville: Eat Smart, Play Hard," also support the use of community-based programs to reduce and prevent overweight and obesity in youth (Economos et al. 2007). This three-year intervention targeted third and fourth graders in a culturally diverse suburban community. The success of this program appears to be its highly collaborative structure teaming community partners, university researchers, families, and schools all working toward building a health-focused environment for children. They incorporated culturally acceptable, manageable, and affordable changes in nutrition and activity behaviors throughout the entire day. For example, the program encouraged:

- school food service to offer healthier meals and promote wise food choices
- after-school programs aimed at cooperative games, field trips, creative cooking, and yoga
- adding in-class curriculum on nutrition and physical activity (e.g., "cool moves") with an emphasis on creativity and fun in learning
- encouraging restaurants to offer healthier menu selections
- working with community services in making their areas more walking friendly
- engaging families in fun, physical, noncompetitive activities.

A third example of a successful community-based program is CHANGE (Creating Healthy, Active, and Nurturing Growing-up Environments) developed and funded by Save the Children (2008). CHANGE adapted the urban-based "Shape Up Somerville" program for use in rural areas. As noted earlier, children from rural, low-income families report some of the highest rates of overweight and obese youth. This three-year program began in the 2007 to 2008 academic year with four sites in Appalachia, Kentucky, the Mississippi Delta, and California's Central Valley with a focus on 6 to 12 year olds. CHANGE is unique for it is one of the few programs aimed at rural American populations who often have less access to parks and recreational facilities.

These three multileveled approaches bring stakeholders from the larger community into the process of enhancing or reducing specific health behaviors. Consider applying a community-based approach to Case 3.3. In this case, the community-based intervention would include working with Julio and his family's social network in learning healthful food selection and preparation along with increasing physical activity. These efforts would be extended by engaging and funding schools to pursue culturally acceptable and affordable strategies for healthier meals and expanding physical activity opportunities for children and their families. The larger community, however, would also become active participants. Thus, restaurants, grocery and convenience stores, and local and state governments would focus on offering products and services that enhance youth behaviors. At the heart of community-based programs is a core value and belief that having healthier youth makes social, ethical, and financial sense for the community. Whether it is lobbying for more after-school activities for youth from low-income families, working with social services to ensure reliable funds for food, offering free community classes on healthy behaviors (e.g., stress management, balancing a budget, healthwise shopping and cooking, learning to be more physically active), or securing safer neighborhoods so families engage in more physical activities, community-based programs are driven by and for the community.

Conclusion

Health behaviors are multifaceted and impacted at several levels. Understanding what drives family members to or not to engage in specific health behaviors requires recognizing what factors impact their behaviors. Using explanatory health behavior theories, such as the HBM, the TPB, and the SCT, along with sociological theories, such as the family systems theory, allow scholars and practitioners to better understand reasons why a problematic health behavior exists. As seen in the cases relating to the complexities of health issues, such as non-vaccination, CVD, and overweight/obese youth, family members' beliefs, attitudes, and perceptions are crucial to their actions and inactions. Effective interventions that enhance healthful behaviors and prevent or reduce the risk of unhealthy behaviors demand inclusion of family members, their social networks, plus the larger community. Community-based programs, such as the Active, Eat Well, Shape Up Somerville, and CHANGE appear to work better than isolated individual or single family interventions in terms of health behaviors, yet such collaborative interventions cannot, by themselves, reverse or prevent youth overweight and obesity. The dynamic nature of family health demands that all five interactive influences (i.e., biology, behavior patterns, social-cultural circumstances, environmental exposures, and policy and services) are recognized and incorporated into defining, enhancing, and maintaining health in families. The following chapter looks at the compelling influence of social circumstances on family health.

Critical Thinking Questions

1. In Case 3.1, outline two strategies you would use to organize a community-based program for educating parents and guardians about the need for and safety of vaccinations such as MMR. What is your rationale for using these?

2. If Simone (Case 3.2) was your mother, summarize your explanation of how her beliefs and attitudes impact her "behavioral intention" and why this is important to her health.

3. Explain how the six central concepts of community-based approaches could be applied to Julio, his social network, and the community (Case 3.3).

4

SOCIAL DETERMINANTS AND FAMILY HEALTH

Health Disparities among Families

Case 4.1 The Injustice of Health Inequities

Ted worked hard to reach his current position of a chief executive officer (CEO) at a major American insurance company. At age 59, he takes pride in his success as well as in his health and that of his family. Ten years earlier he and his wife, Terry, quit smoking with the support of their medical plan. They and their three children strive to maintain healthful diet and exercise behaviors. They live in a lovely, quiet neighborhood with ample biking and walking trails surrounded by a safe and beautiful environment. As college graduates, Ted and Terry are keen that their children attend the best schools and experience a life rich in travel, activities, and health care.

Juanita works as a claims adjustor for the same company where Ted works. She is 37 years old and recently completed her college degree while working full time. She and her partner, Glenda, purchased a house last year, so college debt and mortgage payments are major concerns for Juanita. She enjoys her job and considers herself to be middle class. Her position demands significant responsibility, but she struggles with pressure from her division boss, whose management style is harsh and often disrespectful of Glenda's sex and sexual orientation. Yet, with the job market so tight, Juanita does not want to cause any trouble. She is finally making a decent salary, has health care coverage, and can live away from the Latino projects she grew up in.

Jonathan works as a custodian for this insurance company. At the age 45, he is glad to have a job, but frustrated that his family cannot seem to get ahead. He and his wife, Tiffany, finished high school, but are unprepared for a job market that demands higher skills. Jonathan has a heart condition and Tiffany suffers from type 2 diabetes. They cannot afford the increasing out-of-pocket costs of regular health exams or dental coverage. Their African American neighborhood is plagued with violence and underfunded schools. They and their two sons (aged 12 and 10 years, respectively) are overweight.

Morning Dew, 51 years of age, is unemployed and is living in an American Indian reservation 50 miles from the urban area where Ted, Juanita, and Jonathan live. Her husband is physically disabled and has been out of work for the past 15 years. They live below the poverty line in a crowded two-bedroom apartment in an impoverished rural area with their three teenage children. Morning Dew suffers from depression and both she and her husband have type 2 diabetes. Their children are overweight, smoke, and two of them have dropped out of high school.

Case 4.1 illustrates some of the health disparities found within the American culture. As discussed in Chapter 1, health disparities are disproportionate burdens on or risks of disease, illness, disability, or death found among specific segments of the population. Health disparities fall under the social determinants of health that include features of and channels by which families' social-cultural circumstances impact health and well-being. Social determinants often include income, social status, occupation, housing, geographic location, education, social support, community structure, availability of health services, cultural beliefs and attitudes, discrimination, prejudice, and inequality. If you had to guess from the brief descriptions in Case 4.1 which of these four individuals (Ted, Juanita, Jonathan, and Morning Dew) has the best and worst health circumstances, who would you pick? If you identified Ted and Morning Dew respectfully, you are correct. Would you also say that Juanita and Jonathan enjoy the same level of health opportunity as Ted? If you said yes, you would be incorrect. While Juanita and Jonathan may be healthier than Morning Dew, neither enjoys the full level of health or longevity as that of Ted. Why? Statistically, based on Ted's race and ethnicity (non-Hispanic white), socioeconomic status (SES), education, housing, and geographic location, he will not only live approximately five years or more longer than Morning Dew, but also will have a longer life span than either Juanita and Jonathan. From 1980 to 1982, the life expectancy for the most affluent Americans was 2.8 years longer than that of the most deprived, but by 1990 to 2000 this gap increased to 4.5 years and continues to increase (Singh and Siahpush 2006:975). Consider that, in 2000, the difference in life expectancy between poor black men and wealthy white women was 14 years (2006:975). The quantity and quality of these additional years are important measures of family and population health.

While overall health and life expectancy continues to improve for many Americans, a disturbing number of Americans are not benefiting equally. African Americans, Latinos, American Indians and Alaskan Natives, and Native Hawaiian and other Pacific Islanders suffer greater prevalence of illness and experience higher death rates than the remainder of the U.S. population. Minorities and others living in poverty, therefore, have earlier mortality rates, are in poorer health, often are uninsured, and experience more difficulties accessing quality, effective health care (Mead et al. 2008). According to Sarah Gehlert and colleagues:

> Health disparities occur by race, ethnicity, sex, socioeconomic status, education, geographic location, and sexual orientation, with inequalities in screening, incidence, treatment, and mortality across a number of diseases and conditions, including cancer, diabetes, cardiovascular disease, infant mortality, and HIV/AIDS. (2008:339)

The link between wealth and health has long been recognized as a cause of health disparities in the United States as revealed in Case 4.1. As the SES gap widens, health disparities increase. Even when data are adjusted for income, education, and health care coverage, however, health disparities continue to persist and even increase (Mead et al. 2008). What is less understood, therefore, is the interactive nature of social determinants resulting in health disparities. David Mechanic and Jennifer Tanner (2007) argue that vulnerability to health disparities result from a "social stress process," during which stressors, such as financial downturns, illness, and discrimination, are balanced against resources, such as income and wealth, education, cognitive ability, social networking, and community resources. These authors emphasize that the primary sources of vulnerability are poverty, race, and the "related issues of stigma and discrimination" (2007:1223).

For example, consider the factor of geographic location in Case 4.1. Ted's family lives in a safer neighborhood that provides more healthful opportunities (e.g., recreation and more healthful food options) as compared to Jonathan's or Morning Dew's families. According to scholars (Acevedo-Garcia et al. 2008), even with policy initiatives to reduce poverty and enhance access to medical care, health disparities continue to plague segments of the population along racial and ethnic lines. What is new is their identification of "residential segregation" between minority and white populations as a major determinant of health disparity. They further argue that the SES and affordable housing issues alone do not account for the continued high levels of segregation and note that residential segregation plays a major role. A documentary, *Unnatural Causes: Is Inequality Making Us Sick?"* (California Newsreel and National Minority Consortia of Public Television, 2008) supports a position that discrimination and residential segregation interlinked with issues of poverty, poor education, limited health care access, and lower quality of health services is creating a complex challenge to improving the health of American families. While genetics (Chapter 2), health behaviors (Chapter 3), environmental exposures (Chapter 5), and health care policy and services (Chapter 6) remain crucial influences on family health, social determinants take center stage in understanding and addressing health disparities among families. Scholars urge professionals in medical, social, and related sciences to focus on the impact of this reality (Sankar et al. 2004).

Delores Acevedo-Garcia and her colleagues (2008) report that opportunities for better health are tied to geographical location with disadvantaged neighborhoods struggling with barriers of geography (i.e., limited transportation, poor housing, unemployment, unsafe neighborhoods, limited recreation, and unhealthy food options). Linked to these geographic location issues is the impact of education. Ellen Meara, Seth Richards, and David Cutler (2008) explain that the majority of gains in life expectancy made during the 1981 to 2000 period occurred primarily among highly educated groups with any college education thus exposing an educational gap in life expectancy. From 1990 to 2000, life expectancy increased 1.6 years for the highly educated group, but did not change for the less-educated group. Thus, in 2000, a 25-year-old with some college education had a life expectancy almost seven years longer than a peer with a high school diploma or less education (2008:353). Hence, being educationally disadvantaged, such as Morning Dew's children in Case 4.1, raises the risk of poorer health and earlier death rates. While recognizing education as a powerful factor in health status, however, Rachel Tolbert Kimbro and her colleagues (2008) note that the education gradient appears to vary in its impact with some racial, ethnic, and nativity groups, with foreign-born immigrants enjoying better health and mortality rates than their American-born peers even at lower education levels. There are several rationales for this paradox found within certain racial and ethnic groups. The main point, however, is that in order to better understand and address health disparities, researchers and practitioners need to recognize the important impact of education in conjunction with culture on family health.

Such an eclectic approach is represented by longitudinal studies that provide a solid basis for the vital role of social determinants and their impact on health disparities. One of the premiere studies is the Whitehall I Study that began in 1967 examining the social circumstances of 18,000 British Civil Service men and how these determinants impacted their well-being and health. This initial study was followed by nine waves of data with the latest one occurring in 2007. Whitehall II includes a cohort of over 10,000 women and men employees of the British Civil Service. While this rich study provides extensive data on the important influence of the "social gradient" on health, it also dispelled two myths. The first is that those with the highest status positions have the highest risk of heart disease. In fact, those individuals in jobs with high demand and little control (e.g., office managers, custodians) have a much higher risk of heart disease, as noted with Jonathan in Case 4.1. The second myth is the belief that in developed, industrialized societies, health "is simply a matter of poor health for the disadvantaged and good health for everyone else" (Turnbull and Serwotka 2008:4). The Whitehall and other studies emphasize that health disparities are not solely a matter of poverty, but rather a complex web of social determinants. The social circumstances at home, in the community, and at work (discussed in Chapter 5) all significantly influence family health in general and health disparities in particular.

Healthy People 2010, a nationwide, comprehensive health promotion and disease prevention agenda of the Department of Health and Human Services, serves as a framework for improving the health of the American people. The two primary goals include: (1) an increase in quality and number of years of healthy life, and (2) the elimination of health disparities (U.S. Department of Health and Human Services 2008b). Consistent evidence reveals that "race and ethnicity correlate with persistent and often increasing, health disparities among U.S. populations . . . " and minorities suffer higher rates of mortality and prevalence of most illnesses and diseases (Office of Minority Health and Health Disparities 2007b:1). In 2005, minorities composed over one-third of the U.S. population with Hispanics making up the largest segment of minorities. By 2050, it is estimated that minority groups will make up almost 50 percent of the population as revealed in Table 4.1.

Anticipated demographic shifts during the next few decades raise both ethical and practical concerns over these health disparities. In light of these concerns, six areas have been targeted by *Healthy People 2010*. The following provides a glimpse at the scope of health disparities in these areas.

Infant Mortality

Infant mortality is defined as the proportion of babies who die before they reach their first birthday, and it is often used to compare the health and well-being status across and within countries. In 2008, the United States ranked only 27th among 30 developed nations at 6.9 deaths in 1,000 live births, while the average was only 5.2. Within the nations of the European Union the rate is less than five in 1,000 babies, and in Japan, Singapore, Sweden, and Norway the proportion of babies who die is less than half that of the United States (Organization for Economic Co-Operation and Development 2008:2). When viewed through a minority health

Table 4.1 Projected Change in the Racial and Ethnic Composition Percentages of the United States Population, 2000–2050

Racial and Ethnic Group	2000 Percentage of the Population*	2050 Percentage of the Population*
White, non-Hispanic	69	50
African American	13	15
Hispanic	13	24
Asian	3.8	8.0
Other—includes American Indian and Alaska Native, Native Hawaiian/other Pacific islanders, and two or more races	2.5	5.3

Note: Numbers add up to more than 100 percent due to rounding, and some categories are not mutually exclusive.

Source: Adapted from the U.S. Census Bureau. 2004. "U.S. Interim Projections by Age, Sex, Race and Hispanic Origin." Retrieved May 20, 2008. (www.census.gov/population/www/projections/usinterimproj/natprojtab01a.pdf).

lens, the rate of infant mortality more than doubles (13.7) for non-Hispanic African American families. The mission of the Office of Minority Health and Health Disparities (2007b:1) is to "improve and protect the health of racial and ethnic minority populations through the development of health policies and programs that will eliminate health disparities." Table 4.2 reveals stark disparities in infant mortality on racial and ethnic levels.

This wide variation in infant mortality rates by race and Hispanic origin continues with the highest rate (13.7) for infants of non-Hispanic African American mothers, more than three times higher than the lowest rate of 4.3 for infants of Cuban mothers. Rates of infant mortality for infants of American Indian (8.6) and Puerto Rican (8.1) mothers were also significantly higher than the national rating (National Center for Health Statistics 2007:177). The causes of this higher prevalence of infant mortality remains unclear, but looking at any of a wide variety of risk factors related to infant mortality reveals that non-Hispanic African American, American Indian, and Puerto Rican mothers did not receive adequate prenatal care, often were unmarried or were teenagers, were having a fourth or higher order birth, or had not completed high school. Again, there appears to be a complex web of social determinants such as SES, geographic location, and education level intertwined with poverty (Acevedo-Garcia, Soobader, and Berkman 2005).

Table 4.2 United States Infant Mortality Rates by Race and Ethnicity, 2002–2004

Race and Ethnicity	Infant Mortality Infant Deaths per 1,000 Live Births
All mothers	6.9
Asian or Pacific Islander	4.8
Hispanic or Latino	5.6
Puerto Rican	8.1
Mexican	5.5
Cuban	4.3
Non-Hispanic or Latino white	5.7
American Indian or Alaskan Native	8.6
African American or black	13.5
Non-Hispanic or Latino African American	13.7

Source: Adapted from the National Center for Health Statistics. 2007. "Health, United States, 2007 with Chartbook on Trends in the Health of Americans." Table 19, p. 2. Retrieved February 27, 2008. Hyattsville, MD. (www.cdc.gov/nchs/data/hus/hus07.pdf).

Cardiovascular Disease

Cardiovascular disease (CVD) (i.e., heart disease and stroke) is the leading cause of death in Americans across all racial and ethnic groups and for both sexes. Yet, low-income and minority segments have a disproportional higher level of death and disability rates due to CVD, with African Americans developing high blood pressure earlier and at the highest rate of all groups (Office of Minority Health and Health Disparities 2007c). Black men and women have the highest rates of cardiovascular disease mortality among all races and ethnic groups (see Table 4.3).

The burden of disease borne by minority groups is considerable, "with the greatest evidence of a disproportionate disease burden and disproportionate distribution of risk factors [endured] by African American population (Yancy 2008:276). Medical professionals increasingly recognize that while biological factors are important in this imbalance, "psychosocial and socioeconomic factors" also must be considered and addressed in CVD treatment and preventive care practices (Yancy 2008:283). For example, as the rates of obesity among non-Hispanic African Americans and Hispanic adults climb, so does the prevalence of CVD within these populations.

Table 4.3 Cardiovascular Mortality Rates by Race and Ethnicity, 2003

Race and Ethnicity	Heart Disease Deaths per 100,000 Resident Population	
	Male	Female
Total	287	190
Non-Hispanic white	287	187
Non-Hispanic black	364	254
Hispanic	207	146
American Indian and Alaska Native	203	128
Asian/Pacific Islander	158	104

Source: Adapted with permission from the Commonwealth Fund. Mead, Holly, Lara Cartwright-Smith, Karen Jones, Christal Ramos, Kristy Woods, and Bruce Siegel. 2008. *Racial and Ethnic Disparities in U.S. Health Care: A Chartbook.* Chart 3–11. NY: The Commonwealth Fund.

Diabetes

The Centers for Disease Control and Prevention (2009:1) state that 23.6 million Americans have diabetes. The prevalence rates of diagnosed diabetes, however, show disparities in terms of age, sex, race, and ethnicity with African Americans or blacks, Hispanics or Latinos, American Indian, and Alaska Native adults diagnosed at twice the rate than non-Hispanic whites. From 1980 to 2006, the rate doubled for black men and increased by 69 percent for black women, the highest rate of all racial groups. (Centers for Disease Control and Prevention 2008c:1). The rate of prevalence of diabetes per 100 persons, when measured by age, sex, race, and ethnicity, revealed significant disparities with aged 65- to 75+-year-old black females and 65- to 74-year-old Asian and Pacific Islander males with the highest prevalence rates (see Figure 4.1).

Cancers

In addition, racial and ethnic disparities exist for many cancers (e.g., breast, cervical, colorectal, and prostate) that are amenable to early diagnosis and treatment. Non-Hispanic white women continue to have a higher incidence of breast cancer than minorities, yet non-Hispanic black women have much higher rates of breast cancer mortality. Hispanic women have twice the risk of having cervical cancer than whites, but black women are twice as likely to die from this disease. While poverty and limited access to health care are significant factors in these health disparities, it is vital to note that while black women were just as likely to have had a mammogram as white women; the follow-up communication and treatment regarding their screening results were not as adequate as that provided to white women. Hence,

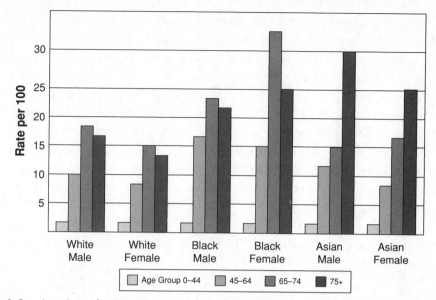

Figure 4.1 Age-Specific Prevalence of Adults Diagnosed with Diabetes by Race and Sex, United States, 2006

Source: Adapted from the Centers for Disease Control and Prevention. 2008c. "Age-Specific Percentage of Civilian, Noninstitutionalized Population with Diagnosed Diabetes, by Race and Sex, United States, 2006." Retrieved July 11, 2009. (www.cdc.gov/diabetes/statistics/prev/national/fig2004.htm).

when considering health disparities, the probe needs to flesh out the complex interactions of social determinants. Similar statistics are found for males in that black men are 50 percent more likely to have prostate cancer than whites, but are twice as likely to die from it (Mead et al. 2008:37–38). Overall, African Americans of both sexes suffer more malignant tumors and have a lower survivor rate than the general population (American Cancer Society 2003). Both Hispanic women and men have higher rates of infection-related cancers such as liver (related to Hepatitis C infections) and cervical (related to human papilloma virus [HPV] infection) than other racial and ethnic groups. American Indians and Alaskan Natives were more than twice as likely to be diagnosed with stomach and liver cancers than non-Hispanic whites (Office of Minority Health and Health Disparities 2008:1).

HIV Infection and AIDS

Chapter 5 discusses the influences of environmental exposures including that of infectious diseases. Human immunodeficiency virus/acquired immunodeficiency syndrome (HIV/AIDS) is noted here to illustrate the dramatic health disparity found within this disease. In 2006, African Americans and Hispanics represented only 27 percent (12 percent and 15 percent, respectively) of the U.S. population, yet they accounted for 68 percent of the HIV/AIDS diagnoses and face more barriers in accessing health care (Kaiser Family Foundation 2008a). The disparity grows even more troublesome when the demographic of sex is considered. While African American men represent 43 percent of all new AIDS diagnoses compared to whites (35 percent) and Hispanics (20 percent), African American women suffered 66 percent compared to whites (17 percent) and Hispanics (16 percent) (Kaiser Family Foundation 2008a:1). African Americans, therefore, are disproportionately affected at all stages of the HIV/AIDS epidemic as compared to other races and ethnicities. The disparity of the epidemic continues to grow with African Americans having the highest rates of those living with AIDS- and HIV-related deaths than any other racial and ethnic group in the United States (Centers for Disease Control and Prevention 2008d). The global impacts of HIV/AIDS are discussed in Chapter 5.

Immunizations

In Chapter 3 the issue of neglecting childhood vaccinations was raised as an introduction to the influence of health behavior patterns in family health. While refusing immunizations cuts cross SES lines, troubling race and ethnic disparities exist that are linked to social determinants over family behavior patterns. Racial and ethnic disparities in completion of vaccinations persist with non-Hispanic African American and Hispanics children significantly undervaccinated as compared to non-Hispanic white children (Smith and Stevenson 2008). A similar trend is found among adults. Michael Link and colleagues (2006) reported that influenza and pneumococcal vaccination coverage (completion) disparities by race and ethnicity persisted for non-Hispanic black and Hispanic adults aged 65 years and older during the period from 2000 to 2005. Vaccination disparities also exist for those less than 65 years old as revealed in Table 4.4.

In addition to these six diseases and conditions, other serious health concerns, such as mental illness, also reveal disparities based on race, ethnicity, gender, age, income, marital status, education, and the very nature of the illness itself.

Mental Illness

In the United States alone, mental illnesses are the second leading cause of disability with mental disorders affecting one in four Americans aged 15 to 44 (National Institute of Mental Health 2008:1). According to the Surgeon General, mental illness reflects a group of diagnosable disorders ranging from "alterations in thinking, mood, or behavior (or combination thereof) associated with distress and/or impaired

Table 4.4 Influenza and Pneumococcal Vaccinations among U.S. Adults, 2007

Vaccination	Population Group	Vaccination Coverage (Percentage completed)
Influenza, 2006–2007 season	*18–49 years of age*	
	High risk*	37.3
	Blacks	30.5
	Hispanics	25.6
	Whites	40.9
	50–64 years of age	
	All	42.2
	Blacks	37.2
	Hispanics	36.1
	Whites	43.1
	65+ years of age	
	All	68.8
	Blacks	54.6
	Hispanics	67.2
	Whites	69.4
Pneumococcal, 2006–2007 season	*18–64 years of age*	
	High risk*	32.8
	Blacks	26.6
	Hispanics	18.8
	Whites	34.0
	65+ years of age	
	All	65.6
	Blacks	52.5
	Hispanics	51.3
	Whites	67.8

*Adults are considered high risk if they had asthma, diabetes, or other lung disease, heart disease, a weakened immune system, kidney disease, sickle cell anemia, or other anemia (Link, Michael W., Indu B. Ahluwalia, Mary L. Euler, Carolyn B. Bridges, Susan Y. Chu, and Pascale M. Wortley. 2006. "Racial and Ethnic Disparities in Influenza Vaccination Coverage among Adults during the 2004–2005 Season." *American Journal of Epidemiology* 163(6):571–578).

Source: Adapted from the Centers for Disease Control and Prevention. 2008e. "Vaccination Coverage among U.S. Adults." National Immunization Survey—Adult, 2007. Retrieved May 15, 2008. (www.cdc.gov/vaccines/stats-surv/nis/downloads/nis-adult-summer-2007.pdf).

functioning" (U.S. Department of Health and Human Services 1999:vii). In Chapter 2, Alzheimer's disease was presented as a mental disorder marked by impaired thinking, in other words, lost memory. Depression represents alternation in mood, while attention-deficit disorder is an example of altered behavior (e.g., inability to concentrate). Impairments in thinking, mood, or behavior contribute to a range of health problems including increased risk of death, disability, pain, distress, impaired functioning, or reduced freedom (American Psychiatric Association 1994).

According to Stephanie Riolo and colleagues (2005), non-Hispanic whites had the highest prevalence of depression (which is clinically termed *major depressive disorder*) as compared to African Americans and Mexican Americans, but minorities who suffered depression were less likely to receive medical care, which may contribute to their higher rates of "lingering depression," "dysthyma disorder."[1] This difference was partially explained by poverty and lower education; however, not speaking English may also play a key role. Violent neighborhoods, such as Jonathan's in Case 4.1, has a direct (e.g., victims of violence) and indirect (e.g., fear and perceptions of neighbor as disordered) connection to distress and depression of their residents (Curry, Latkin, and Davey-Rothwell 2008).

Gender reveals significant disparity in mental illness. While the overall rates of psychiatric disorders are somewhat similar for men and women, there are striking differences in the patterns of mental illness with women experiencing depression twice than that of men. On a global scale, depression is the most common mental health problem for women, and it remains more persistent in females than males. It is estimated that 20 percent of women seeking primary health care in developed countries suffer from anxiety and/or depressive disorders. According to the World Health Organization (2008a:2):

> Pressures created by [women's] multiple roles, gender discrimination and associated factors of poverty, hunger, malnutrition, overwork, domestic violence and sexual abuse, combine to account for women's poor mental health. There is a positive relationship between the frequency and severity of such social factors and the frequency and severity of mental health problems in women.

While the diagnostic criteria for depression are similar for both sexes, women with depression more frequently experience higher levels of anxiety and guilt, along with increased appetite and sleep, weight gain, and eating disorders (Bhatia and

---

[1] Dysthymic disorder is a type of mild or moderate depression that lasts at least two years causing difficulty in functioning at home, school, or work. This "lingering depression" includes symptoms of over or undereating, difficulty in sleeping or over sleeping, low energy, frequent fatigue, and feelings of hopelessness [(American Academy of Family Physicians. 2008. "Dysthymic Disorder: When Depression Lingers." Retrieved May 3, 2008. http://familydoctor.org/online/famdocen/home/common/mentalhealth/depression/054.html)].

Bhatia 1999). According to Phyllis Moen and Kelly Chermack, gender and health are both biological, yet are dependent on social determinants, for while women tend to live longer than men, females often endure poorer health, greater stress, and more disabilities (2005). Gender imposes critical influence on mental health and mental illness since gender is related to power and control over the social determinants of individuals' lives including social status, treatment, and exposure to specific mental risks. Gender risk factors for common mental disorders include lower SES, gender-based violence, genetic (family health history), and persistent psychosocial stressors (e.g., loss of job, discrimination) (Bhatia and Bhatia 1999).

Many women, some time during their lives, develop depression at a rate almost twice that of men. According to Mayo Clinic's researchers "[a] woman's unique biological, psychological, and cultural factors may increase her risk of depression" (2008a:1). In addition to hormonal shifts and physical changes, social and cultural determinants play a role in female depression. The stressors of balancing work and family responsibilities along with increased rates of female sexual abuse and domestic violence increase the depression gender gap. American women, as with most women globally, often earn less than men and enjoy lower SES. Stressors include, but are not limited to, an uncertainty about the future, community support, economic down-turns, and limited access to health care that all increase women's vulnerability. Single, divorced, or widowed women living alone in rural areas also report greater instances of depression than their married peers, which may be due to isolation, lower SES, and general fears about the future (Mayo Clinic 2008b). Some minority women also face the additional stressor of discrimination. When depression prevalence for women is examined by race and ethnicity, Hispanic-Latina women have the highest lifetime rate of depression (24 percent) among women. While the rate of depression among women for non-Hispanic white women (22 percent) is higher than that for non-Hispanic African American women (16 percent), almost half (47 percent) of non-Hispanic African American women suffer with severe depression. Finally, 14 percent of American Indians and Alaskan Native female adolescents report feeling extremely sad and hopeless (Women's Health 2003). In Case 4.1, Morning Dew's depression may have a genetic component, but when combined with SES, educational and geographic location disparities a risk of mental illness significantly increases among her children.

While race, ethnicity, age, and gender offer greater insight to the health disparities surrounding mental illness, the concept of "healthy immigrant effect" raises a core issue of social relationships. Healthy immigrant effect occurs when foreign-born populations enjoy better mental and physical health than their native-born peers as revealed in the literature (Kennedy, McDonald, and Biddle 2006; Lincoln et al. 2007). This advantage erodes after 10 years of living in their adopted country, which focuses attention on the potential harm of discrimination, prejudice, and isolation. Karen Lincoln and her colleagues (2007) report that SES alone did not account for the variation between Caribbean-born blacks living in the United States for 10 or fewer years who had lower levels of depression, when compared with U.S.-born blacks and Caribbean-born blacks living in America for more than 10 years. The factor of nativity is linked to social networking and relationships within families as well as within the larger community. Perceived discrimination may be "one of the most endemic and enduring stressors facing minority groups in the US [United States]" (Lincoln et al. 2007:202). The issue of the negative impact of perceived discrimination also is documented in international studies in which black participants reported much higher levels of psychological distress and depressive symptoms than whites even after adjustments were made for SES (Williams et al. 2008).

Discrimination, Stigmatization, and Health

Overt and recently more covert forms of discrimination and prejudice, therefore, remain factors in health disparities (Institute of Medicine 2003). Discrimination tends to focus on disparities related to race, ethnicity, gender, age, and social class as discussed earlier (Phelan, Link, and Dovidio 2008). Yet, stigmatization of health conditions, such as mental illness and HIV/AIDS (covered in Chapter 5), also marginalizes individuals and their families; thus negatively impacting prevention and treatment efforts (U.S. Department of Health and Human Services 2003; Stuber, Meyer, and Link 2008). Stigma labels a person as different from his or her peers and leads to a devaluation of the individual. In Erving Goffman's classic work, stigma is defined as "an attribute that links a person to an undesirable stereotype, leading other people to reduce the bearer from a whole and usual person to a tainted, discounted one" (1963:3). Building on Goffman's efforts, Bruce Link and Jo Phelan (2001) identified five specific aspects of stigmatization that help hone the concept to better understand its presence with medical conditions such as mental illness and HIV/AIDS. Stigmatizing a person due to an illness means:

- labeling the medical difference as less important as other more acceptable conditions, such as cancer or diabetes;
- linking those afflicted with the undesirable illness to negative stereotypes;
- separating "them" from "us";
- perpetuating a loss of status for those with this trait (illness) through discrimination (employment, health insurance coverage, etc.);
- societal elements (social, economic, and political) that allow this stigma and prejudice to exist and continue.

One who suffers stigmatization not only suffers from the "[n]egative social attitudes [stereotypes] and even enacted discrimination [prejudice]," but often engages in "self-discrimination, concealment, withdrawal and other forms of stigma management" due to the overriding societal stigma (Burris 2008:474). The issue of mental illness stigma remains a serious personal, familial, and population health concern with families playing a crucial role in providing support to members with mental illnesses or disorders. Scholars currently are reaching across disciplines and various levels of society to better understand the causes of stigmatization, prejudice, and discrimination arguing "that stigma is defined in and enacted through social interaction . . . [that] takes place in a context where organizations and institutions structure norms that create the possibility of marking [labeling] and sharing notions of 'difference'" (Pescosolido et al. 2008:432).

While the battle for parity between mental and physical health continues at local, state, national, and international levels, families remain at the forefront. Consistent and positive family support in the face of persistent stigmatization provides vital elements in both mental health promotion and particularly mental illness treatment and recovery.

Family Relationships and Mental Health

Mental health and mental illness are points on a continuum. Mental health is mental functioning that results in the ability to cope with stressors and to adapt to change, engage in productive activities (e.g., work), and have fulfilling interpersonal relationships. "Mental health is indispensable to personal well-being, family, and interpersonal relationships, and contribution to community or society" (U.S. Department of Health and Human Services 1999:8). While the importance of mental health is often voiced, mental illnesses continue to receive inadequate respect and understanding, medical treatment, and even acceptance as a serious medical condition. The vital merging of the biological, psychological, and social aspects of human health is recognized in the biopsychosocial approach discussed in Chapter 1. Unfortunately, in the United States, with its long history of separating physical and mental health, the delivery of care and mental illness services often are not equal to that experienced by those with physical illnesses. Strikingly, several years ago other developed nations, such as Canada, the United Kingdom, and the Scandinavian countries, removed much of the stigma or "second class" treatment of mental illnesses, thus providing complete treatment on par with physical ailments.

Imagine if those with cancer, cardiovascular disease, or diabetes had to suffer the same discrimination and stigmatization as those with depression or other mental illnesses. People would be outraged and demand swift legislative and legal actions to protect those who are ill. Remember, no one asks to be mentally ill, nor do they deserve medical illness any more than those who suffer a physical disease or condition. Human health should not be artificially segmented with some ailments, such as cancers and cardiovascular disease, that receive greater respect and care than others such as depression or addiction. Here, genetics and scientific advances play significant roles in revealing the biology and neurology of mental illnesses, which strengthens the call for parity in respect, treatment, and health insurance coverage for mental and physical ailments.

Progress to gain parity for mental illness was not gained until late in 2008 when the Paul Wellstone and Pete Domenici Mental Health Parity and Addiction Equity Act of 2008 was signed into law that would ensure that health insurance companies could no longer discriminate against people with mental illness (Library of Congress 2008). While this bill does not completely protect people with mental illness from health care discrimination, it is a start. Failure to provide parity between mental and physical illnesses reinforces myths that somehow those with mental illness did something to deserve this ailment and that if they really tried or wanted to try, they could "snap out of it" and be "normal." Such negative attitudes and false notions cause tremendous harm to not only the afflicted, but to their families and the larger communities. According to the National Institute of Mental Health, 26.2 percent of Americans aged 18 and older have a diagnosable mental disorder, and this same report identified depression as the main cause of disability in the United States for those who are 15 to 44 years of age (2008:1). Mental illness touches the lives of many families and is a national health concern.

This battle for parity in America came not only from the medical community and some members of Congress (e.g., the late Minnesota Senator, Paul Wellstone), but primarily from families with loved ones suffering serious illnesses while struggling with employers and health insurance providers for treatment coverage. Hence, it is often within families where mental health promotion and detection of mental disorders and illnesses occurs. While the composition and nature of families vary, it is universally true that the family influences an individual's core identity. It is through family that we may experience profound support and joy or antagonism and sorrow. Because families are such a driving force in defining who we are, families remain at the heart of mental health promotion and partners in mental illness treatment. Thus, it is at the family level that mental health education and promotion is most vital.

Families: Overcoming Mental Illness Stigma and Discrimination

Families with members experiencing mental illnesses are painfully aware of the stigma attached to mental illness that results from ignorance and prejudice. Stigma means labeling someone with a condition, stereotyping those who are afflicted, creating a division and devaluing "them," and basically discriminating through reduced social and medical treatment, payment for services, and/or access to health care. While some labels result in support and encouragement, such as "breast cancer," others such as "depression," do not enjoy positive messages or actions (Mayo Clinic 2008c). Stigmatizing beliefs also exist within the medical field. Steve Chin and Richard Balon (2006) report that the most significant factor in reducing stigmatizing attitudes toward mental illness among resident physicians was when the physician had a family member with a psychiatric illness. Likewise, other researchers report that perceptions of stigma and coercion were even found within mental health treatment programs in the treatment of outpatients (Link, Castille, and Stuber 2008). The passage of the landmark Paul Wellstone and Pete Domenici Mental Health Parity and Addiction Equity Act of 2008 was a first step toward reducing ignorance, stigma, and prejudice attached to mental illness and moving the United States toward a more biopsychosocial approach to health and well-being. Mental illness is a major local, national, and global health concern, thus the "stigma of mental illness needs to be eliminated at individual, family, societal, and structural levels (Ping Tsao, Tummala, and Roberts 2008:2).

Families need to be proactive in supporting members with mental illnesses and speaking out against this stigma forwarded by peers, employers, insurers, health care providers, insurers, and the larger community. According to the medical community (Mayo Clinic 2008c), consequences of such unbridled stigma not only negatively impact the afflicted family member, but often lead to harmful behaviors and consequences for the ill person such as:

- pretending he or she is "fine," nothing is wrong;
- refusal to seek medical treatment and concealment of condition;
- rejection by friends, coworkers, and family due to untreated illness;
- discrimination and difficulties at work, and denial of or limited disability leave;
- difficulty finding suitable housing;
- subjection to harassment or even physical violence;
- lack of or inadequate health insurance coverage of mental illnesses.

These added burdens interfere with recovery, generate increased anxiety, and often cause greater isolation. While the stigma pushes many depressed individuals to attempt to conceal their condition, disclosing aids not only the afflicted, but also helps in reducing the stigmatization and stereotyping (Garcia and Crocker 2008). Increasing familial involvement in the care of those with mental illnesses is not only crucial to reducing stigma and prejudice, but also to the "social and health outcomes of patients and providing support to family members" (Ping Tsao, Tummala, and Roberts, 2008:1). The stigma of mental illness reflects deeply engrained social attitudes that allow discrimination that if the same was aimed at "respectable illnesses" would not be tolerated.

> The inability to discuss mental illness in an informed and straightforward way, to deal with it as the major public health concern that it is, is unjustifiable. There is a very large group that I think of as the silent successful—people who get well from psychiatric illness, but who are afraid to speak out. This reluctance is understandable, very human, but it is unfortunate because it perpetuates the misperception that mental illness cannot be treated. (Jamison 2006:533)

Elimination of this stigma, therefore, hinges on open discussion of mental health promotion as well as mental illness intervention and treatment. Mental illnesses and disorders are real ailments worthy of discussion that increases family and public understanding and support. Families and/or their members who attempt to hide or deny mental illness often make the condition worse by delaying treatment and recovery. Unlike family members with somatic diseases, those with mental illnesses need to be reminded that they have a "real medical condition" that is not their fault, and that effective treatments are available and it is their right to engage in them without shame or scrutiny from insurers or employers. Case 4.2 offers a story of an "informed" teen with depression and her conversation with her family.

Case 4.2 Sarah: What a Depressed Teenager Wished She Could Say by Chris Gonzalez[2]

Sarah was 16 years old and struggling with depression. She felt hopeless, isolated, and did not know what was happening to her. All she knew was that she was falling deeper and deeper into a dark hole. Most people do not understand the complexities of a mood disorder, such as depression, especially when they are experiencing it. As a result, depressed people have difficulty communicating that experience to the people who could help them. In the following piece of creative nonfiction, we explore what the family conversation would be like if Sarah was extremely self-aware and highly knowledgeable about her mood disorder.

SARAH: Mom, dad, little Timmy, I have gathered you all together here in the living room because I need to make a very important mental health announcement. For the past four weeks, I have been experiencing a loss of appetite, I have lost 8 percent of my body weight, I have had an inability

---

2 Chris J. Gonzalez, M.MFT, LMFT, University of Minnesota. Chris is a practicing marriage and family therapist and is engaged in research on parent–adolescent relationships and adolescent mental health. Interviewed by Janet Grochowski, August 3, 2008.

to sleep, have been irritable, which I am sure you are all aware, and I have had a significant loss of energy as well. On top of all of that, I have had a nasty spell of anhedonia (i.e., an inability to find pleasure, to enjoy) like you wouldn't believe. Seriously, I am not interested in doing anything but staying in bed and looking at the ceiling. In short, I am experiencing a major depression disorder.

MOM: Well Sarah, I had no idea.

DAD: Yes, and what caused this depression?

TIMMY: I know that I am only five and a half years old, but I am afraid that you caught depression from me.

SARAH: Mom, dad, Timmy, thanks for your concern. Timmy, I didn't catch this from you. You can't catch depression like you catch a cold. It's not your fault. Depression is a mood disorder with a biopsychosocial etiology.

DAD: Bio what?

MOM: What's an etiology?

SARAH: Etiology means the cause or origin and biopsychosocial means that there are many contributing factors relating to my own biology, psychology, and my social environment. And if that were not complicated enough, these three influences do not work independently to result in depression, they interact in various ways.

DAD: Ok, so that means . . . uhm . . . nope, you lost me.

SARAH: Let's begin with our family history. There are many cases of depression and mental health problems that have gone unchecked and undiagnosed in our family. Aunts, uncles, grandparents—mom, even you have had some bouts of depression that you have not ever admitted to.

MOM: Well, I am sure I don't know what you are talking about.

SARAH: It's OK mom, you don't have to admit it. But, please understand, your denial of your own mental health issues actually models for me what to do with my mental health problems, offers me fewer coping skills, and leaves me isolated, afraid, and left to fight depression all by myself—just like you.

DAD: Oh, I get it. So a biological predisposition or vulnerability to become depressed interacts with environmental factors, such as relationships, to act as an instigator of depression. And the psychology comes in when the patterns of thinking are consumed in hopelessness and self-condemnation. And then once someone is depressed, their social network can either serve to fight against the depression, serve to maintain it, or even increase the symptoms.

SARAH: Wow dad, you so get it and so don't get it at the same time (spoken in a tone of stock teenage sarcasm). Although you verbalized the complexities of depression well, I also want to point out that you just learned that mom has been depressed and you acted like it didn't even happen. The truth is that you've always known, but have ignored it. That kind of interpersonal denial can reinforce the beliefs mom has that she is worthless because now she has more evidence to support these thoughts of worthlessness. So, when mom models for me this kind of thinking and helplessness, it is hard for me to know what to do. But then again, it's hard to blame mom, the family pattern is to ignore mental health problems like depression. Remember how the family responded to Uncle Louie who had "the blues?" We ignored him and just let him drink himself to sleep during holiday gatherings. Well, what do you think he was dealing with? It was depression. When the whole family colludes to maintain depression, it's pretty tough for anyone to shake it off all on their own.

MOM: (crying) It's all my fault. I should have done more, had more courage. I've failed you. (Timmy gives mom a hug and she clings to him.)

SARAH: I wish it were that simple, but depression is a complex thing. And by the way, your enmeshed relationship with Timmy as a response to dad's workaholic tendencies and emotional distance from you results in a family imbalance that doesn't leave me with a lot of security. You see, depression is a complicated . . .

MOM (LEAPING TO HER FEET): We should drop everything and focus all of our attention on Sarah. She needs our help so badly. Nothing is more important than getting her better. Everything we do from now on must be focused on her depression.

SARAH: Mom, I'm glad you said that, but not for the reason you are thinking. Ignoring depression is one way of maintaining it, but so is centralizing it.

DAD: What do you mean?

SARAH: Underreacting to a mood disorder, such as depression, is not helpful, but neither is overreacting. Here is what I mean: If the family communication patterns reorganize from total denial of a problem to total focus on a problem, then what will keep the family's attention when the depression goes away? In a strange sort of way, if I get better, then the family reverts back to the previously most familiar pattern, but if I stay depressed, then the family maintains its reason to focus on the problem. What we need is balance, not a new kind of family dysfunction.

DAD: Now, wait a minute, all this influence of depression makes sense, but you're the depressed one. The depression is in your brain. Can't we just get a prescription or send you to a shrink?

SARAH: Oh, I guess you don't really get it at all. That's the strictly biological or strictly psychological approach. Medication often does help to relieve symptoms, but not always. And it is true that talk therapy can help me with my thinking patterns, building coping skills, and dealing with my feelings. So, yes, we do need professional help. But most therapists don't take into account how systemic family patterns serve to maintain depression. If we do therapy, we need to find a therapist who can deal with the whole family, our patterns of interaction, and what each of our roles is. That person also needs to know the psychological aspects of depression and be able to prescribe medications or refer us to someone who can.

MOM: (looking up through her tears, now with a glimmer of hope) Depression is a family problem?

SARAH: I didn't get depressed all by myself and I am not going to beat it all by myself. Are you all willing to fight depression with me?

MOM, DAD, TIMMY: Yes.

Sarah and her family engaged in an open, informed discussion about a complex illness. While the dialogue was meant to be a bit over the top in terms of how candidly this family discussed mental illness, its point was to illustrate how families require knowledge, skills, and support in learning to encourage mental health and care for mental illness. Prior to the implementation Paul Wellstone and Pete Domenici Mental Health Parity and Addiction Equity Act of 2008 (scheduled for late 2009 or 2010), most health insurance companies only covered the first 20 mental health sessions per year, after which time the patient, Sarah in Case 4.2, and her family would have to pay the entire cost of all sessions. Another parity issue, especially found in non-group plans, is that the insurer may only pay for sessions with psychiatrists and not counselors, and then only cover a fraction of the medication costs. The tragedy is that under these financial demands, patients may discontinue medications and/or therapy, thus risking slipping into deeper depression or anxiety.

Elimination of all forms of stigmatization and prejudice begins within families. Helping them learn to recognize and avoid such negative beliefs and behaviors are the responsibility of local, state, national, and global communities. Increased understanding, awareness, and openness reduce stigmatization and discrimination. Schools collaborating with families emerge as important avenues to dispelling myths and learning accurate information and healthful strategies. Globally, schools hold a vital position in health education and health promotion. While their role has been clearly outlined for conditions such as cardiovascular health and reducing childhood obesity, increasingly schools are also being called on to aid in mental health promotion as well as sexuality education (British Medical Association 2008).

Health Education: Family, School, and Community Collaborations

The primary purpose for educating children is to prepare them for a healthful and productive life. This includes learning skills such as reading, computation, problem solving, critical and creative thinking, accessing and assessing information, as well as social and communication skills. Schools in the United States are also charged with strengthening the well-being of children and youth through health programs that address issues such as depression, teen suicide, tobacco use, asthma management, childhood obesity, and teen pregnancy (Center for Health and Health Care in Schools 2008).

Scholars argue that schools in the 21st century need expanded school-based health care programs to better aid in developing, enhancing, and/or maintaining the health and well-being of children and youth (Lear 2007). This call for increased collaboration among families, schools, and communities (i.e., medical and political) focuses on reducing current (e.g., childhood obesity, diabetes, teen pregnancy, sexually transmitted diseases [STDs]) and future (e.g., avian flu epidemics, unmet dental and vision needs) health concerns. Unlike many areas of health (e.g., nutrition, exercise), sexuality education continues to be bombarded by significant social influences in which culture, values, politics, and science play key roles. Restrictive programs that gained political favor in 2000, had been proven to be ineffective by mid-decade which resulted in increasing numbers of American families turning their support toward comprehensive approaches in helping their children prepare for their sexual health (Bleakley, Hennessy, and Fishbein 2006). Case 4.3 reveals a situation in which an adolescent and her boyfriend become victims of unintended sexual consequences due to ignorance and inadequate support from their families, school, and community.

Case 4.3 Mia: The High Price of Ignorance

Mia fidgeted in the waiting room awaiting the test results. Certainly these blisters on her lips were just cold sores, but the accompanying fever, aching muscles, and headache resulted in her mother sending her to the clinic. "Mia, you have genital herpes, a sexually transmitted disease," the nurse calmly told her. "How can that be?"

pleaded Mia. "I'm a virgin, well a "renewed virgin." I mean Nat and I had intercourse few times last year, but not since we took the "virginity pledge"[3] as part of the abstinence-only-until-marriage program at school," Mia sobbed. The nurse gently placed her hand on Mia's shoulder trying to comfort the crying 16-year-old and asked, "Mia, have you and Nat had oral or anal sex recently?" Mia turned away; her parents are going to kill her she thought. "Yes, but that isn't really sex, I mean you can't get pregnant or any disease, right?" "I am sorry, Mia, but the reality is that people can contract common STDs especially herpes, chlamydia, and genital warts through any sexual contact, including oral and anal sex," the nurse stated. "OK, so what can you do to cure me? Please, my parents and Nat simply can't find out about this," Mia pleaded. The nurse gently took both of Mia's hands in hers and said, "Mia, this is a viral disease and cannot be cured. We can treat the symptoms, but it is a lifelong disease. Nat and any other sexual partners he and you have had will have to be tested right away. As for notifying your parents, I recommend that you do talk to them, but it is not required that I notify them.[4] Of course, if you use your health insurance coverage, your parents may find out, so if you want confidentiality you will need to use the Title X supported clinic that I can refer you to."

Alarms over adolescent sexual health spiked in 2007 as birth rates and incidents of teenagers with STDs escalated. Birth rates for adolescents increased 3 percent from 40.5 live births per 1,000 in 2005 to 41.9 live births per 1,000 in 2006 after a 14-year decline in teen birth rate (Hamilton, Martin, and Ventura 2007:1). Non-Hispanic black teens experienced the greatest increase with a rate increase of 5 percent as compared to increases within other racial and ethnic groups such as 4 percent for American Indian or Alaskan Native, 3 percent for non-Hispanic whites, and 2 percent for Hispanic teens (2007:1).

In addition to climbing teen birth rates, unacceptably high rates of STDs among teens also caught the attention of families, the medical community, and

---

[3] Virginity pledge: delaying sexual intercourse until marriage. While virginity pledges appear to delay sexual intercourse for some 15- to 17-year-olds within certain ethnic groups, they are not a panacea since pledgers often engage in first sex at the same rate as non-pledgers (Bearman, Peter S. and Hanah Brückner. 2001. "Promising the Future: Virginity Pledges and the Transition to First Intercourse." *American Journal of Sociology* 106(4):859–912). Other major findings include: (1) As the proportion of students who take the pledge increases the effectiveness decreases, hence virginity pledge is not a vaccination against teen sex, and more comprehensive programs are needed; and (2) Those who do take the pledge are at higher risk for unintended pregnancy and STDs, because such abstinence-only programs often fail to provide accurate and complete sexuality information such as safe-sex practices (Brückner, Hannah and Peter Bearman. 2005. "After the Promise: The STD Consequences of Adolescent Virginity Pledges." *Journal of Adolescent Health* 36(4):271–278).

[4] Title X, the only federal program dedicated to family planning services for low-income women and teenagers provides contraceptive services and other reproductive health care to minors on a confidential basis, although they encourage minors to involve their parents in their decision to seek services. Several conservative groups have worked to reinstate parental notification, but the American Medical Association and other professional groups have countered these efforts to keep the statute in place. For more information visit The Center for Health and Health Care in Schools. 2000. "Minors and the Right to Consent to Health Care." Retrieved March 9, 2008. (www.healthinschools.org/static/papers/guttmacher.aspx) and Guttmacher Institute. 2003. "New Medical Records Privacy Rule: The Interface with Teen Access to Confidential Care." Retrieved March 9, 2008. (www.guttmacher.org/pubs/tgr/06/1/gr060106.html).

researchers. The Centers for Disease Control and Prevention (2008f) reported that more than one in four (26 percent) adolescents aged 14 to 19 years were infected with at least one of the more common STDs, that is, herpes, HPV, chlamydia, and trichomoniasis. The racial and ethnic disparities are found here as well, with almost half (48 percent) of the African American women were infected with a STD as compared to 20 percent of the non-Hispanic whites (2008f:1). Scholars note that the 2006 increases in teen birth rates and the prevalence of STDs in teens coincided with declines in contraceptive use, due in part to a prevalence of restrictive sex education programs (Santelli 2008).

Case 4.3 illustrates a situation in which Mia's health and well-being needs were unmet in that she was ignorant of the risks and precautions needed when engaging in oral sex. Although the perception that adolescents (aged 15 to 19 years) frequently substitute oral sex for vaginal intercourse is a myth, both oral and anal sex are more common among teens who have already had vaginal intercourse, such as Mia (Wind 2008). Mia and Nat's ignorance regarding safe sex is the primary concern. While the responsibility for their actions remains with adolescents themselves (e.g., Mia and Nat), others also bear responsibility, including their families, schools, community, and society in general. How to best prepare adolescents for lifelong sexual health includes providing clear, complete, and accurate sexual health information so as to reduce the risk of unintended and lifelong health consequences. Starting in the 1980s, delivering sexual information to youth became a battleground between abstinence-only and abstinence-plus programs[5] in the American schools. The battle seems to be over, however, for the majority of American families, but not for families such as Mia's. Christopher Trenholm and his colleagues (2007; 2008) supported additional research (Underhill, Montgomery, and Operario 2007; Hauser 2008) that abstinence-only programs were ineffective in changing sexual behaviors (e.g., vaginal sex, number of sexual partners, and condom use) and failed to reduce teen pregnancy and STD levels. Family health concerns over abstinence-only programs are not only in their ineffectiveness, but additional poor health behaviors they appear to have spawned. Youth, such as Mia and Nat, who took the "virginity pledge" also engaged in unhealthy behaviors in which they:

- Were much less likely to use contraception when they did become sexually active than their peers who did not pledge (Bearman and Brückner 2001).

---

[5] Comprehensive sexuality education "promotes abstinence but includes information about contraception and condoms to build young people's knowledge, attitudes and skills for when they do become sexually active." Abstinence-only-until-marriage programs "provide no information about contraception beyond failure rates" [Hauser, Debra. 2008:1. "Five Years of Abstinence-Only-Until-Marriage Education: Assessing the Impact." Retrieved June 20, 2008. (www.advocatesforyouth.org/publications/stateevaluations/index.htm)].

- Had significantly higher rates of STDs for those coming from communities with a larger proportion of virginity pledgers than in communities with a smaller proportion of virginity pledgers (Brückner and Bearman 2005).
- Were much more likely to have engaged in unprotected anal and oral sex than nonpledgers, with male pledgers being four times more likely to have anal sex than those who did not pledge (SIECUS 2007).

Parents and guardians mean well in wanting to keep their children safe and healthy, but increasingly American families realize that keeping adolescents ignorant and unprepared often results in unintended and/or unhealthy results. In 2004, national surveys conducted by the National Public Radio, the Kaiser Family Foundation, and the Harvard University's Kennedy School of Government revealed that 93 percent of American adults stated that sexuality education should be taught in schools. There was some disagreement over the kind of sexuality education with over 46 percent supporting abstinence-plus agreeing that while abstinence is best, teens who choose not to abstain should know about condoms and contraception. Another 36 percent disagreed that abstinence was the most important thing, stating that the sexuality education should focus on teaching teens how to make responsible decisions about sex through having accurate and complete information and skills. Another 15 percent believed that schools should teach abstinence-only programs and not provide any information on how to obtain and use condoms and other contraception or any other information on sexual decision making (National Public Radio et al. 2004:1). The vast majority of American families, therefore, did not the support abstinence-only programs and believed providing teens with information on how to obtain and use condoms would not encourage early onset of sexual intercourse with 77 percent stating that such information would aid in teens practicing safe sex. Within this same survey, families identified oral sex (27 percent) and homosexuality (25 percent) as controversial topics. Interestingly, 52 percent of these families want homosexuality to be taught, but without labeling it as wrong or acceptable as compared to 18 percent who want it labeled as wrong and another 8 percent who said it should be taught as acceptable (2004:2).

While the majority of evangelicals oppose sexuality education in schools, there was some variation between white and non-white evangelical families' positions. For example, 23 percent of white evangelicals believe it is inappropriate to teach about contraception, but only 13 percent of non-white evangelicals believe this. As for adherence to the abstinence-only program, 27 percent of white evangelicals prefer it compared to only 12 percent of non-white evangelicals and 10 percent of non-evangelicals (National Public Radio et al. 2004:2). Such divisions reflect to some extent that when families have confidence in the data regarding health information, in this case adolescent sexual health statistics, the majority will vie for what is effective in preparing their children for healthful lives. Support for comprehensive sexuality education cuts across social and political divisions with approximately 82 percent in favor of inclusive and complete programs that include abstinence but also must include other effective methods to prevent STDs and unintended pregnancy (Bleakley, Hennessy, and Fishbein 2006:1154).

Comprehensive sexuality education works as revealed in the findings comparing teen pregnancy, birth, abortion, and STD rates in the Unites States to those in Western European nations where comprehensive sexuality education is supported and universally taught. The rate of teen pregnancy in America (72.2 per 1,000) was more than twice that in France (22.6 per 1,000) and significantly more than that in Germany (16.3 per 1,000) or the Netherlands (12.8 per 1,000) (Advocates for Youth 2008:1). The rate of STDs among American teens is also more than double that of many Western European nations. Sexuality education is vital to family health, and families remain foundational in not only serving as children's primary "health educators," but also as supporters of effective health education programs offered through schools, clinics, and other venues. Sexuality health, which often suffers the stigma of a "controversial" health topic, continues to require positive social influences.

Conclusion

While health disparities are not new, current studies regarding social and political attitudes, practices, and policies define a culture by continuing to impact and "get under the skin" of individual, family, and population health (Aronowitz 2008). Social determinants, therefore, play pivotal roles in family health. Recognizing this reality allows individuals, families, communities, societies, and nations to understand that health is not a static state dictated solely by genetics, behaviors, environmental exposures, and political policy (see Figure 1.1 Family Health Determinants Model), but rather a dynamic process in which social determinants (i.e., the heart, soul, and will of society) can foster or hinder health disparities, which in turn intertwine with genetics, behaviors, environments, and health policy and services.

There is no shame in being ill. The only shame falls on those who deny full respect, care, and coverage based on race, ethnicity, gender, age, SES, education, geographic location, or type of illness. The goals of the *Healthy People 2010* initiative include: (1) increase length and quality of healthy life, and (2) eliminate health disparities. Health disparities on national and global levels, however, provide formidable obstacles. The disproportionate toll on racial and ethnic minorities, women, the urban and rural poor, and other medically underserved individuals and their families result in poorer health status not only for the afflicted individual, but also for their families, communities, and nations. As discussed in Chapter 1, the United States spends more on health care than any other nation and yet is ranked only 24th out of 33 developed nations in life expectancy (Organization of Economic Co-Operation and Development 2008). This low ranking was due in large part to health disparities. These disparities reveal themselves in unequal and unfair rates of infant mortality, cardiovascular diseases, cancers, diabetes, HIV/AIDS, and immunizations, thus serving as rallying points. Yet, areas related to stigma toward classes of diseases and illnesses, such as mental illness and HIV/AIDS, remain relatively underrecognized and undertreated. Here the illness itself suffers from stigmatization, discrimination, disregard, and disrespect.

Using mental illness as an exemplar, the issue of mental illness and family relationships reveals the importance of boldly working toward the elimination of the stigma attached to mental illness as well as the crucial need to aid families in fostering mental health. "Mental health and mental illness are dynamic, ever-changing phenomena. At any given moment, a person's mental status reflects the sum total of that individual's genetic inheritance and life experiences" (U.S. Department of Health and Human Services 1999:13). Science continues to race to better understand the neurobiological and genetics of brain processes, behaviors, and life experiences that either strengthen mental health or foster mental illness. A significant challenge in the early 21st Century is elevating mental health in the minds and actions of societies around the world to higher levels of recognition, awareness, and respect, thus providing care on parity with somatic conditions. This calls for increased collaboration among families, medicine, and social scientists in fostering mental health as well as developing more effective means of supporting and aiding families in caring for members with mental illnesses. Eliminating the stigma of mental illness remains a major challenge for families and their communities. Teaching effective communication and supportive relationships, and social networking within families and larger communities are promising ways to promote mental health and aid those with mental illnesses.

This chapter on social determinants concludes with an important area of family health, human sexuality, which has been underserved due to social divisions and ignorance. In order to avoid future mishandling of health-related controversies, individuals and their families need to be well-informed on current, accurate, and complete health information presented in a culturally sensitive manner. Other developed nations, such as Western Europe, have significantly lower rates of teen pregnancy and STD as compared to teens in the United States. Why? The answer is complex, but basic to the success of these nations in the area of adolescent sexual health is their comprehensive sexuality education programs and society's relatively calm, realistic approach to sex and sexuality in general. This means that health education, including sexuality education, requires multiple venues in addition to the primary sites of families and schools.

Where one is born holds dramatic impacts on health. According to the World Health Organization's Commission on Social Determinates of Health (CSDH), the life expectancy of those living in Sweden or Japan is more than 80 years, in Brazil 72 years, India 63 years, and in several African countries less than 50 years. Plus "[i]n all countries at all levels of income, health and illness follow a social gradient: the lower the socioeconomic position, the worse the health" (CSDH 2008:1). Promoting healthful living and eliminating health disparities are everyone's concerns and in the best social and economic interests of all. Awareness of social determinants and their impacts along with proactively engaging in reducing social inequities that lead to poorer and unequal health care and treatment form a foundation of resilient family health and well-being. Environmental exposures, Chapter 5, picks up on the determinants of biology, behavior, and social circumstances to reveal how especially interrelated we are in terms of our global family health.

Critical Thinking Questions

1. Consider Jonathan's and Morning Dew's neighborhoods in Case 4.1 in terms of health concerns. For each one (Jonathan and Morning Dew) identify, two recommendations that would improve the health potential in that neighborhood using two of the six areas (infant mortality, CVD, diabetes, cancer, HIV/AIDS, immunizations) discussed in the health disparities section. Also provide a rationale for why you selected each of these recommendations.

2. The stigma of mental illness remains a serious health concern for many families. Outline four talking points that you would want to raise with your sister if you were concerned that she or her 16-year-old daughter (your choice) was struggling with depression but feared the stigma of seeking medical help.

3. While the battle between abstinence-only and abstinence-plus sexuality programs appears over, outline three lessons we should take away from such a controversial period in terms of how to best prepare our youth and their families for healthful lives in terms of physical, mental, social, and sexual health.

5

ENVIRONMENTAL
EXPOSURES AND GLOBAL
FAMILY HEALTH

The Global Burden of Infectious Disease

Case 5.1 Aisha: Malaria—A Disease of Poverty

Four months ago, Aisha and her four-year-old son were displaced due to a devastating combination of drought, which left their small farm barren, and violence, which not only took her husband's life, but forced Aisha and her child to flee with little more than the clothes on their backs. They joined tens of thousands of other displaced Somalis who relocated to a refugee camp in the south near the capital Mogadishu. Those living in these camps often suffer from a lack of clean water, food, shelter, and access to medical treatment (Doctors Without Borders 2008:1). These harsh living conditions increase these victims' vulnerability to easily treatable diseases and conditions, such as malnutrition, malaria,[1] respiratory infections, diarrhea (e.g., cholera),[2] and obstetrical complications. The heavier than normal monsoons, due in part to climate change, accelerate exposure to malaria epidemics. Aisha was six weeks pregnant when they fled the violence, but her main concern

---

[1] Malaria is a mosquito-borne disease caused by a parasite. The symptoms include fever, chills, sweats, fatigue, and other flu-like concerns. Severe complications and even death can occur if left untreated [Centers for Disease Control and Prevention. 2008g. "Malaria: Topic Home." Retrieved July 20, 2008. (www.cdc.gov/malaria/)].

[2] Cholera is an acute, diarrheal illness caused by the cholera bacterium transmitted when drinking contaminated water. The symptoms of cholera include watery diarrhea, vomiting, and leg cramps, but approximately one in 20 infected victims suffer severe symptoms and even death within hours without medical treatment. Cholera infections are rare in developed nations, but are still common in developing parts of the world [Minnesota Department of Health. 2008. "Causes and Symptoms of Cholera." p. 1. Retrieved July 20, 2008. (www.health.state.mn.us/divs/idepc/diseases/cholera/basics.html)].

was simply to feed her son and herself. She did not think she was at risk for malaria because she was an adult, but she did worry about her son and tried to be consistent in giving him the malaria drugs provided by the "Roll Back Malaria Initiative" that passed through the camp each month (2005). Living as a widowed, single-mother refugee, however, sapped her strength and health. Aisha was rail thin, with flu-like symptoms including fatigue, fever, chills, sweats, and vomiting. After several weeks of this agonizing condition, a friend who shared their tent took her to the camp clinic. Aisha stumbled into the camp's Doctors Without Borders emergency tent and through an interpreter, tried to explain her symptoms including recent vaginal bleeding. She was rushed into the modest surgery tent where they scrambled to save not only her fetus, but Aisha. Her elevated vulnerability, however, due to malnutrition, overcrowding, exposure to infectious diseases, and the accumulative stressors of displacement overcame the doctors' best efforts. Aisha and her unborn child died leaving only her orphaned son as a legacy. The postmortem tests revealed that Aisha had malaria. If Aisha had been semi-immune (due to past exposures) to malaria infections (i.e., asymptomatic), her untreated malaria would have contributed to severe maternal anemia and parasitic infection of the placenta impairing the fetus' growth resulting in low birth weight and an increased risk of infant mortality. The situation was worse for Aisha, however, since she had no malaria immunity. Her untreated malaria elevated her risk for developing severe maternal anemia two to three times higher than for pregnant women who were semi-immune. This severe maternal anemia and underdevelopment of her fetus directly and indirectly resulted in her death and the spontaneous abortion of the fetus (Roll Back Malaria 2005:31).

Aisha's story (Case 5.1) reveals complex interactions of environmental exposures negatively impacting family health. Note that environmental exposures, such as safe clean air and water,[3] safe food, peace in the neighborhood, health education, medical access, and so on, have highly positive impacts on family health. In Case 5.1, however, several troubling aspects of negative environmental exposures are active. Malaria is a disease of poverty, with more than 2.3 billion individuals (35 percent of the world's population) living in areas of high risk for a deadly form of malaria, such as the type that infected Aisha (Guerra et al. 2008:e38). Globally, each year between 350 to 500 million cases of malaria are reported along with over 1 million deaths, with the majority occurring in sub-Saharan Africa (Bloland and Williams

---

[3] The World Health Organization (WHO) initiative, "Water for Life—2005 to 2015," calls on the global community to address the critical issue of scarcity of clean, safe water. This scarcity leads to increased prevalence of contaminated drinking water (e.g., cholera), favorable breeding for mosquitoes (e.g., malaria, dengue haemorrhagic fever), and decreased sanitation conditions (e.g., plague, typhus) [United Nations. 2008. "The International Decade for Action—Water for Life, 2005–2015." Retrieved May 9, 2008. (www.un.org/waterforlifedecade/issues.html#scarcity)].

2002:3). Aisha's story serves as an example of how complex conditions, including natural disasters (e.g., floods, droughts, tsunamis, earthquakes) and human-made tragedies (e.g., war, genocide, violence, climate change), often result in the displacement of populations. As cautioned by population health experts, "[w]ar, poverty, environmental degradation and misallocation of resources are the greatest root causes of worldwide mortality and morbidity" (Cohen, Gould, and Sidel 2004:1670). Migrations of displaced people, especially in areas of poverty, often increase risks of epidemics due to contamination of water and food, crowding and homelessness, plus exposure to pathogens from insects, humans, and other animals (Watson, Gayer, and Connolly 2007). The impacts of such displacements, however, are not isolated to the affected nation. We are indeed a global community and as Meg Karraker (2008) notes, we are "global families." Globalization is reflected in our rapid mobility, electronic interconnectedness, transnational commerce and food production, economic interdependence, dependence on chemicals, worldwide revolutions, and the ominous trend of antimicrobial-resistant (i.e., drug-resistant) strains of infectious diseases (e.g., MRSA [methicillin-resistant *Staphylococcus aureus*] staph bacteria)[4] that render all of us globally linked. Those, such as Aisha, who experience tragic environmental exposures, deserve humanitarian concern and action. Yet such global situations also serve as a warning that "[v]ulnerability is universal" and that "any emergency with international repercussions for health, including outbreaks of emerging and epidemic-prone diseases, outbreaks of foodborne disease, natural disasters, and chemical or radionuclear events" touches all of us (World Health Organization 2007:2). Another example of such a far-reaching preventable disease, HIV/AIDS, further illustrates the global burden of infectious disease epidemics and pandemics challenges that demand a truly universal response.

The HIV/AIDS Pandemic

When a disease or infectious agent is constant or spreads rapidly among a certain population group, such as the spread of malaria in Case 5.1, it is termed an *epidemic*. When this epidemic is global, impacting a wide geographic area and large numbers of people, it is termed a *pandemic*. Human Immunodeficiency Virus (HIV) that causes acquired immunodeficiency syndrome (AIDS),[5] is an insidious epidemic of global or pandemic proportions. According to projections of the

---

[4] MRSA bacteria are resistant to common antibiotics, such as penicillin, oxacillin, and amoxicillin. For more information, see the Centers for Disease Control and Prevention. 2008h. "Community-Associated MRSA Information for the Public." Retrieved August 1, 2008. (www.cdc.gov/ncidod/dhqp/ar_mrsa_ca_public.html#2).

[5] AIDS is the last stage of a progressive disease that begins with HIV infection. The obliteration of the immune system caused by HIV leaves an untreated individual prone to opportunistic infections (e.g., tuberculosis) that take advantage of the weakened immune system.

"Global Mortality and Burden of Disease from 2002 to 2030", global HIV/AIDS deaths are projected to increase from 2.8 million in 2002 to approximately 6.5 million in 2030 to become the "leading cause of burden of disease in middle- and low-income countries by 2015" (Mathers and Loncar 2006:e442). While the HIV/AIDS epidemic raged in the 1980s, the response was muted at best, as seen in the United States, due in large part to the stigma and discrimination surrounding this highly infectious disease. In a little over a decade, HIV/AIDS spread throughout North America, Europe, South America, Asia, and Africa becoming a worldwide pandemic by 2000 (Perlin and Cohen 2002).

In July 2008, the United Nations published its "2008 Report on the Global AIDS Epidemic." This was the halfway point of the 2015 target of the "Millennium Development Goals" that aimed to reverse the HIV/AIDS pandemic by 2015. While some progress had been made in reducing new HIV infections and AIDS deaths, the results were uneven, with sub-Saharan Africa remaining the most seriously affected by HIV with 67 percent of all people living with HIV and 72 percent of all AIDS deaths in 2007 occurring in the sub-Saharan Africa region (UNAIDS 2008a:5). Table 5.1 presents data from this groundbreaking report. As you review these data, consider the extensive impacts the sub-Saharan Africa region and imagine how such a massive environmental disaster negatively affects the social and economic well-being of families. For example, life expectancy fell from 60 to 67 years in 1995 to only 36 to 47 years by 2007 in the sub-Saharan region due to this HIV/AIDS pandemic (Population Reference Bureau 2007:6).

Why is HIV/AIDS more prevalent in sub-Saharan Africa than in other parts of the world? There are complex responses to this frustrating question including (*The Economist* 2008; Weijing et al. 2008):

- *Biological-genetic* (e.g., gene variation, which is common in those of African descent, increases the susceptibility to HIV infection, however, since the HIV-affected person remains symptom-free longer, he or she does not seek medical aid sooner)
- *Social, cultural, and behavioral* (e.g., high rates of poverty, which have been made worse by the HIV/AIDS pandemic in sub-Saharan Africa, gender inequality, limited safer sex educational opportunities, higher incidents of formal and informal polygamy)
- *Geographic location* (e.g., position that AIDS began in Africa and has had more time to spread there)
- *Policy and services* (e.g., plagued by stigma and discrimination, response to this global pandemic has only recently received significant global attention and financial support)

Table 5.1 Global HIV/AIDS: Prevalence Rates in Adults and Children by Region, 2007

Region	Adults and Children Living with HIV	New HIV Infections among Adults and Children	Deaths Due to AIDS in Adults and Children	Prevalence for Adults (15–49 years) (Percentage)
Global				
Total	33 million	2.7 million	2.0 million	0.8
Adults	30.8 million	2.3 million	1.8 million	—
Women	15.5 million	—	—	—
Children under 15 years	2.0 million	370,000	270,000	—
Sub-Saharan Africa	22.0 million	1.9 million	1.5 million	5.0
South/Southeast Asia	4.2 million	330,000	340.000	0.3
Latin America	1.7 million	140,000	63,000	0.5
Eastern Europe/central Asia	1.5 million	110,000	58,000	0.8
North America	1.2 million	54,000	23,000	0.6
East Asia	740,000	52,000	40,000	0.1
Western/central Europe	730,000	27,000	8,000	0.3
Middle East/North Africa	380,000	40,000	27,000	0.3
Caribbean	230,000	20,000	14,000	1.1
Oceania	74,000	13,000	1,000	0.4

Sources: Compiled from the UNAIDS. 2008a. "2008 Report on the Global AIDS Epidemic. Executive Summary." Retrieved July 30, 2008. (www.unaids.org/en/KnowledgeCentre/HIVData/GlobalReport/2008/2008_Global_report.asp); and the UNAIDS. 2008b. "Core Slides." Retrieved August 1, 2008. (http://data.unaids.org/pub/GlobalReport/2008/2008_globalreport_core_en.ppt).

The complex nature of the global HIV/AIDS pandemic is also revealed in the increasing "feminization" and "youthfulness" of this pandemic. The prevalence of young women (15 to 24 years) living with HIV and children (under 15 years) dying from AIDS-related opportunistic diseases, such as tuberculosis (TB), continues to frustrate efforts to reverse the course of the insidious disease. The complexity deepens, however, when those infected with HIV appear to be more prone to other diseases, such as wherever HIV prevalence is high, so too is TB. This HIV–TB combination is deadly. The United Nations HIV/TB Global Leaders Forum noted that in 2008, a person with HIV/TB dies from TB every three minutes, even though most TB cases are preventable and treatable (Smith 2008:1). Case 5.2 offers a story of one "face" of the global HIV/AIDS pandemic.

Case 5.2 Mandisa: The Youthful, Feminine Face of HIV/AIDS

Mandisa is 20 years old and "living positively" as she struggles with being HIV positive in a society where the stigma and discrimination toward those who carry the illness is cruel and at times violent. She hides the fact that she is HIV positive from her husband. "He would divorce me and leave me with nothing," sobs Mandisa, adding "I hide my antiretroviral (ARV) medicine and can only take it when he is out of the house." She explains, "My friend, Naledi, told her husband and he not only left her, but took all their possessions, including clothing, mattresses, sheets, dishes, food, money, everything! Naledi was disowned by her own family, just for having HIV." "I understand Mandisa, but you must keep taking the medicine," the nurse cautioned. "I know, but sometimes I can't buy the drugs since my husband would ask why I need the money. I don't know what to do," Mandisa sobbed. The nurse softly told her, "Mandisa, you have a drug-resistant form of tuberculosis and that with your HIV is very serious. We need to begin treating both for your sake and your children's." The empathetic nurse then asked, "Has your husband hit or hurt you, forced you to have sex?" Mandisa blushed, "Husbands don't rape, they take. He has hit me, but I can't say he raped me, yet I am sure that he would kill me if he knew I was HIV positive." "Mandisa, your husband is HIV positive, that is how you became infected," the nurse said as she calmly placed her hand on Mandisa's shoulder. "But you don't understand. If I tell him why I need the money he will know and leave me. Without him I have nothing, no home, no children, plus I would be shunned by my family and the entire village. No, I simply can't tell him."

Mandisa's story is not unique as the HIV/AIDS pandemic increasingly victimizes youth (15 to 24 years) and women as revealed in Table 5.2. Based on the findings revealed in Table 5.2, consider the ramifications that women account for

Table 5.2 Global HIV/AIDS: Prevalence Rates of Women, Young Adults, and Children, by Region in 2007

Region	Percentage of Adult Women Living with HIV/AIDS	Prevalence of Young Women (15–24 years) (Percentage)	Prevalence of Young Men (15–24 years) (Percentage)	Children (under 15 years) with HIV/AIDS
Global	50	0.6	0.4	2.0 million
Sub-Saharan Africa	59	3.2	1.1	1.8 million
Middle East/North Africa	54	0.3	0.2	26,000
Caribbean	50	0.4	0.5	11,000
South/Southeast Asia	37	0.5	0.3	140,000
Latin America	32	0.2	0.7	44,000
Eastern Europe/central Asia	31	0.1	0.9	12,000
Oceania	30	0.6	0.4	1,100
East Asia	27	<0.1	<0.1	7,800
Western/central Europe	27	0.2	0.2	1,300
North America	21	0.7	0.6	4,400

Sources: Compiled from the UNAIDS. 2008a. "2008 Report on the Global AIDS Epidemic. Executive Summary." Retrieved July 30, 2008. (www.unaids.org/en/KnowledgeCentre/HIVData/GlobalReport/2008/2008_Global_report.asp); and the UNAIDS. 2008b. "Core Slides." Retrieved August 1, 2008. (http://data.unaids.org/pub/GlobalReport/2008/2008_globalreport_core_en.ppt).

50 percent of the adults living with HIV globally, nearly 60 percent in sub-Saharan Africa, 54 percent in the Middle East/North Africa region (location for Case 5.2), and 50 percent in the Caribbean (UNAIDS 2008a:33).

The youthfulness and feminization of the HIV/AIDS pandemic has significantly affected the health and well-being of families in those regions, as well as having global implications in terms of worldwide health, land use, global economies, environmental and conservation concerns,[6] and political instability. In sub-Saharan Africa, death rates among children under age five are substantially higher than they would be without HIV. Without ARV treatment, approximately one-third of the children who are born infected with HIV (transmitted through their mothers) die before their first birthday, and about 60 to 75 percent die by age five, but with effective ARV treatment this figure is reduced to below 20 percent (International HIV/AIDS Alliance 2008:1).

This young female "face" of the HIV/AIDS pandemic also means that besides the significant health and financial burden placed on the poorest households, these young women often suffer ostracism and destitution due to HIV/AIDS-related stigma and discrimination. As Mandisa, in Case 5.2, points out, she believed that she would lose everything plus would be labeled as a virtual outcast if her husband and family found out about her being HIV positive. The stigma of being HIV positive in Africa not only fuels the spread of the disease, but further disenfranchises women. William Rankin and his colleagues (2005) report that this stigma often results in individuals being isolated from their family, community, and even medical aid. The cultural subordinate position of women in sub-Saharan Africa allows husbands to beat and abandon their HIV-positive wives, even if the husband infected his wife. This deadly mix of stigma and sexism further disempowers women as they are blamed as the vectors of HIV and other STDs that are wrongly considered "women diseases" (Rankin et al. 2005). As seen in Mandisa's situation (Case 5.2), poverty, violence, and gender discrimination have helped change the face of the HIV/AIDS pandemic to young and female.

Mandisa also suffers from the HIV–TB coinfections combination that is a major health catastrophe in developing regions. In India, recent studies (Mahajan et al. 2008) sound the alarm over HIV–TB coinfection rates and call for international mandatory screening and treatments for HIV–TB coinfections. The United Nations 2008 Report on AIDS notes that the HIV/AIDS pandemic is "a generation-long challenge that requires persistence, vision, and flexibility" (UNAIDS 2008:28). In order to make progress in reducing AIDS deaths and preventing new HIV infections, a "social norm" needs to be instilled about HIV prevention that must include reduced gender inequalities, along with the stigma, discrimination, and social marginalization associated with HIV/AIDS.

---

[6] Judy Oglethorpe and Nancy Gelman (2007) warn that the HIV/AIDS epidemic in Africa has resulted in dramatic loss of skilled staff (e.g., 14 percent decrease in Malawe Kasungu National Park staff due to AIDS-related deaths). In addition to fewer caretakers, there is a loss of traditional knowledge regarding healing plants and an increase in poverty leading to mismanagement of water, plant, and animal resources (e.g., domestic and native species, such as elephants, lions, etc.). World Wildlife Fund officials warn that these losses are resulting in long-term effects on local and global scales [Oglethorpe, Judy and Nancy Gelman. 2007. "HIV/AIDS and the Environment: Impacts of AIDS and Ways to Reduce Them." Retrieved May 1, 2008. (www.worldwildlife.org/what/whowehelp/community/phe/WWFBinaryitem7051.pdf)].

HIV/AIDS-Related Stigma and Discrimination

Stigma toward a disease or illness, as discussed in Chapter 4, not only harms the immediate family, but also has impacts on national and global levels. HIV/AIDS was once considered a "gay disease" as well as associated with intravenous drug abusers and sex workers.[7] Horrific repugnance and hostility toward AIDS patients occurred in developed and developing countries alike (Keusch, Wilentz, and Kleinman 2006). Stigmas die hard, but the physical and social costs of continuing or ignoring the plight of those who are afflicted because of prejudice and discrimination are significant. For example, the current costs of fighting the global HIV/AIDS pandemic, in terms of treatment for the afflicted, care for those orphaned, loss of productivity, reduced conservation of land and resources, and programs to prevent new infections, are higher than if HIV/AIDS had been treated as the serious, common disease (i.e., we all are vulnerable and those who are ill are just like us) and not stigmatized due to social discrimination and ignorance.

While the scourge of the global HIV/AIDS pandemic remains centered in developing regions, such as sub-Saharan Africa, developed regions are not "immune" to this global pandemic. In 2008, the Centers for Disease Control and Prevention (CDC) announced that they had underestimated the prevalence of HIV and AIDS within the United States by 40 percent, noting that there were 56,300 new HIV infections in 2006 (2008i:1). While the prevalence of HIV/AIDS is lower in the United States than in low- and middle-income nations, there remain disparities in which Americans become infected. Table 5.3 offers data on HIV/AIDS in the United States in 2006 based on the CDC's updated findings.

These new estimates reveal that the prevalence of HIV/AIDS in the United States was worse than previously believed. Rates of HIV infection remain unacceptably high among gay and bisexual males and also females exposed to high-risk sexual contact. However, for African Americans, especially young women, the trends in new HIV infections are disproportionately high. According to the CDC, the rate of new HIV infections for African Americans was seven times that of non-Hispanic whites (83.7 versus 11.5 new infections per 100,000) while the rate for Hispanics was three times higher than non-Hispanic whites (29.3 versus 11.5 per 100,000) (2008j:4). Reasons attributed to these disparities include socioeconomic barriers (e.g., poverty, poor education), stigma directed at those with HIV/AIDS, discrimination, and geography (i.e., where you live) and available resources (2008j). African Americans and Hispanics also faired poorer on measures of

---

[7] The increased victimization and violence experienced by sex workers heightens their exposure to HIV infection. There is a global call for environmental interventions to reduce this risk by creating "enabling environments for HIV prevention" (Shannon, Kate, Thomas Kerr, Shari Allinott, Jill Chettiar, Jean Shoveller, and Mark W. Tyndall. 2007. "Social and Structural Violence and Power Relations in Mitigating HIV Risk of Drug-Using Women in Survival Sex Work." *Social Science and Medicine* 66:911–921).

Table 5.3 New HIV Infections in the United States, 2006

Categories	Percentage (56,300 New HIV Infections)
Sex	
Females	27
Males	73
Age (years)	
13–29	34
30–39	31
40–49	25
50 and over	10
Race/ethnicity	
Non-Hispanic African Americans	45
Non-Hispanic whites	35
Hispanics	17
Asians/Pacific Islanders	2
American Indians/Alaska Natives	1
Transmission Category	
Male-to-male	53
High-risk heterosexual contact	31
Injection drug use (IDU)	12
Male-to-male and IDU	4

Source: Compiled from the Centers for Disease Control and Prevention. 2008i. "Estimates of New HIV Infections in the United States." CDC HIV/AIDS Facts. Retrieved August 3, 2008. (www.cdc.gov/hiv/topics/surveillance/resources/factsheets/pdf/incidence.pdf).

having access to health care including health insurance, transportation, follow-up care, which negatively influenced prevention and early intervention (Kaiser Family Foundation 2008a).

Women of color, especially African American women, represent the majority of new HIV and AIDS cases among women. While they represent only 12 percent of the United States female population, African American women were 66 percent of the new AIDS diagnoses among all U.S. women in 2006, compared to white women (17 percent) and Latina women (16 percent) (Kaiser Family Foundation 2008b:1). A combination of biological, social, cultural, and economic factors contribute to women's increased vulnerability. In particular, gender inequalities prevent women from asserting power over their own lives and controlling the circumstances that increase their vulnerability to infection. Women are also physiologically more susceptible to becoming infected with HIV than men. Thus, as heterosexual transmission patterns grew from 3 percent in 1985 to 32 percent in 2006, so too did the feminization of HIV/AIDS (Kaiser Family Foundation 2008c:2). While preventing HIV infections remains a primary focus, reducing HIV infections also means identifying those who are HIV positive, providing treatment, and encouraging them to practice safer sex behaviors. According to the CDC, 250,000 Americans are living with HIV and are not aware of their infection, thus risking the transmitting of HIV and contributing to the HIV/AIDS pandemic (2005:601). Part of the reason for this frightening situation is linked to the reduction in HIV testing during 2001 to 2006 (Duran et al. 2008:845). Reasons for this trend in HIV testing may partly be due to social and political ambivalence along with a faulty belief that HIV/AIDS only affects men who have sex with men, and intravenous drug users, while the changing face of HIV/AIDS around the world is increasingly younger, heterosexual, and female.

The initial lukewarm global response to the HIV/AIDS pandemic is beginning to improve in scope and depth, yet "despite increased efforts, most people living with HIV and those at risk do not have access to prevention, care, and treatment" (Kaiser Family Foundation 2008d:2). The human, environmental, and economic costs of this pandemic threaten not only the security of the hardest hit regions, such as sub-Saharan Africa, but on a global scale as well. The HIV/AIDS pandemic affects global security by weakening economies along with social and governmental structures. Public health and national security experts warn that the HIV/AIDS pandemic not only presents a humanitarian crisis in sub-Saharan Africa, but also impacts security individuals (e.g., soldiers, peacekeepers), undermines the security of entire regions, and threatens to destabilize entire nations (Feldbaum, Lee, and Patel 2006). Recognizing the links between population health and global security demands greater attention and investment by developed nations. HIV/AIDS is our global concern for just as the health status of a family member impacts the entire family unit, so does the health status of our global family members influence the entire global community, regardless of the geographic and socioeconomic factors that separate us. The world is growing smaller in terms of telecommunications, mobility, and globalization. This is also true when it comes to most environmental exposures; indeed we are in this together. The next section of this chapter focuses on another shared environmental exposure, which is a breath away for each of us.

The Global Reach of Pollution

According to the World Health Organization (WHO), negative environmental exposures cause 24 percent of all global diseases and 33 percent of all diseases in children four years or younger (Osseiran and Hartl 2006:1). These negative environmental factors also account for a significant percentage of deaths including 23 percent of all deaths, and 36 percent of children's deaths (zero to four years), with the leading causes of death for children (0 to 14 years) being diarrhea, malaria, and respiratory infections (World Health Organization 2002:1). Of increasing global concern are human-driven environmental exposures, such as population displacement, climate change, and pandemics, that impact family health on a global scale with consequences that are not evenly distributed, as illustrated in Aisha's and Mandisa's stories (Cases 5.1 and 5.2, respectively).

While environmental exposures to infectious disease agents and acute illnesses are more readily recognized, what is increasingly gaining attention among those interested in family health are the interactions between genes and unhealthy environmental factors that influence chronic illnesses, such as cardiovascular disease (CVD), cancers, chronic obstructive pulmonary disease (COPD),[8] and asthma. Chapter 2 discussed the vital role of genetics in understanding human health and illness. In Chapters 3 and 4, the influences of family behavior patterns and social-cultural circumstances on family health and well being were explored. Differences in genetic makeup, behavior choices, and health disparities impact our risk of developing various illnesses. Yet, these three influences alone do not provide a complete picture of why some individuals get sick and others do not, and why some enjoy thriving health, while others suffer poorer health. Unhealthy environmental exposures, therefore, not only play direct roles in increased risks of acute diseases (e.g., malaria, cholera), but they also directly and indirectly influence the prevalence and severity of chronic illnesses (e.g., CVD, asthma). The National Institutes of Health's "Genes and Environment Initiative" 2007 to 2010 program aims to measure biological responses to multiple environmental exposures, during and after they occur (National Institutes of Health 2006). While these interactions are not well understood, it is agreed that the quality of environmental exposures, such as the air we breathe, the water we drink, the food we eat, the space we live in, the atmosphere we work in, and the climate that envelopes us, are vital contributors not only to the global burden of diseases, but a global gift of healthful living. Francesca Valent and her colleagues noted that almost a third of the complete burden of disease for European children 0 to 19 years of age was due to "indoor and

---

[8] *Chronic obstructive pulmonary disease* refers to a group of conditions "that cause airflow blockage and breathing-related problems. It includes emphysema [enlargement and destruction of the air sacs within the lungs], chronic bronchitis [i.e., inflammation and scaring of the bronchi] and is some cases asthma" [Centers for Disease Control and Prevention. 2008k. "Chronic Obstructive Pulmonary Disease." Retrieved July 2, 2008. p. 1. (www.cdc.gov/nceh/airpollution/copd/copdfaq.htm)].

outdoor air pollution, unsafe water conditions, lead exposure, and injuries" (2004:xi). Case 5.3 explores how environmental exposures, such as indoor and outdoor air pollution along with a decline in a normal gestational bacterium, may influence a child with asthma.

Case 5.3 Leon: Uneasy Breaths of Pediatric Asthma

Leon Jones' mother, Jasmine, heard the lamp next to her son's bed break as it hit the floor. She dashed into his bedroom and found her five-year-old son covered with sweat and gasping for air. "Leon, Leon," she cried, "what's wrong baby?" The panic in Leon's eyes raged as his ragged breathing emitted a shrill wheezing sound. He coughed as his chest tightly squeezed and ached for oxygen. His heart raced and the room seemed to spin as he heard his mother's anxious call to 911, pleading that they send an ambulance. Leon continued to gasp and wheeze. The frequency of Leon's breathing attacks had increased these past two years, but his mother had hoped that he would "grow out of it." Unfortunately, his breathing and these attacks just seemed to be getting worse. "Hold on Leon. I hear the sirens. Hold on baby," she wept. She met the paramedics at her door literally dragging them toward Leon's bedroom. Leon lay still, his thin lips a sickly blue-grey color. Jasmine screamed and rushed to Leon. "Let us do our job," the taller of the two men said as he pushed the frantic mother aside. "Has he recently used a bronchodilator?"[9] the other paramedic asked as they quickly began a resuscitation process. "A what? No, no, it's just a breathing thing Leon has. Please help him!" she pleaded. After administering an emergency dose of steroids and bronchodilators, the paramedics whisked Leon off to the emergency room. An hour later, the physician approached Jasmine, who smoked as she paced the cold tile floors of the nonsmoking waiting room. "Ms. Jones, your son has suffered a serious asthmatic attack, one of the most severe I have witnessed in my eight years as an emergency department physician," Dr. Henderson said shaking her head. "Leon needs regular medical care and long-term medications," she added. "Can you cure him, doctor? I mean like they did when he had his chronic ear infections and they put him on amoxicillin [antibiotic] all those times while he was a baby," Jasmine sighed. "No, Ms. Jones. Leon has asthma, which cannot be cured, but can be treated to reduce symptoms and attacks. Tell me, has anyone in your family ever had such breathing problems? Does Leon have any allergies?" Dr. Henderson inquired. "Well, I had some trouble breathing whenever I would play outside, as a kid, but I outgrew it. Don't most kids outgrow these things?" sobbed Jasmine. "As for the allergies, Leon complains about not feeling well whenever he plays on the sidewalk in front of our apartment building. He only

---

[9] Bronchodilator (inhalers) are short-term medications used to relieve symptoms (e.g., wheezing, gasping for breath, tightness in the chest, rapid attempts at breathing, and sweating) during an asthma attack [U.S. National Library of Medicine. 2008d. "Pediatric Asthma." Retrieved July 8, 2008. (www.nlm.nih.gov/medlineplus/ency/article/000990.htm)].

stays out for a few minutes before he starts wheezing and has to come inside. I know the air is bad, but what can I do? I can't afford to move. I just thought he was not as strong as the other kids, something he could overcome, like those ear infections, right?" asked Jasmine as she slumped into an olive green plastic chair.

Asthma is a chronic disease in which the inside walls of the bronchial tubes (airways) become inflamed and swell causing these tubes to narrow. Symptoms often include wheezing, coughing, chest tightness, and general discomfort due to the reduced flow of oxygen (National Heart, Lung, and Blood Institute 2008). The Global Initiative for Asthma (GINA) states that the prevalence of asthma is increasing worldwide, estimating that globally 300 million people currently have asthma with an additional 100 million by 2025 as the world population becomes increasingly urbanized and adopts Western lifestyles (Beasley et al. 2004:1). Within the United States, approximately 20 million citizens have asthma, of which 9 million are children (National Heart, Lung, and Blood Institute 2008:2). As noted in Chapter 2, genetics plays a role in many complex illnesses, such as asthma. Genetics studies reveal that asthma is not one disease, but several diseases with early (childhood) onset varying from later onset asthma, particularly when children live with smokers (Bouzigon et al. 2008). In Case 5.3, Leon has pediatric asthma, the most common chronic childhood illness. Inner-city children with asthma, such as Leon, may be especially vulnerable to the impacts of air pollution as revealed in the findings from the Inner-City Asthma Study that children from low-income families in seven American inner cities had "significantly decreased lung function following exposure to higher concentrations of the air pollutants sulfur dioxide, airborne fine particles, and nitrogen dioxide [from motor vehicle exhaust]" (National Institute of Allergy and Infectious Diseases 2008:1).

The historically high prevalence of asthma for Americans began in the 1980s impacting all age, sex, and racial groups, though in varying degrees of severity. While factors fueling this increase are not fully understood, the interplay of health determinants (see Family Health Determinants Model, Figure 1.1) appears to provide the best explanation. Research findings reveal links between genetic mutation and asthma (Thakkinstian et al. 2005). Yet, the dramatic rise during the past two or more decades, a period too brief to reflect any significant genetic pool change, underscores the vital roles of behaviors, socioeconomic disparities, health care (e.g., physician diagnostic procedures), and especially environmental (e.g., air pollution, allergens, irritants) influences (Szeftel 2007).

As indicated in Table 5.4, asthma is more common among children (0 to 14 years) than adults (35 years and above) with male children experiencing a higher prevalence than female children (Asthma and Allergy Foundation of America 2008:2). This sex difference switches once individuals reach adulthood (especially after age

Table 5.4 Asthma Prevalence by Age Group and Sex, United States, 2006

Age and Sex	Percentage
All ages	
Total	8.0
Female	8.8
Male	7.1
0–14 years	
Total	9.6
Female	7.5
Male	11.6
15–34 years	
Total	8.0
Female	9.5
Male	6.4
35 years and over	
Total	7.4
Female	9.0
Male	5.6

Source: Adapted from the Centers for Disease Control and Prevention. 2007b. "Data Table for Figure 15.5. Prevalence of Current Asthma among Persons of all Ages, by Age Group and Sex: United States, 2006." p. 96. Retrieved July 7, 2008. (www.cdc.gov/nchs/data/nhis/earlyrelease/200706_15.pdf).

34 years), when the prevalence of asthma for adult females is significantly higher than that for adult males. This sex–age interaction appears to have biological sex (e.g., genetics, sex hormones, airway physiology), social-cultural determinants (e.g., pre-existing obesity, poverty, geographic location), and environmental exposures (e.g., air pollution, infections, displacement) as factors (Carey et al. 2008; Melgert et al. 2007).

As noted in Chapter 4, health disparities are common in the United States, which also is true regarding the prevalence of asthma. Table 5.5 illustrates the racial and ethnic disparities in terms of the prevalence of asthma with non-Hispanic African Americans and American Indians/Alaskan Natives experiencing significantly higher rates of asthma at all age groups.

When the data are focused on childhood asthma, however, the health disparities become increasingly blatant. Table 5.5 reveals that for American children aged

Table 5.5 Asthma Prevalence by Race and Ethnicity, United States, 2005

Race and Ethnicity	Percentage
Total	7.7
Non-Hispanic African American	9.4
American Indian/Alaska Native	9.2
Non-Hispanic white	7.6
Hispanic/Latino	6.2
Asian American	4.9

Source: Adapted from Akinbami, Lara. 2006a. "Asthma Prevalence, Health Care Use and Mortality: United States, 2003–2005." Figure 1. Retrieved July 7, 2008. (www.cdc.gov/nchs/products/pubs/pubd/hestats/ashtma03-05/asthma03-05.htm#fig1).

0 to 17 years, the prevalence of asthma for African American children was 60 percent higher and for American Indian or Alaskan Native children it was 25 percent higher than for white children. Less well known is that when race and ethnicity are considered, Puerto Rican children (0 to 17 years) had the highest prevalence of asthma of all groups, 140 percent higher than non-Hispanic whites. In addition to the prevalence of asthma, rates of ambulatory visits, emergency visits, and mortality rates deepen the clarity of the health disparity for non-Hispanic African American children with asthma (Akinbami 2006b:8). These findings suggest that compared to non-Hispanic white children, non-Hispanic African American children, such as Leon in Case 5.3, may be underutilizing ambulatory care,[10] suggesting that minority children may not receive the same quality of ambulatory care for asthma and have limited health care coverage. Likewise, minority children have a 260 percent higher rate of emergency department visits and a 500 percent higher mortality due to asthma than non-Hispanic whites (Akinbami 2006b:9). Table 5.6 presents comparisons among racial and ethnic groups regarding the type of health care they access and mortality rates among youth with asthma.

According to the Asthma and Allergy Foundation of America, of the over 20 million Americans who suffer from asthma, 50 percent of asthma cases are "allergic asthma" or "allergy-triggered asthma" (2008:1). Allergic asthma is commonly found in children with allergic reactions to dust mites, pollen, or animal dander, with estimates that 75 to 85 percent of children with asthma also have some allergy (2008:1). The role of environmental exposures in asthma and allergic

---

[10] Ambulatory care is "medical care including diagnosis, observation, treatment and rehabilitation that is provided on an outpatient basis" [MedicineNet. 2008a. "Definition of Ambulatory Care." p. 1. Retrieved July 8, 2008. (www.medterms.com/script/main/art.asp?articlekey=2218)].

Table 5.6 Asthma Prevalence, Health Care Use, and Mortality among Children 0–17 Years of Age, by Race and Ethnicity, United States, 2003–2005

Race and Ethnicity	2004–2005 Prevalence Percentage	2003–2004 Ambulatory Visits per 1,000	2003–2004 Emergency Room Visits per 10,000	2003–2004 Deaths per 1,000,000
Non-Hispanic African American	12.7	71.5	251.6	9.2
Non-Hispanic white	8.0	100.2	65.8	1.3
American Indian or Alaskan Native	9.9	*	*	*
Asian American	4.9	*	*	*
Hispanic or Latino	7.8	83.3	108.1	1.8
Puerto Rican	19.2	*	*	*
Mexican American	6.4	*	*	*

*Data not available or estimates not considered reliable.

Source: Adapted with permission from Commonwealth Fund. Akinbami, Lara J. 2006b. "The State of Childhood Asthma, United States, 1980–2005." Advance Data from Vital and Health Statistics; No. 381, Hyattsville, MD: National Center for Health Statistics. Table B, p. 9. Retrieved July 7, 2008. (www.cdc.gov/nchs/data/ad/ad381.pdf).

asthma includes external triggers (e.g., dust, pollen, temperature) and possible internal changes to the body's reactions and/or to the genes themselves.

Internal Environmental Exposures: Imbalances in Biological Flora

While scientists remain unsure about exactly what causes asthma, the condition does appear to be familial, suggesting a genetic link. As noted earlier, approximately 10 million Americans have allergic asthma meaning that their asthma attacks are triggered by allergens, such as dust mites, mold, pollen, exercise, viral infections, animals (dander), tobacco smoke, chemicals in the air or in food, changes in weather (cold temperatures), strong emotions, and some medications (Medline Plus 2008b:1). Allergic asthma is an expanding global problem. In a global study that reviewed 54,000 children in 22 nations ranging from urban Europe to rural Africa, the findings revealed that affluent countries had four times the rate of allergic asthma as that of less affluent countries (*Science Daily* 2007:1). In trying to understand these data, scientists began to look at other possible causes including the "hygiene hypothesis." The *hygiene hypothesis* means that perhaps children and their families living in affluent environments have a lower level of common gestational bacteria (i.e., *Helicobacter pylori*) due in part to more sterile homes and the overuse of antibiotics, as compared to less affluent nations (*Science Daily* 2007). Yu Chen and Martin Blaser (2007) were the first to report that indeed an inverse relationship between *H. pylori* bacteria (*H. pylori*) and pediatric asthma exists, noting that without this bacterium the prevalence of pediatric asthma rises. They also stated that a reduction in normal gut flora (*H. pylori*) appears to be one explanation for the increases of childhood allergic sensitivity and allergic asthma in affluent nations. In their findings they found that youth (3 to 19 years of age) who did have *H. pylori* in their gut were 25 percent less likely to have asthma than those with less *H. pylori*. The statistics were even stronger for younger children (3 to 13 years of age) in which those with *H. pylori* were 59 percent less likely to have asthma. Likewise, both children and teens who carried the *H. Pylori* bacteria in their systems were 40 percent less likely to have hay fever or other related allergies as well. Chen and Blaser explain that "if a child does not encounter *Helicobacter* early on, the immune system may not learn how to regulate a response to allergens. Therefore, the child may be more likely to mount the kinds of inflammatory responses that trigger asthma" (*Science Daily* 2008b:2). Such findings may aid families and the medical community in wiser use of antibiotics and deeper recognition of the need to "work with the body's immune system." This position of working with the body in times of health and illness does not support the brazen ignoring of recommended immunizations as discussed in Chapter 3, but rather suggests a more prudent use of antibiotics in our food sources, and recognition that the human species continues to evolve in terms of immunity and vulnerability to infectious agents. In Case 5.3, Leon had internal (e.g., low levels of *H. pylori*) and external (e.g., indoor tobacco smoke and outdoor vehicle exhaust air pollution) environmental exposures that may have added to a hypersensitivity resulting in his allergic asthma. Both internal and external environmental exposures could have been improved in the name of securing better family health. This need for reducing harmful environmental exposures is especially true for the tobacco smoke, identified as the number one cause of preventable death in the world.

External Environmental Exposures: The Global Tobacco Epidemic

Renewed concerns over climate change and poor air quality have surfaced on local, national, and global levels. In early 2008, the Environmental Protection Agency (EPA) identified approximately 345 out of 700 American counties as having air "too dirty to breathe" (Meersman 2008:A7). Globally the issue of air pollution moved to centerstage with the 2008 Summer Olympics, which were held in Beijing,

China. Questions about athletes' safety focused less on terrorism and more on poor air quality in the weeks prior to the opening ceremonies. Despite Chinese officials' efforts to reduce air pollution, the American Lung Association warned that anyone with asthma or other respiratory diseases attending the 2008 Olympics to be prepared for "flare ups" both in ambient air (due to extreme air pollution) and inside air (due to excessively high prevalence of cigarette smoking in China) (Fernandez 2008). This issue of the polluting impact of tobacco smoke received significant notice in 2008 when the WHO estimated that tobacco use will kill 1 billion people globally in this century, which is 10 times as many as the 100 million who died from tobacco-related illness in the last century (2008b:9). This WHO initiative, financed by the Gates and Bloomberg philanthropies, embraces six policies (MPOWER) to counter the tobacco epidemic including: (1) Monitor tobacco use and prevention policies, (2) Protect people from tobacco smoke, (3) Offer help to quit tobacco use, (4) Warn about the dangers of tobacco, (5) Enforce bans on tobacco, and (6) Raise taxes on tobacco (WHO 2008b:23–39). For such global initiatives to succeed, however, families must play the primary role in working with organizations, such as the Johns Hopkins Bloomberg School of Public Health and the CDC, in promoting and supporting programs to eliminate tobacco use in families throughout the world.

External environmental exposures, such as outdoor air pollution, also have insidious impacts beyond recognized relationship between pollution and CVD, cancers, respiratory illnesses (e.g., COPD, asthma), and so on. Recent research sheds light on the devastating burdens of damage to the structure and function of our DNA caused by air pollution.

Deeper Health Impacts: Air Pollution and DNA

Another troubling family health question related to external environmental exposures, such as air pollution, asks if harmful pollutants not only irritate and damage human biological systems (e.g., cardiovascular, respiratory), but also impact the genetic system. If this link exists, and it appears to, then families and the governing bodies that represent them would have greater scientific leverage in demanding that our external environments, such as air, water, and food supplies, need to be much safer and more healthful. Earlier work, such as that of Frederica Perera and her colleagues, found that those families living in polluted neighborhoods (e.g., New York, United States; and Krakow, Poland) were exposed to high levels of "polycyclic aromatic hydrocarbons" (PAH) (i.e., incomplete combustion of organic sources, such as coal, cigarettes, vehicle exhaust, and barbecued meats), that can bond to DNA and cause somatic gene mutation in newborns (Perera et al. 2002). In 2008, additional evidence emerged from research in China in which an epidemiological study identified the impacts of air pollution on the structure and/or activity of DNA in fetuses that appear to cause growth and developmental problems in children. Each year, 656,000 Chinese citizens die of diseases triggered by air pollution (Fabin 2008:77). In a highly polluted industrial city of Tongliang in south-central China, Perera and her colleagues studied the changes in the bodies of the city's children both before and after the closing of a pollution-belching coal power in 2004. Their findings revealed that children born in 2002 to mothers who breathed the more polluted air suffered greater damage to their DNA while in the womb that resulted in lower developmental scores after birth and higher risks of cancer as they age. Children born in 2005 to mothers in the same city, but who breathed cleaner air (only one year after the plant's closing) had less damage to their DNA, better developmental scores and lower risks of cancer. The message from this powerful study was that "PAH are a ubiquitous pollutant capable of affecting children even at relatively low concentrations" for even "[i]n New York City, where airborne PAH levels are more than 10 times lower than in Tongliang, we have been able to measure the effects in reduced fetal growth and neurodevelopmental impacts" (Fabin 2008:79). Environmental exposures, such as air pollution, are powerful and sweep across our globe at ever-increasing amounts. Dirty air, wherever and however it is produced, is every global family's concern. While the impacts of environmental exposures, such as infectious diseases or air and water quality, capture global attention, the work environment also plays a crucial role in the health and well-being of families. Unhealthy physical environmental exposures in the workplace (e.g., air, water, and food contamination; hazardous chemical or radiation exposure; carcinogenic concerns; combustible material dangers; harmful noise levels; electrical mishaps; construction or manufacturing accidents; harmful ergonomic[11] conditions) remain significant health concerns for workers and their families. Psychological and social environmental exposures, however, also demand attention due to their impacts on stress responses and health. The next section of this chapter explores how location and nature of "work" have shifted in recent history for both women and men and how the "psychosocial work environment" impacts families' health and well-being.

Work Environments and Global Family Health

For most families, work is essential for economic and social well-being. What is only recently being appreciated are the impacts of the work environment on physical, psychological, and social health of employees and indirectly for their families.

---

[11] "Ergonomics, a relatively new science, looks at the application of physiological, psychological, and engineering principles to interactions between people and machines. Ergonomics attempts to define working conditions that enhance individual health, safety, comfort, and productivity. This can be done by recognizing three things: the physiological, anatomical, and psychological capabilities and limitations of people; the tools they use; and the environments in which they function" (Hannah, Kathryn J., Marion J. Ball, and Margaret J.A. Edwards. 2006. *Introduction to Nursing Informatics*. p. 234. NY: Springer).

Workplaces are complex ecologies, therefore, changes in any aspect of the workplace often has a ripple effect on those in that work environment. Progressive businesses recognize that developing and maintaining physically, psychologically, and socially healthy work environments increase productivity, reduces attrition, and lowers costs (e.g., sick days) (Partnership for Workplace Mental Health 2006). Throughout human history, families have been engaged in the multiple tasks of "making a living" and raising the next generation. The stressors of balancing family and work have grown more complicated as the work environment changed in locations, demands, and composition. Several themes surface from the family and work literature, including impacts of maternal employment, changing workplace locations and conditions, and balancing roles as worker, partner/spouse, parent, coworker, and community member. This section of the chapter discusses the impacts of several of these themes in the context of work environments and family health.

Women in the Workplace

With the Industrial Revolution large numbers of men began to work away from the farm and outside of the home. In 2007, the proportion of American families with at least one employed member was 82.6 percent with a race and ethnicity range of 89.6 percent of Asian, 87.6 percent Hispanic, 82.7 percent of non-Hispanic white, and 78.9 percent non-Hispanic African American families (U.S. Department of Labor 2008:1–2). While this movement of men into wage and salaried work impacted families, women entering the workforce, especially during the last half of the 20th century onward, changed the rhythm and relationships of family life. In 1950, 34 percent of American women 16 years and older worked outside of the home, but by 2000 this demographic swelled to over 60 percent (Toossi 2002:15). With the increase in women in the labor force, the demographic of working women with children struggled with the shifting nature of the work environment, which was increasingly productivity focused. By 2007, 71 percent of all American women with children[12] under 18 years, 63.3 percent of those women with children under six years, and 56 percent of women with infants (under one year) were in the workforce (U.S. Department of Labor 2008:11–13). Globally, women continue to enter the workforce in greater numbers as they comprise 40 percent of all employed adults, but increases in employment have not substantially narrowed the gender gap in the workplace with higher percentages of women in "vulnerable employment"[13] rather than wage or salaried work as their male peers (International Labour Office 2008:2–6). The Global Employment

---

[12] These percentages may understate how many women are raising children in the paid labor force for these data only reflect women raising "own" children and do not include those raising grandchildren, nephews, nieces, or other children.

[13] Vulnerable employment means either unpaid contributing family workers or own-account workers and is at risk to economic cycles [International Labour Office. 2008. "Global Employment Trends for Women—March 2008." Retrieved August 10, 2008. p. 3. (www.ilo.org/wcmsp5/groups/public/---dgreports/---dcomm/documents/publication/wcms_091225.pdf)].

Trends for Women—March 2008 cautions that for women who do find work "they are often confined to work in the less productive sectors of economies and in status groups that carry higher economic risk and a lesser likelihood of meeting the characteristics that define decent work including access to social protection, basic rights and a voice at work" (International Labour Office 2008:1). This gap in parity with male peers means that women are more likely to work in service and agriculture jobs resulting in lower pay, decreased control of their work and family lives and increased conflicts between work and family demands. Earlier in this chapter, data on regional disparities related to environmental exposures to disease (i.e., malaria epidemic and HIV/AIDS pandemic) and chronic illness (i.e., asthma) were linked to global conditions. The work environment also holds regional disparities in terms of employment opportunities as noted in Table 5.7.

Table 5.7 presents data reflecting high employment-to-population levels for women living in poverty regions, such as sub-Saharan Africa. Caution is needed in understanding these data for they are not necessarily positive developments as they would be in developed regions of the world. In developing regions, such as sub-Saharan Africa, families also struggle with burdens of overwhelming poverty, epidemics, pandemics, and civil conflicts. Women living in poverty work to subsist, often enduring low job quality, lack of flexibility, long hours, and minimal social support. This high employment ratio also may mean that significant numbers of young women are forced into paid labor instead of enrolling in school. Women's employment in many regions remained burdened by troubling working conditions, limited social protection, and high levels of under- and unemployment along with external and internal brain drains.[14] Even though women in developed economic regions did not struggle with the complexities of high poverty, civil conflicts, or nutritional and disease concerns, they still endure gender wage gaps and difficulties in trying to balance family and work demands and overall work-related stress as noted in the concerns of Table 5.7. Globally, therefore, the work environment increasingly means that adults (women and men) work away from home with less control over their time and work responsibilities plus added concerns over family health and child care. The work environment is more than its physical, chemical, or other material conditions, however, for psychological and sociological dimensions also play vital roles in creating healthful or sick work environment exposures.

Psychosocial Work Environment

The narrow definition of "work environment," has broadened to the "psychosocial work environment" (Siegrist 2004). Chronic work stress can develop into "job strain," which, while not a disease, is related to serious health concerns (e.g., CVD,

---

[14] Brain drain: when educated and skilled workers leave the country for job opportunities abroad (external) or the local area such as migrating from rural to urban areas (internal).

Table 5.7 Ratios of Employment-to-Population by Sex, Region, and Concerns, 2007

Region	Female 2007 (Percentage)	Male 2007 (Percentage)	Work Related Concerns
East Asia	65.2	78.4	Job quality, social protection, long hours Job security Inequality in rural and urban development Child labor Brain drain* (external and internal)
Sub-Saharan Africa	56.9	79.7	Underemployment skill mismatch Job quality Develop nonfarm jobs in rural areas High poverty Civil conflicts, child soldiers Child labor Need to improve education enrolment Infrastructure Nutrition and disease (e.g., HIV/AIDS) Job creation Brain drain (external and internal)
Southeast Asia and the Pacific	55.1	78.1	Underemployment skills mismatch Job quality Need to improve education enrolment Child labor Develop nonfarm jobs in rural areas Job creation Brain drain (external and internal)
Developed economies and the European Union (EU)	49.1	64.0	Job quality Hours of work Balancing, flexibility Gender wage gaps
Latin America and the Caribbean	47.1	73.7	Barriers for young females Need to improve education enrolment Need for investment and job creation Job quality Child labor

(continued)

Table 5.7 (*continued*)

Region	Female 2007 (Percentage)	Male 2007 (Percentage)	Work Related Concerns
Central and Southeastern Europe (non-EU)	45.6	63.8	Unemployed women Balancing, flexibility Discouragement Child Labor Underemployment skills mismatch Brain drain (external migration)
South Asia	34.1	78.1	Unemployment Job quality Underemployment skill mismatch Child labor Barriers for young females Job creation Brain drain (external and internal) High poverty Need to improve education enrolment Develop nonfarm jobs in rural areas
Middle East	28.1	70.3	Barriers for young females Poverty Job quality, informal job search networks Civil conflicts Underemployment skill mismatch Child labor Need to improve education enrolment Unemployment Brain drain (external and internal) Job creation
North Africa	21.9	69.1	Same as found in the Middle East

* Brain drain: when educated and skilled workers leave the country for job opportunities abroad (external) or the local area such as migrating from rural to urban areas (internal).

Sources: Compiled from the International Labour Office. 2008. "Global Employment Trends for Women—March 2008." p. 5. Retrieved August 10, 2008. (www.ilo.org/wcmsp5/groups/public/---dgreports/---dcomm/documents/publication/wcms_091225.pdf); and the International Labour Office. 2007. "Global Employment Trends for Women—2007." p. 17–20. Retrieved August 10, 2008. (www.ilo.org/public/english/employment/strat/download/getw07.pdf).

depression). Job strain is experienced when work demands exceed the employee's ability to cope with or control the demands of work and home. Description of this work demand–control–support imbalance first appeared in the Robert Karasek model (Karasek 1979; Karasek and Theorell 1990). "Karasek's job strain model states that the greatest risk to physical and mental health from stress occurs to workers facing high psychological workload demands or pressures combined with low control or decision latitude in meeting those demands" (Landbergis et al. 1993:1). Based on this model, Table 5.8 presents five areas and related factors that play crucial roles in the creation of job strain.

Job strain is not the same as work challenge for when one is challenged it motivates, energizes, and allows for feelings of accomplishment. Unlike a challenge, job strain results in decreased self-efficacy, increased depressive symptoms, fatigue, suppressed immune system, increased risks for physical and mental illnesses, injuries, and even job failure (Bianchi, Casper, and Berkowitz 2005; Sauter et al. 2008). In 2007, a study of Danish employees found that adverse psychosocial work environment factors caused 10 to 15 percent of the disability cases after controlling for smoking, overweight, and ergonomic issues (Christensen et al. 2007:235). Case 5.4 serves as an example of some of the factors related to job strain as revealed in Table 5.8.

Case 5.4 Theresa and David: Stress . . . at Work, by Steven Sauter et al. (2008:1)

The longer he waited, the more David worried. For weeks he had been plagued by aching muscles, loss of appetite, restless sleep, and a complete sense of exhaustion. At first he tried to ignore these problems, but eventually he became so short-tempered and irritable that his wife insisted he get a checkup. Now, sitting in the doctor's office and wondering what the verdict would be, he didn't even notice when Theresa took the seat beside him. They had been good friends when she worked in the front office at the plant, but he had not seen her since she left three years ago to take a job as a customer service representative. Her gentle poke in the ribs brought him around, and within minutes they were talking and gossiping as if she had never left.

"You got out just in time," he told her. "Since the reorganization, nobody feels safe. It used to be that as long as you did your work, you had a job. That's not for sure anymore. They expect the same production rates even though two guys are now doing the work of three. We're so backed up. I'm working twelve-hour shifts six days a week. I swear I hear those machines humming in my sleep. Guys are

Table 5.8 Job Strain Components and Related Factors

- **The design of tasks and roles ("work latitude"):**
  - imbalance in effort–reward, low pay, disrespect
  - unsuitable demands: too high or too low demands, monotonous work
  - long hours, hectic pace, or infrequent breaks
  - shiftwork
  - low control, skill discretion, or decision authority over work
  - conflicting or confusing work expectations
  - too much responsibility in terms of "too many hats" to wear

- **Career concerns:**
  - job insecurity, limited growth, or advancement or promotion
  - unprepared for rapid change
  - limited work-related learning opportunities, isolation

- **Work interpersonal relationships:**
  - limited support from colleagues and management
  - limited lightheartedness (little humor or joy)
  - discrimination, prejudice: racism, sexism, homophobia, other stigmas

- **Work environmental conditions:**
  - hazardous, unsafe work space or materials
  - uncomfortable temperature, too hot, too cold, too humid, too dry
  - noisy, loud, unpleasant, poor lighting
  - non-ergonomic work stations, crowded, cluttered work stations
  - unclean, dirty, dusty, unpleasant surroundings, needs upkeep, remodeling
  - poor air or water quality, unpleasant smells

- **Work organization and management:**
  - limited information about the job
  - limited feed back from supervisors
  - inflexibility in scheduling and family-friendly policies
  - poor communication between management and employees
  - limited concern for workers' and their families' health and well-being
  - limited lightheartedness (little humor or joy)
  - job insecurity, downsizing

Source: Adapted from Sauter, Steven, Lawrence Murphy, Michael Colligan, Naomi Swanson, Joseph Hurrell, Jr., Fredrick Scharf, Jr., Raymond Sinclair, Paula Grubb, Linda Goldenbar, Toni Alterman, Janet Johnston, Anne Hamilton, and Julie Tisdale. 2008. "Stress . . . at Work." National Institute for Occupational Safety and Health. Publication No. 99-101. p. 3–4. Retrieved August 2, 2008. (www.cdc.gov/Niosh/stresswk.html).

calling in sick just to get a break. Morale is so bad they're talking about bringing in some consultants to figure out a better way to get the job done."

"Well, I really miss you guys," she said. "I'm afraid I jumped from the frying pan into the fire. In my new job, the computer routes the calls and they never stop. I even have to schedule my bathroom breaks. All I hear the whole day are complaints from unhappy customers. I try to be helpful and sympathetic, but I can't promise anything without getting my boss's approval. Most of the time I'm caught between what the customer wants and company policy. I'm not sure who I'm supposed to keep happy. The other reps are so uptight and tense they don't even talk to one another. We all go to our own little cubicles and stay there until quitting time. To make matters worse, my mother's health is deteriorating. If only I could use some of my sick time to look after her. No wonder I'm in here with migraine headaches and high blood pressure. A lot of the reps are seeing the employee assistance counselor and taking stress management classes, which seems to help. But sooner or later, someone will have to make some changes in the way the place is run."

Review Table 5.8 as you consider Case 5.4. David and Theresa (Case 5.4) represent a common and costly problem of job strain that plagues workers in the United States and other nations. In terms of "the design of tasks and roles," David works to exhaustion with long hours and an overload of demands. Overtime and extended work shifts are related to lower perceptions of health, increased risk of injuries, fatigue, and decreased physical activity often contributing to elevated risks of CVD (Caruso et al. 2004). For David's colleagues who are transitioning into parenthood, the overload especially increases risks of depressive symptoms and relationship conflicts (Neal and Hammer 2006; Perry-Jenkins et al. 2007). Workers who do not get sufficient sleep, whether due to job strain (aggravated by prolonged workdays, anxiety, taking work home, etc.) and/or family sleep disruptions, risk nodding off at work, and/or in their cars. For example, in 2007, the National Sleep Foundation's (NSF) findings from the "Sleep in America" survey of 1,000 randomly selected adults reveal that Americans on average are working 4.5 extra hours from home per week in addition to their regular 47.5-hour workweek and were coping by sleeping too little and too poorly (Francini and Tumminello 2008:1). Even though the adults in this study reported averaging 6 hours and 40 minutes of sleep per weeknight, they did not sleep soundly enough, with 49 percent stating that they wake up feeling unrefreshed, and another 42 percent waking during the night a few nights per week (2008:2). Negative results of this unhealthy sleeplessness include (2008:1):

- 36 percent nodded off or fell asleep while driving;
- 29 percent became very sleepy or fell asleep at work in the past month;

- 20 percent had sex less often or have lost interest in sex due to exhaustion and sleepiness;
- 14 percent missed family events, work functions, and leisure activities in the past month due to sleepiness;
- 12 percent were late for work in past due to sleepiness.

Impacts of prolonged work hours and additional job strain meshed with family demands, therefore, often result in interrupted and poor sleep that in turn negatively affect personal and work lives.

The overload and frustration of Theresa's job (Case 5.4) also means fewer needed breaks, and while she is sympathetic to customers' concerns, she has no authority to do anything to help them. In 2004, a study of the sociodemographic factors (i.e., sex, age, and marital status) of Swedish general practitioners' stress levels revealed that the highest rates of job strain were observed among younger married females, especially when work interfered with family demands (Vanagas, Bihari-Axelsson, and Vanagienė 2004). It appears that to some extent, development of job strain, anxiety, and low job satisfaction are directly related to social context. The work–family conflict for Theresa trying to meet family care needs, therefore, significantly contributes to her job strain, but the pressure could be more pronounced if Theresa (and David) worked nonstandard schedules (shift work). Researchers argue that workers engaged in shift work suffer increased risks of depressive symptoms as well as decreased levels of effective parenting than their peers working standard schedules (Strazdins et al. 2006). It appears that indeed paid work greatly affects individual's health and that of their families.

Both Theresa and David (Case 5.4) appear frustrated over their limited career options within the company. David's "career concerns" are particularly high with the company's reorganization and employees' worries over what will happen next. These career concerns are linked with troublesome interpersonal relationships at work. The "work interpersonal relationships" for both David and Theresa are limited as the demands to do more in less time keep workers somewhat isolated. Some of David's colleagues end up using sick days just to get a much needed break from the pressure of too few workers doing too much. Neither Theresa nor David mentioned getting support or encouragement from coworkers much less management, which means morale may be low, adding to the job strain and related ill health effects. A positive social climate in the workplace is vital to health in terms of providing support, communication, and reducing feelings of isolation, thus reducing anxiety, absenteeism, turnover, and lost productivity. Ilan Meyer (2003) and Ilan Meyer, Sharon Schwartz, and David M. Frost (2008) argue that employees exposed to race, ethnicity, and/or sexual orientation discrimination and prejudice risk additional job strain and resulting ill health effects. If David was non-Hispanic African American and gay while Theresa was Hispanic and lesbian, the job strain they experienced may have been intensified in a bigoted workplace thus creating even greater spillover effects on family health (Bond et al. 2008). For example, Clifford Broman (2001) states that job strain has serious health implications not only on the personal health of African American workers, but also on their family life for as job strain increased, marital harmony decreased.

The excessive noise that David was exposed to at work also speaks to "work environmental conditions" factors. Crowding, air pollution, and ergonomic problems also impact the worksites for both David and Theresa. While neither is working with "hazardous waste," they are being exposed to environmental conditions that are not healthy or pleasant. Such conditions not only negatively impact health and safety, but also extend into employees' family lives and work productivity in terms of missing work due to work-climate–related illness (e.g., hearing loss, carpal tunnel syndrome).

The overall "work organization and management" of David's and Theresa's employer sorely needs improvement. According to Eileen Appelbaum, Annette Bernhardt, and Richard Murnane (2003), deregulation, and de-unionization have impacted all businesses as they compete on the global stage. These powerful social and economic forces are changing the face of the workplace in terms of employment relationships, trust, commitment, demands, control, responsibilities, support, leadership, compensation (pay), and communication among employees and employers. The downsizing of staffs plus increased workloads contributed to rising levels of job strain resulting in both David and Theresa seeking medical help for their own ill health. In addition to the lack of meaningful participation in work-related decision authority, the company appears to lack a family-friendly policy for workers with family health concerns as seen with Theresa's need to help her ailing mother. David and Theresa are not alone in their job strain struggles. In 2000, 80 percent of American workers reported feeling stressed on the job with almost half stating that they needed help in learning how to manage the stress, 35 percent noted that their job was harming their physical or emotional health, and another 42 percent claimed that work pressures interfered with their personal relationships (Harris Poll 2001:1). Workers who experience low job control, support, and/or security, therefore, endure greater risks for ill health. For example, several European studies have found that workers who experience high job demands and low job decision-making authority experienced greater risks for depressive symptoms (Rugulies et al. 2006), coronary heart disease (Belkic et al. 2004; Karasek and Theorell 1990), and emotional exhaustion (Santavirta, Kovero, and Solovieva

2005). Poor work organization and management combined with economic recession and labor downsizing often pit employers against employees with damaging impacts on the psychosocial work environment that negatively affect workers' health and spill over into their families' health and well-being. When family demands clash with work requirements, workers may experience chronic stress responses that manifest into physical, psychological, emotional, and social ill health. The work–family conflicts, therefore, are of vital concern to family health.

Work-to-Family and Family-to-Work Conflicts

Scholars explain that Americans are viewed as overworked and overstressed, scrabbling with a time deficit ("time divide"[15]) as they barter child care and lower personal health behavior expectations, such as sufficient sleep, healthy diet, exercise, and relaxation (Jacobs and Gerson 2004). This perceived time-deficit divides often cause friction between work and family lives. Conflicts between workplace and home are often separated as "work-to-family" and "family-to-work" concerns. Work-to-family conflicts occur when work demands interfere with roles of parent, caregiver, or spouse/partner, such as David's job strain caused him to be short-tempered and irritable at home. Family-to-work conflicts, such as Theresa's need to care for her mother, may interfere with work responsibilities and demands. In addition to the usual factors considered in the psychosocial work environment, such as job demands, control, and social support, there are also "workplace norms," such as a drive for higher productivity, constant job attendance, work-comes-first type commitment to an organization, and/or a covert message that "only the strong will survive" (Hammer et al. 2004:84, 95). Boundaries between family life and work life blur as workplace norms "encroach on nonwork life and relationships, contributing to conflicts between demands at work and family roles" (2004:85). Naturally, work–family conflicts vary among firms, but when workplace norms are rigid and management is unapproachable, job strain escalates. For example, the unfriendly family policies and practices contributed to Theresa's (Case 5.4) high job strain and negatively impacted her mental and physical health.

Increases in the wage and salaried work force, rising urbanization, and shifting workplace norms challenge work–family relationships and child care demands. These burdens are especially felt in developing regions of the world, where incomes are far lower and resources more sparse, resulting in greater impacts on families' health. Yet, working families, regardless of region, appear to have common

---

[15] The time divide(s) include: work–family conflicts between workplace and home, occupation-growing gap in the workforce in terms of hours worked, parenting competition between parents and childless/childfree workers, gender gap in job flexibility and pay, and aspiration gap in control and flexibility in decision making at work (Jacobs, Jerry and Kathleen Gerson. 2004. *The Time Divide: Work, Family and Gender Inequality*. Boston, MA: Harvard University Press).

work–family worries. The project on Global Working Families[16] by Jody Heymann, Stephanic Simmons, and Alison Earle (2005) explored this aspect. They conducted in-depth interviews of families, schools, child-care centers, shelters, and medical personnel from six diverse countries including the United States, Mexico, Botswana, Vietnam, Honduras, and Russia. This project explored how families' work–social conditions impacted the health and development of their children. While the socioeconomic circumstances varied, surprisingly parents from these varied regions had common concerns. While at work, all of the adults worried about their children's health and how to help them with schoolwork in the face of limited contact time at home. Similar workplace concerns emerged as well, such as inflexibility, long hours, lack of paid leave, no or limited health care access, and working uncommon shifts (i.e., evenings and weekends). In each participating country, families struggled with leaving minor children with substandard care while they worked due to inadequate supports, low wages, and/or poor working conditions. All families recognized the importance of parental involvement in their children's health and education, yet conflicts between work and home often interfered, especially for single parents. Families across the world, therefore, face similar tough choices and conflicts in balancing demands of work and home environments and echo common themes of needing more time for caregiving at home for children and other ill, disabled, or elder family members. Within the United States, 70 percent of children (under 16 years), as well as most elders and sick and disabled adults, rely on the caregiving of working adults (Harvard School of Public Health 2008:1). Family needs for greater flexibility in work schedules, more quality childcare resources, and access to health care coverage and treatment are global concerns. A national survey of employers reveals that they recognize the negative impacts of job strain and desire that their employees be more engaged in and satisfied with their jobs, have less negative stress spillover from work to family and vice versa, and enjoy better mental health (Galinsky et al. 2008). It appears, therefore, that employers' desire to reduce work–family conflicts, not only for the health of their workers and their families, but also for the health of their businesses.

While both work-to-family and family-to-work conflicts contribute to job strain, defining the factors that comprise the work–family interface demand greater study. For example, it is suggested that families with a healthful "work–family fit" are better able to balance and weather the demands of work–family strains and reduce conflicts. The concept of work–family fit is dynamic for it reflects a family resilience framework, as described in Joan

---

[16] For more information on "The Project on Global Working Families," see Institute of Health and Social Policy. 2009. "The Project on Global Working Families." Retrieved July 30, 2009. (www.hsph.harvard.edu/globalworkingfamilies/).

Patterson's (2002) integration of family resilience and family stress theory, in which demands are balanced with family coping skills and resources. It is further argued that "work-family fit is more than the absence of work-family conflict. As the workforce and labor market continue addressing the challenge of the work-family interface, increased attention needs to be given to work-family facilitation, how it can be cultivated and exploited, and how it operates in conjunction with work-family conflict in shaping desirable individual, family, and work-related outcomes" (Grzywacz and Bass 2003:259).

Smart Workplaces: Just for the Health of It

Reducing job strain is a global aim as stated by the 2007 World Health Assembly's "Workers' Health: Global Plan of Action," in which psychological and social health work concerns are rated equally in importance with physical and occupational issues. Likewise, the Whitehall II Study on "Work, Stress, and Health," explained that workers worldwide require balance of demands and control balance, support for social networks, fairness in effort–reward, and reasonable job security (e.g., job retraining coverage) (Ferrie 2004). A comprehensive approach to preventing job strain is one that ensures fair work design and roles, supports healthful interpersonal work relationships, creates sound environmental climate conditions, and supports humane management approaches. Employers and employees need to cooperate and work together in creating healthful work–family relationships and worksites. For example, when employers offer health incentives, such as stress management classes during the regular workday, employees need to actively engage in these opportunities. Similarly, when employees offer strategies to better meet work–family demands, employers need to listen and work toward mutually beneficial solutions. An area of significant importance in reducing job strain is developing an approachable, lighthearted work (and family) environment. Adrian Gostick and Scott Christopher (2008) argue that humor also helps in reducing job strain. Medical studies found that laughter may be good for the heart, (Crawford, Levitt, and Newman 2000; Seiler and Levitt 2005), positively influence overall physiological and psychological well-being (Bennett and Lengacher 2008), and reduce chronic stress responses and improve immune response (Bennett et al. 2003). Thus, sharing a laugh at work and at home improves both the health and productivity of workers and their families. Some countries have enthusiastically embraced this idea, such as Australia's National Humor Foundation. Yet, significant attention is placed squarely on the act of laughing for its physiological, psychological, and sociological health benefits. By mid-June 2008, it was estimated that there were over 8,000 "laughing clubs" in

60 nations (Kavanaugh 2008:1). Increasingly, individuals, families, businesses, and health care facilities are getting serious about the need to laugh and inserting doses of laughter, humor and lightheartedness into our vital environments of work and home, just for the health of it.

Conclusion

Environmental exposures hold significant influence on the health and well-being of families. While some of these exposures, such as tsunamis or earthquakes, cannot be controlled, others can. For example, many infectious diseases are preventable and treatable, yet vast numbers of families continue to suffer the ravages of epidemics, such as malaria, and pandemics, such as HIV/AIDS, that devastate our collective youth and future. Human actions (e.g., war, genocide, violence, stigmatization and discrimination, waste, pollution, destruction of natural resources) and inactions (e.g., inadequate allocation of resources toward those in need, limited access to effective health care, weak response to epidemics and pandemics) frequently have devastating ramifications. These negative actions and inactions lead to complex conditions such as population displacement, urban crowding, poverty, increased spread of disease, and/or climate change (draughts, floods, storms) with devastating effects on family health and well-being. Unhealthy environmental exposures not only play a role in increased risks of acute diseases (e.g., malaria, HIV/AIDS), but also directly and indirectly influence the prevalence and severity of chronic illnesses (e.g., CVD, asthma). The prevalence of asthma rose dramatically worldwide over the past decades, particularly in developed countries, as experts puzzled over the cause of this increase. The mechanisms that cause asthma are complex and vary among population groups and even from individual to individual. Yet evidence linking external (e.g., air pollution) and internal (e.g., low *H. pylori* bacterium levels) environmental exposures and respiratory illnesses continues to mount. These data, along with the findings that document the damaging impacts of air pollution on DNA structure and activity, raise additional arguments and challenges in the pursuit to secure more equitable global family health. Environmental exposures also include the changing nature of the workforce, which is increasingly female and technologically connected, and a workplace that is global, fast-paced, and continually engaged (i.e., operating 24/7). Globally, women still struggle with inequities in wages and with balancing family and work. As more coupled and single women enter the workforce, issues of quality child and medical care surface as universal family concerns. Due to social and economic pressures, the workplace often creates job strain, which occurs when work demands exceed workers' decision-making control and social supports. Job strain surfaces in work–family conflicts (i.e., work-to-family and family-to-work) often resulting in physical, mental, and/or social ill health for workers and their families. Reducing and preventing job strain is in the best interest of employees and employers, since healthy workers are more productive, incur few health care costs, and are more effective in their nonwork roles. Redesigning the workplace to better support the workforce means balancing job demands and control, encouraging positive social networking and support, making worksites safer and more pleasant, providing effective flexible leadership that offers workers and their families healthful opportunities (e.g., quality health care, incentives to engage in fitness programs), and creating a lighthearted environment where laughter is respected as seriously healthy. This work–family fit, however, also demands that families engage in high levels of family facilitation to enhance family resilience and healthful coping strategies.

The quality of environmental exposures, such as the air we breathe, the water we drink, the food we eat, the space we live in, the climate that envelopes us, and the place we work can be part of the burden of illness or gift of healthful living. A powerful lesson from environmental exposures is that "we are indeed in this together." These words are no truer than when the determinant of health policy and services is considered. Chapter 6 explores why health care reform is needed and what a redesign of policy and services might look like.

Critical Thinking Questions

1. Global family health has emerged as a major area for professionals working with and studying families. In your own words, explain how two specific human actions negatively contribute to the malaria epidemic (Case 5.1) and how two different actions affect the spread of the HIV/AIDS pandemic (Case 5.2).

2. You are working with families in Leon's (Case 5.3) neighborhood where the prevalence of pediatric asthma has soared. Outline four talking points you believe are vital for families to understanding the impacts of external and internal environmental exposures on asthma. Why these points?

3. You work in the human resources department of the company that employs David and Theresa (Case 5.4). Management is concerned about the escalating health care costs as ever-increasing numbers of workers seek health care for physical and mental illnesses. You are asked to come up with a plan to reduce job strain and smooth out the work–family conflicts. However, you are limited to identifying only three strategies. Describe the three you believe are paramount at this point in time. Why did you select these strategies?

6

HEALTH CARE AND FAMILIES

✛

Underinsured Families: Paying Too Much and Getting Too Little

Case 6.1 Ed: Medical Tourism and American Health Care

Ed and Ellen enjoyed living in their small Midwest rural community where Ed ran a hardware store and Ellen worked at the local coffee shop. With their combined annual income at $59,000, they considered themselves "middle class," but these last few years they often were living paycheck to paycheck. One reason for this financial shift was the cost of health insurance. Being self-employed, they purchased a private plan that demanded high monthly premiums and an escalating deductible that together resulted in ever-increasing out-of-pocket health care costs. Apart from the occasional bout with the flu, Ellen's high blood pressure, and Ed's diabetes, they thought that they were fairly healthy for 60-year-olds. For the past few weeks, however, Ed complained about an aching jaw and bleeding gums that the over-the-counter pain relievers simply couldn't relieve. Overruling his protests of "we can't afford this," Ellen drove him to the nearest dentist's office located 45 miles away. "Mr. Gray, you have serious periodontal[1] infections in 10 areas of your mouth. I think we can save four of the decayed teeth with crowns, but the periodontal disease in the other six is too advanced and has caused the bone to erode. These teeth will have to be extracted and replaced with implants," Dr. Knight stated. "Geees, this doctor looks

---

[1] For more information on gum disease, see MedicineNet. 2008b. "Gum Disease." Retrieved September 8, 2008. (www.medicinenet .com/gum_disease/page4.htm#tocg).

younger as my son," thought Ed as he asked, "How much are we talking about?" "The crowns run about $925 each and the surgery and implants run about $3,800 per tooth, so the total would be approximately $26,500; your dental insurance should pick up some of the cost for the crowns, but maybe not the implants," said Dr. Knight as he handed Ed the oral surgery number. Ed looked at Ellen and shook his head, "Look, we don't have dental insurance, so we will have to think about this." "Oh, I understand," Dr. Knight sighed, "but I can't tell you enough how serious your dental condition is, Mr. Gray. It is not only the health of your teeth, but periodontal disease is associated with increased health risks including stroke, heart disease, and worsening diabetes." The trip back home was a quiet one for Ed and Ellen. "We could take out a home equity loan," Ellen suggested. "No we can't, not in this lousy economy," Ed whispered. They avoided the subject the next few days as Ed continued to swallow double and triple the recommended dosage of pain reliever. Responding to a call from Ellen, their son Charles drove up from a large metropolitan area in the next state that weekend. "Dad, you got to take care of this," Charles said adding, "Have you looked into having the dental work done outside of the country, like Mexico?" "MEXICO, you can't even drink the water there and that's where you want me to have oral surgery?" Ed retorted. "Look, my girlfriend Sophie's mother had her dental work done there and said it was high quality, fast, and at one-fourth the cost in the United States," Charles argued, adding, "It's called 'medical travel' or 'medical tourism.' I read about it at work and it makes sense. Here is some material Sophie sent along that includes contact information and the dental clinics and hospitals that have Joint Commission International (JCI) accreditation.[2] Naturally we have to be sure to pick one with the best standards, but the fact remains that this is a reasonable way to get the medical attention you need without the high price tag. Besides, mom and you would even get a vacation out of the deal. So, what do you think?"

Case 6.1 serves as an example of the more than 25 million American adults (19 to 64 years old) who had inadequate health insurance coverage in 2007, up 60 percent from the 16 million in 2003 (Schoen et al. 2008a:w298). According to Cathy Schoen and her colleagues approximately 42 percent or 75 million[3] Americans were uninsured or underinsured in 2007 while suffering from both health care

---

[2] JCI accreditation standards for hospitals establish worldwide benchmarks for quality, cleanliness, and service [The Joint Commission. 2008. "Facts about the Joint Commission International." Retrieved July 9, 2008. (www.jointcommission.org/AboutUs/Fact_Sheets/jci_facts.htm)].

[3] In mid-2008, the U.S. Census Bureau reported that 45.7 million Americans were uninsured, which is a decrease from 47 million in 2006. This statistic reflected the 1.3 million children who were added to Medicaid and State Children's Health Insurance Program (SCHIP) coverage due to the efforts at the state level. What the 45.7 million figure fails to capture, however, was a dramatic spike in unemployment and subsequent lost health care coverage during the second half of that year. The statistic of 42 percent or 75 million uninsured or underinsured, therefore, is argued as being more accurate [Commonwealth Fund Commission. 2008. "Why Not the Best?: Results from the National Scorecard on U.S. Health System Performance, 2008." p. 9. Retrieved August 3, 2008. (www.commonwealthfund.org/usr_doc/Why_Not_the_Best_national_scorecard_2008.pdf)].

access problems and financial strains (2008a:w298). A lesser-known fact is that 89.5 million (i.e., one out of three) Americans under age 65 lacked health insurance for at least one month or more during 2006–2007 (Families USA 2009:1). While the plight of the uninsured remained troubling, the rapidly increasing rates of "underinsured families" pushed the urgency of the health care reform and redesign discussions to higher levels.

Employer-sponsored health insurance is the leading source of coverage for approximately 158 million nonelderly Americans. The average premium for family insurance, however, increased 119 percent from 1999 to 2008 resulting in employers shifting more of the expense on to their employees through cost-sharing measures (Kaiser Family Foundation 2008e:1). These out-of-pocket expenses, such as high deductibles, co-payments of office visits, prescriptions, hospital stays, and surgeries, plus full payment for noncovered services (e.g., restorative dental needs as in Case 6.1) place a significant financial strain on families. According to the Kaiser Family Foundation study, larger percentages of employers who do offer benefits will continue to increase the amount that workers contribute to premiums, deductibles, and/or co-payments (2008e:6). This shift toward greater cost sharing without regard for income or cost containment of medical costs spur escalating rates of "underinsured families," who are getting less coverage at higher prices.

Families who are underinsured shoulder out-of-pocket medical, prescription, dental, and/or vision expenses that amounted to 10 percent or more of their total household income or 5 percent if they were low-income families (i.e., less than 200 percent of the federal poverty level). Underinsured families also include those with deductibles equal to or greater than 5 percent of their income because of their potential financial exposure (Schoen et al. 2008a:w299). The upward trend in the underinsured rate reflects how much rising health care costs have outpaced wage gains. Insurance premiums for family coverage increased 78 percent in 2001 to 2007, while wages only rose 19 percent and general inflation 17 percent (Kaiser Family Foundation 2007:1). From 2007 to mid-2008, health insurance premiums increased another 5 percent, yet wages only grew by 3.5 percent (Claxton et al. 2008:w493). Underinsured families suffer not only financially, but in terms of the utilization of health care. Cathy Schoen and her colleagues (2008a:w304) report that 68 percent of uninsured and 53 percent of underinsured American adults aged 19 to 64 years went without needed care, such as not filling prescriptions, not seeking medical aid when sick, and/or failing to get recommended follow-up treatments or diagnostic tests. These trends appear to be linked to findings revealing that 51 percent of uninsured and 45 percent of underinsured adults (19 to 64 years) faced significantly greater financial burdens, such as difficulty paying medical bills, changing their way of life to pay for health care costs, and/or being contacted by bill collection agencies, as compared to 21 percent of insured (but not underinsured) adults (2008a:w304). Uninsured and underinsured Americans, therefore, face a number of obstacles to both their medical and financial well-being. This includes higher out-of-pocket costs for care, poorer health outcomes than their higher-income, fully insured counterparts, and a greater likelihood that easily treatable ailments will go untreated and become serious medical problems. Geography plays a role with poor urban and rural communities often having fewer health care options as seen with Ed in Case 6.1.

In 2007, the rate of underinsurance nearly tripled among middle- and higher-income families, those with at least $40,000 of family income (Schoen et al. 2008a:w299). According to Karen Davis of the Commonwealth Fund, "[l]ack of insurance is only one part of the problem, as even the insured have serious gaps in coverage . . . Insurance coverage is the ticket into the health-care system, but for too many, that ticket doesn't buy financial security or genuine access to care" (Reinberg 2008:1). As discussed in Chapter 1, young adults (19 to 29 years old) are at the greatest risk of being uninsured, but adults aged 50 to 64 were more likely to be underinsured. These underinsured middle-aged adults who struggle with chronic disease and ill health stumble into Medicare coverage at age 65 with health conditions that could have been prevented or reduced in severity if they had received earlier and more complete health care coverage (Schoen et al. 2008a).

Dental Health Coverage, Not a Frill

Ed and Ellen in Case 6.1 are underinsured, unable to adhere to sound medical advice related to Ed's needed dental work. Their case raises several issues including the often neglected area of oral health and the growing trend of "medical travel" or "medical tourism," when patients from wealthier nations seek treatments and medications in developing countries often due to the high costs at home and/or underinsurance. Being uninsured or underinsured is particularly evident in the area of oral health. In 2000, the Surgeon General reported that policymakers, providers, and the public needed to recognize the importance of oral health, a point driven home in 2007 with the death of a 12-year-old due to untreated dental disease.[4] Untreated bacteria from diseased gums and teeth often cause inflammation in the body that can eventually lead to heart and coronary artery diseases and/or even brain infection. Most traditional dental insurance plans offer very limited or no coverage for orthodontic or restorative dental care resulting in dramatic out-of-pocket expenses for families, as Ed in Case 6.1 discovered. Approximately

---

[4] Deamonte Driver's death due to brain infection caused by an untreated abscessed tooth [The Center for Health and Health Care in Schools. 2007. "Pediatric Oral Health—New Attention to an Old Problem." Retrieved June 7, 2008. (www.healthinschools .org/News-Room/EJournals/Volume-8/Number-2/Pediatric-Oral-Health.aspx)].

7 out of 10 (i.e., over 130 million) Americans lacked dental health coverage in 2007 (American Dental Education Association 2007:1). In some ways, the under-insured can be worse off than the uninsured, as they think and even act, like they have coverage, only to find themselves financially ruined or betrayed when a medical calamity hits. Ed in Case 6.1 was among those who were fortunate enough financially to afford medical travel to secure necessary dental treatment. This often is not an option for lower-income families (200 percent or less of the federal poverty level) with 58 percent of lower-income adults aged 19 to 64 years without dental insurance coverage (Haley, Kenney, and Pelletier 2008:1). What is this medical travel trend and is it a wise health care choice?

Globalization of Health Care and Medical Travel

The globalization of health care is not a recent phenomenon, but it has taken on some unique characteristics in the past few decades with increasing numbers of families seeking health care for treatments and medications they no longer can afford or wait for in their home nation. The outsourcing of medical information, such as the reading and storing of X-rays, to developing nations as well as a more controversial practice of recruiting medical personal from developing to developed nations remain commonplace. Yet, the outsourcing of patients from wealthy to developing nations is an emerging phenomenon with an estimated 750,000 Americans traveling abroad for medical care in 2007 and an anticipated 6 million, a 700 percent increase, by 2010 (Deloitte Center for Health Solutions 2008:4). The rate of the "medical migration" out of the United States is now faster than the number of patients coming in for treatments. Josef Woodman (2008) argued that while the term *medical tourism* has exploded across the medical treatment landscape, a better term is *medical travel* for the focus is on medical treatment, not just a vacation. He also reported that the cost of quality JCI accredited health care remains substantially higher in American hospitals when compared with 28 other nations, such as India, Malaysia, China, Thailand, Taiwan, South Korea, Singapore, Mexico, Costa Rica, and Brazil. Americans and millions of others from developed countries are engaged in medical travel for a wide range of medical treatments, such as restorative dentistry in Mexico (Case 6.1), hip resurfacing in India, fertility diagnosis and treatment in South Africa, heart valve replacements in Thailand, or plastic surgery in Brazil. The savings to families are quite substantial. For example, "[a] $50,000 hip replacement in the U.S. can cost as little as $9,000 in Singapore" (McCulloch 2008:2). Engaging in medical travel results in savings of 30 to 85 percent due in part to "both the economy of scale and simpler health care reimbursement systems that feature fewer middlemen and a greater orientation toward cash payment or a single-payer insurance model [that] help keep the cost of care overseas significantly lower than typically found in the U.S." (Rhea 2008:3). Cost alone, however, is not the sole issue driving American "medical refugees." Two additional factors spurring this surge include the increased quality of health care (e.g., state-of-the-art facilities and medical personnel) in Asia and Latin America and the unsettling fact that the fraying American health system often results in more middle-class families experiencing similar health care access problems as the uninsured (Bergstrand 2008). As noted in Chapter 1, the majority of uninsured or underinsured families have at least one full-time working adult. Medical travel is just one sign of an ailing American health system. The United States, the only developed nation without universal health insurance, struggles with a complex health system of public–private insurance that is more than twice expensive as other developed countries, yet ranks last in all but one performance indicator. Table 6.1 presents comparisons of health system performance ranking for six developed nations.

Table 6.1 Health Care Performance Rankings for Six Nations

	Australia	Canada	Germany	New Zealand	United Kingdom	United States
Overall ranking	3.5	5	2	3.5	1	6
Health care expenditures*[a]	$2,999	$3,578	$3,371	$2,448	$2,766	$6,714
Healthy lives[b]	1	3	2	4.5	4.5	6
Access[b]	3	5	1	2	4	6
Equity[b]	2	5	4	3	1	6
Quality care[b]	4	6	2.5	2.5	1	5
Efficiency[b]	4	5	3	2	1	6

Note: Highest = 1, lowest = 6; *Per capita and adjusted for differences in cost of living in 2006.

Sources: [a] Compiled from the Organization for Economic Co-operation and Development (OECD). 2008a. "OECD Health Data 2008: How Does the United States Compare" Retrieved July 9, 2008. (www.oecd.org/dataoecd/46/2/38980580.pdf).

[b] Adapted with permission from the Commonwealth Fund. Davis, Karen, Cathy Schoen, Stephen C. Schoenbaum, Michelle M. Doty, Alyssa L. Holmgren, Jennifer L. Kriss, and Katherine K. Shea. 2007. "Mirror, Mirror on the Wall: An International Update on the Comparative Performance of American Health Care." The Commonwealth Fund, May 29, Figure 2. Retrieved June 2, 2008. (www.commonwealthfund.org/usr_doc/1027_Davis_ mirror_mirror_ international_update_final.pdf? section=4039).

Table 6.1 reveals an American health system falling short of what is possible and necessary for a high-performing health system. Clearly, American families are spending too much and getting too little in return for their health care dollars. Gaining a better understanding of what constitutes high-performing health systems, begins with an examination of the performance dimensions of health systems. The following discussion on the performance dimensions of an ailing American health system serves as a foundation to the final section on reform and redesign options.

An Ailing Health System

While the American health system retains exceptional medical technology and innovation, it struggles with an inefficient, disjointed delivery system. One of the first steps in improving a health system clearly in trouble is acknowledging that there are problems. In 2001, the Institute of Medicine published a pivotal document, "Crossing the Quality Chasm" calling for change in the delivery of the American health care system, which it argued had fallen short in six core elements: safety, effectiveness, patient-centeredness, timeliness, equitability, and efficiency. Often putting a human face on a troubled system helps illustrate the severity and complexity of the situation. Several authors, such as Jonathan Cohn (2007), helped raise awareness of a troubled American health care system through their unflinching stories of patients and their families struggling not only with an illness or injury, but with the system that is supposed to aid them. Case 6.2 offers a story of how a middle-class woman struggles with acute and chronic health issues in a fragmented, underperforming health system revealing problems in these six core elements.

Case 6.2 Isabella: Unhealthy Health Care

Isabella Gonzalas often biked to her job as a mathematics teacher at Oak River Middle School. At 45 years old, she was proud to be one of the first in her Hispanic community to complete college and return to help students from diverse backgrounds. Isabella was not feeling well this Friday morning. "Just one of those urinary tract infections again," sighed Isabella "I do not want to go in to the clinic since my high deductible means I end up paying out-of-pocket for the entire office visit and any meds. Anyway, I won't even be able to get in to see a doctor today. I'll just wait until Monday or maybe try one of the "retail clinics" at the grocery store. Anyway, it will probably go away after a weekend of rest." Besides, she promised one of her students she would be there before school and a little infection was not going to prevent Isabella from fulfilling that promise. While pedaling faster so as not to be late, she never saw the car that rolled through the stoplight. When she regained consciousness, the paramedics gently placed her on the stretcher. Isabella tugged the sleeve of one of the paramedics, Donna, and asked "Please take me to St. Michael's. I don't want to end up at County General, please," Isabella gasped. Isabella had heard stories of medical errors and long wait times for those who end up at County General. Donna glanced at her colleague knowing that they had little choice since it all depended on emergency department (ED) congestion. The ambulance raced toward St. Michael's, but on route it was informed that they couldn't take Isabella to St. Michael's, so they diverted her to County General, 20 minutes further. "They have good doctors at County, it will be fine," Donna said trying to comfort Isabella. Once they arrived at County General, however, Isabella's concerns escalated as she saw the overly crowded ED waiting area. Donna found a nurse and confirmed that Isabella seemed stable, but her blood pressure was quite low. "She will be seen as soon as we can get to her, maybe 20 to 30 minutes," the nurse said after a quick triage of Isabella's wounds. "Donna," Isabella grabbed her arm. "Please call my partner, tell her to pick up Gab after basketball practice." "I will tell the nurse, don't worry," Donna added as she left. Isabella shivered as she waited, but no one was checking on her or called her partner. Twenty five more minutes passed before Dr. Aims appeared. He calmly examined Isabella's injuries saying, "You have a few cracked ribs, a broken left arm, some nasty scraps, but luckily no concussion. You must have been wearing your helmet. Anyway, we should have you out of here soon." Isabella merely nodded, but then passed out. Dr. Aims quickly rechecked Isabella's vitals and discovered she had dangerously low blood pressure or hypotension (e.g., below 50/33 mmHg). "There must be some internal bleeding. Get an IV going and start a unit of blood now!" Dr. Aims demanded adding, "See if we can get her into the operating room immediately." The staff worked frantically trying to stabilize Isabella's blood pressure. When an operating room was available, Dr. Aims worked carefully on the internal, although minor, wounds caused by the cracked ribs, but Isabella's blood pressure failed to stabilize. "She might be on some sort of medication or other drugs," the nurse offered and added, "We don't have any electronic medical records on any of our patients, much less those brought into the ED." "Where are the results of her blood tests? Has anyone contacted her next of kin yet?" barked Dr. Aims. The intake nurse said "The tests aren't back yet. There is a delay in the lab due to all the strep throat testing demands from other ED patients. Ms. Gonzalas only had a driver's license and her insurance card, but when I called the insurance company all I got was an answering machine so I couldn't find out where her medical records were or her next of kin. The paramedic who brought her in did ask us to call Isabella's partner, but we were so busy with all those uninsured flu patients, so no one called yet." "Well, call now!" demanded the nurse practitioner, Pam. Four hours after Isabella entered the ED, her partner, Elaina, raced into the ED. "I am looking for Ms. Isabella Gonzalas. What happened? How is she?"

Elaina asked. "Isabella is recovering from surgery, but her blood pressure isn't stabilizing. Can you tell us the name of her primary care physician?" Pam asked. "She doesn't have a primary care physician, but she has seen Dr. Jien, over at St. Michael's Hospital and Clinic," Elaina said. After several minutes and numerous phone transfers, Pam reached Dr. Jien's nurse and explained the situation with Isabella. "Dr. Jien's patient load is very heavy these days, so I'll have to review and send over Ms. Gonzalas'electronic medical file," offered Dr. Jien's nurse. "Look, we don't have that technology, just tell me which medications Isabella is on that might impact her blood pressure," Pam sighed. "I see, let me contact Dr. Jien and get back to you." After 30 minutes, Dr. Jien was on the phone to Pam. "As a primary care physician I see so many patients each day, I don't really remember Ms. Gonzalas, but according to my records she was in twice. Six months ago I prescribed an antidepressant, for her mild depression and anxiety, which might be contributing to the lower blood pressure. I had suggested that she seek additional care, but I have no idea if she did. I also treated her two weeks ago for a urinary tract infection, a nasty one at that, but she never came back for a recommended follow-up or refill on the antibiotics I prescribed. My concern is that urinary tract infection may have become more serious." "I will confer with the physician here," Pam added as she thanked Dr. Jien and hung up. Several more hours and additional blood tests later, it was confirmed that Isabella was suffering from severe sepsis,[5] a serious blood infection, that demands immediate treatment including fluid resuscitation and broad-spectrum antibiotics. Isabella was moved to the intensive care unit (ICU) for treatment. Later that afternoon, Elaina visited Isabella in the ICU and was shocked at how pale and unresponsive Isabella was. Unknown to anyone, Isabella's condition was not improving as the infection continued to rage throughout her system. "Why isn't she getting better?" Elaina asked. "Surely the antibiotics should have turned the tide. It has been over six hours since she has been on that IV." The nurse, Ben, nodded, but when he checked Isabella's blood pressure and pulse he became concerned and double-checked her chart while glancing at the list of medications added to Isabella's IV. Ben did a double take and dashed out to find the ICU doctor on duty. "It's the patient in Bed A, Room 319, she has been given the wrong antibiotic spectrum!" Ben hurriedly explained to Dr. Black. Dr. Black rushed into Room 319 pushing past Elaina and asking her to wait in the lounge as a medical team feverously worked to save Isabella who was slipping into septic shock.[6] Their heroic efforts in the end saved Isabella's life, but

[5] Sepsis and severe sepsis: caused when bacteria that leave the infected area, such as abdomen or urinary tract, enter the bloodstream and produce toxins that impact the blood vessels causing life-threatening decline in blood pressure as well as organ failure, such as lung, kidney, and liver [Mayo Clinic. 2007. "Sepsis." Retrieved July 7, 2008. (www.mayoclinic.com/health/sepsis/DS01004)].

[6] Septic shock can occur if there is delayed or no treatment for severe sepsis. The death rate for those suffering septic shock is 45 percent [Wenzel, Richard P. 2002. "Treating Sepsis." *New England Journal of Medicine* 347(13):966–967].

her health care experience resulted in significant avoidable physical, emotional, and financial costs including permanent kidney damage due to delays and incorrect medication, slower recovery from her biking injuries, seven extra days in the hospital, additional missed workdays, and a shocking medical bill of over $28,000.

In Case 6.2, Isabella's story reflects an ailing health care system. While the medical staff members at the fictional County General were skilled and dedicated professionals, the health system failed Isabella. In order to begin to improve health care performance, however, core elements need to be understood, measured, and reported. Based on the Institute of Medicine's (2001) core elements as noted earlier, the Commonwealth Fund Commission (2008) produced a comprehensive "National Scorecard on U.S. Health System" measuring 37 core indicators on five overlapping dimensions (healthy lives, access, equity, quality, and efficiency) of health system performance. While there were pockets of excellence, the overall score of only 65 affirmed that the American health system was falling behind in consistently providing access to high-quality and efficient care (Commonwealth Fund Commission 2008:9). Table 6.2 displays the scores for these five overlapping dimensions, which include the six core elements as discussed in the following.

Table 6.2 reveals a decline in three of the five scores from 2006 to 2008. According to these researchers, "[t]he U.S. continues to perform far below what is achievable, with wide gaps between average and benchmark performance across dimensions" (Commonwealth Fund Commission 2008:10). The gaps in health care performance were especially evident when comparing geographic areas within the United States. According to Joel Cantor and his colleagues, the "State Scorecard on Health System Performance" revealed substantial room for improvement in

Table 6.2 United States Health System Performance Dimension Scores,* 2006 and 2008

	Overall Score	Healthy Lives	Access	Equity	Quality	Efficiency
2006	67	75	67	70	72	52
2008	65	72	58	71	71	53

*Performance score out of possible 100.

Source: Adapted with permission from the Commonwealth Fund. Commonwealth Fund Commission. 2008. "Why Not the Best?: Results from the National Scorecard on U.S. Health System Performance, 2008." p. 9. Retrieved August 3, 2008. (www.commonwealthfund.org/usr_doc/Why_Not_the_Best_national_scorecard_2008.pdf).

terms of healthy lives, access, quality, and costs when comparing high- and low-performing states[7] with all states performing below achievable levels of health care (Cantor et al. 2007).

Healthy Lives

On this dimension of long, healthy, and productive lives, the United States ranked last out of 19 nations on the issue of "amendable mortality" or deaths of those under 75 years of age from causes that are potentially preventable with effective and timely health care interventions. It is estimated that 101,000 deaths per year could be avoided if the United States reached the levels of amendable mortality as Japan, France, or Australia (Nolte and McKee 2008:59–69). These findings are consistent with other cross-cultural studies (Davis et al. 2007) that reveal an under-performing American health system. The last thing Isabella (Case 6.2) wanted to hear as she was wheeled into the ED was that she would have to wait before getting treatment. According to a study by Andrew Wilper and colleagues, of over 92,000 adult ED visits between 1997 and 2004, there was an 18 to 26 percent rise in ED adult visits and a median ED wait time increase of 36 percent for all patients, but especially for African Americans, Hispanics, women, and patients in urban settings (2008:w92). Such delays are especially life-threatening for those suffering from serious conditions, such as heart attacks, strokes, pneumonia, trauma, sepsis, and septic shock. Causes for these longer ED wait times appear to be linked to increased congestion, shortages of inpatient beds, growing numbers of uninsured and underinsured (who have delayed primary care, such as Isabella), an aging population with chronic illnesses, staff shortages, reduction in the number of ED units, and limited access to interpreters (Wilper et al. 2008:w92–w93). Isabella (Case 6.2) was a trauma patient whose delayed sepsis diagnosis and error in medications progressed into life-threatening sepsis shock. The amendable results of her health care experience (e.g., damaged kidney, slowed recovery, increased loss of workdays, high medical costs) detracted from her healthy life dimension. The following dimensions, access, equity, quality (including effectiveness, coordination, safety, patient-centeredness, and timeliness), and efficiency also directly impact families' healthy lives.

---

[7] Based on 32 measures across five dimensions (i.e., access, quality, potentially avoidable use of hospitals and costs of care, equity, and healthy lives and living long), the top 13 health system performing states in 2006 were Hawaii, Iowa, New Hampshire, Vermont, Maine, Rhode Island, Connecticut, Massachusetts, Wisconsin, South Dakota, Minnesota, Nebraska, and North Dakota. The bottom 13 were California, Tennessee, Alabama, Georgia, Florida, West Virginia, Kentucky, Louisiana, Nevada, Arkansas, Texas, Mississippi, and Oklahoma [Cantor, Joel C., Cathy Schoen, Dina Belloff, Sabrina K.H. How, and Douglas McCarthy. 2007. "Aiming Higher: Results from a State Scorecard on Health System Performance." Retrieved August 3, 2008. (www.commonwealthfund.org/usr_doc/StateScorecard.pdf?section=4039)].

Access

As discussed in this chapter and in Chapter 1, increasing numbers of uninsured and underinsured families significantly add to the erosion of the American health system. While Isabella had health coverage, it was inadequate due to a "health consumerism" approach that increased her out-of-pocket costs, such as rising deductibles and co-pays for office visits and medications, making family health care less affordable for her and increasing numbers of middle-income Americans. The concept that using commercial incentives (e.g., shifting the burden of health care from business and onto families) as a means to rein in health care costs has faltered in its initial applications because "medicine—with its third party payers and partly social mission—does not lend itself to market discipline," but such cost shifting does heavily contribute to reducing health care access for families (Kuttner 2008:549). Health consumerism undermines health care access and erodes families' financial health. Case in point, Karen Seccombe and Kim Hoffman's (2007) timely study examined the lack of health care in the shadows of post-welfare reform. When families moved from welfare to work, the children might be covered by State Children's Health Insurance Program (SCHIP), but the adults often were uninsured, which proved detrimental to their physical and mental health. All families deserve fair and uninhibited access to health care, thus access to consistent, complete health insurance. "Health insurance is crucial to successful welfare reform. Without it, families cannot adequately transition from poverty to self-sufficiency—health problems are always present, but the ability to pay for care is elusive" (Seccombe and Hoffman 2007:170). Health care is not a luxury, it is a necessity.

Another sign of an ailing health system, or some may argue a welcomed response to it, is the emergence of the "retail clinic" as Isabella (Case 6.2) referred to while thinking about how to get relief from her infection. Retail clinics, located in stores (e.g., Target, Walmart, Walgreens, grocery chains), are predicted to increase from 450 in 2008 to over 6,000 by 2013 (Mehrotra et al. 2008:1272). These clinics arose out of a demand for more convenient locations, shorter wait times for same-day service, and after-hour care (weekends, evenings, holidays) for families who want quick medical service at affordable out-of-pocket prices. Since the first retail clinic opened in 2000, controversy has surrounded this trend as the medical community raised concerns over accuracy of diagnosis, appropriate triage decisions, and if such clinics interrupt existing patient–physician relationships (Mehrotra et al. 2008:1273). Findings dispelled several of these concerns, such as (1) young adults (18 to 44 years old) often without coverage are the most frequent users of retail clinics, (2) these clinics treat acute problems (e.g., flu) and provide preventive services (e.g., immunizations), (3) three-fifths of retail patients do not have a primary care physician (PCP), (4) most retail clinics provide patients with a printed summary of each visit from the clinic's electronic medical records, and (5) most conditions treated at retail clinics do not require physician's training (Mehrotra et al. 2008:1279). Retail clinics appear to provide an outlet for patients during a period of shortages of PCPs and overburdened EDs as seen in Case 6.2. Yet, retail clinics are an example of an intermittent change in health care that promises some relief, but they alone do not correct the shortcomings in the national health system. Perhaps retail clinics will become part of the needed reform and redesign of health care delivery.

By 2005, affordable comprehensive health care was out of reach for increasing numbers of Americans as escalating out-of-pocket costs (premiums, co-pays, direct spending for services not covered) were not matched by increases in wages, with medical debt impacting 41 percent of American adults 19 to 64 years old in 2007 (Commonwealth Fund Commission 2008:30). Closely paired with access to health care is equity of care. A high-performing health care system provides equal opportunities for all to enjoy healthy, productive lives as a right, not a privilege.

Equity

Chapter 4 discussed health disparities across age, sex, socioeconomic, racial, ethnic, educational, and geographic groups. Such inequities also exist in health care performance. According to the Commonwealth Fund Commission report (2008), there was no improvement in reducing the gap in health care performance as experienced by vulnerable populations. Thus, women, minorities, and poor families remained less likely to secure preventive, required, and/or recommended health care. For example, minorities had higher risks than non-Hispanic whites of untreated dental caries. Likewise, non-Hispanic African Americans and Hispanics were less likely to receive comprehensive mental health care for depression than non-Hispanic whites. As discussed in Chapter 4, health disparities include the stigma and discrimination toward specific diseases and illnesses, such as mental illness. Isabella (Case 6.2) had insurance, but due to soaring employer premiums, her employer opted for coverage with inadequate mental health treatment options. Because the new mental health parity bill, The Paul Wellstone and Pete Domenici Mental Health Parity and Addiction Equity Act of 2008,[8] was not

---

[8] The Paul Wellston and Pete Domenici Mental Health Parity and Addiction Equity Act of 2008 was signed into law on October 3, 2008 after a 12-year fight with a resistant federal administration to get parity for mental illness, behavior health issues, and addiction.

passed until late 2008, generally it would not take effect until 2010. Since her insurance would pay only for physician visits and not counseling, Isabella couldn't afford to follow her doctor's recommendation of seeking additional mental health care. This disparity in health care services is especially evident for those with chronic conditions, such as diabetes, with non-Hispanic African Americans and Hispanics having the higher rates of hospitalization and death due to diabetes-related complications (Commonwealth Fund Commission 2008:36–38). Making health care more accessible, therefore, also demands that a health delivery system is more affordable and equitable. Studies (Cantor et al. 2007; Commonwealth Fund Commission 2008; Daniels 2008) reveal that states and nations with greater access and equity to health care also had higher levels of health system quality and efficiency, all at a lower cost.

Quality

This dimension of the health system is measured by five core elements including *effectiveness, coordination, safety, patient-centeredness*, and *timeliness*. The Commonwealth Fund Commission (2008) reported that inadequate health system quality results in preventable loss of lives and health and costs in the billions of dollars in lost productivity and medical expenses. Providing *effective* care for acute, chronic, and preventable health concerns is vital to the delivery of quality health care. While acute issues (e.g., Isabella's accident injuries) must receive immediate attention, a quality health system needs to better respond to demands of increasing rates of chronic conditions (e.g., heart disease, stroke, cancer, diabetes, asthma) as well as rising numbers of aging Americans. Each year, chronic diseases result in 70 percent of the deaths and cause major limitations in activity for approximately 25 million Americans (Centers for Disease Control and Prevention 2008l). According to the Medical Research Council, 80 percent of heart disease, stroke, and type 2 diabetes plus 40 percent of cancer would be prevented if families eliminated poor diets, inactivity, and smoking behaviors (2007:1). Preventive care, therefore, aims to prevent, delay, or alleviate chronic conditions through fostering healthful family behaviors, as discussed in Chapter 3, including vaccinations, hypertension treatment, reducing rates of obesity, diabetes, and effectively treating acute conditions, such as urinary tract infections. Effective care also includes mental health diagnosis and treatment, yet a third of American adults with depression did not receive effective care and even those who did receive care, the care may have been inadequate, too brief due to out-of-pocket costs, such as the situation with Isabella who had a prescription for antidepressants but no follow-up care (Wang, Demler, and Kessler 2002).

Quality family health care must also have *coordination* in the transitions within and among hospitals, clinics, and other medical settings. Isabella's (Case 6.2) health care experience reflected the often fragmented nature of the American health system where communication between different medical centers, departments, and even among medical colleagues contributed to the delay and confusion in treatment. The exploding science of "biomedical and health informatics"[9] provides a foundational role in the "acquisition, maintenance, retrieval, and application of biomedical knowledge and information to improve patient care, medical education, and health sciences research" (Gennari 2002:1). This interdisciplinary science interfaces health information, technology, and health care in the quest of improving the quality and efficiency of health delivery systems. For example, if Isabella's health records regarding previous illnesses and medications had been readily available to the ED medical staff (through a universal electronic medical records system), the life-threatening delay in treatment, amendable injury, and higher expenses most likely would have been avoided. Closely linked to such coordination of care, therefore, is safety.

The area of patient *safety* emerged as another troubling item with the United States having the highest medical error rate as compared to other developed nations. Patient congestion, inadequate staffing levels, insufficient quality control standards, and a lack of complete medical information at point of care increase the risk of medical errors, further eroding the quality and efficiency of American health care. In 2007, almost a third (32 percent) of American adults aged 19 to 64 with chronic conditions reported a medical, medication, or lab test error (Schoen et al. 2007b:w717). The medication error that Isabella experienced falls under the area of "never events." That is, serious, highly preventable adverse events resulting in the death, injury, or disability of patients. The National Quality Forum has identified 28 never events, that is events that should never occur during health care.[10] These never events fall under six categories including: surgical errors (e.g., surgery on wrong patient or body part), product or device events (e.g., air/gas embolism), patient protection events (e.g., infant discharged to wrong person, patient suicide), care management events (e.g., death or serious disability due to medication error [wrong drug, dose preparation, or route of administration]), environmental events (e.g., death or disability due to patient falling), and criminal events (e.g., impersonating a licensed health care provider) (Agency for Healthcare Research and Quality 2008:1). Accurate

[9] For more information see, American Medical Informatics Association. 2008. "Biomedical and Health Informatics," Retrieved June 12, 2008. www.amia.org/files/shared/What_is_Informatics__Fact_Sheet_03_24_09_0.pdf

[10] For a complete list of the 28 never events, see Agency for Healthcare Research and Quality. 2008. "Never Events." Retrieved August 3, 2008. www.psnet.ahrq.gov/resource.aspx?resourceID=5363

reporting of never events is an important part of ensuring safety, but so too is providing meaningful options for medical professionals to share and learn from never events so as to reduce errors and enhance health care quality. While numerous reporting systems are in place, "systematic, national improvement in patient safety still remains uncoordinated and based on efforts that are driven by individual health care organizations, systems, or states, and improvement is not occurring in a unified, national fashion" (National Quality Forum 2007:v). Another safety concern within family health care involves the 37 percent (42 percent of those with chronic conditions) of adults under age 65 years who skip follow-up appointments, do not take their medications, or fail to obtain recommended care because they could not afford it (Schoen et al. 2007b:w717). Isabella not only suffered the never event of receiving the wrong medication, but she also did not follow up on either her mental health or acute urinary infection conditions due to cost and availability concerns.

Along with effectiveness, coordination, and safety, higher health system quality also demands *patient-centered* and *timely* responses. Focusing on the patient and not solely on the injury or illness is crucial to high-quality health care. A patient-centered health system reflects a more biopsychosocial approach to health care and is core to integrative medicine as discussed in Chapter 1. In Case 6.2, Isabella needed a PCP who could provide patient-centered and timely health care in terms of building a collaborative patient–physician relationship that included follow-up and consistent care for her mental health and acute infection medical needs. Dr. Jien (Case 6.2) could not provide the patient-centered, timely care Isabella required due to a health system in which patient–physician collaboration was not supported or encouraged. This lack of patient-centeredness also appeared in the ED where the sheer numbers of patients overwhelmed the staff which resulted in poor communication between medical settings, departments, and providers. Getting timely medical aid when one needs it demands a health system that is highly responsive and flexible. For Isabella, not being able to receive needed care for her infection due to office hours limitations contributed to the severity of her condition. Less than 50 percent of American adults with health problems were able to get a same-day appointment with a physician with 73 percent reporting difficulty obtaining health care after hours (i.e., evenings, weekends, holidays) without going to the ED (Commonwealth Fund Commission 2008:12). Isabella did not follow up on her mental health needs due to concerns over inadequate coverage and affordability. She delayed medical treatment for the urinary infection in part out of resignation that she could not get same-day or after-hour care and would have to wait until after the weekend. Closely hinged on improving the complexity of quality of the health system is enhancing efficiency.

Efficiency

This area had the lowest score of the five areas measured in the scorecard (Table 6.2). An efficient health system strives to maximize health quality and results through wise use of resources and increasing value, in other words, great care at a fair price. The American health system suffers from incomplete coverage, waste, and fragmentation. In 2007, the United States spent $2.2 trillion on health care or 16.3 percent of the Gross Domestic Product (GDP), which is estimated to almost double ($4.3 trillion) or 19.5 percent GDP in 2017 (Centers for Medicare and Medicaid Services 2008:1). Yet, this high price did not bring the full measure of high-performance health care that is possible and needed. According to the scorecard, compared to patient-peers in other developed nations, American patients not only had more duplicate tests, but also had unavailable medical records and tests at the time of their appointments. Inefficiency also was evident in unnecessary hospitalizations, health insurance administrative costs that were 30 to 70 percent higher than in other nations, and lagging use of electronic medical record systems (EMRs) as compared to the percentage of physicians using EMRs in leading countries, such as Netherlands (98), New Zealand (92), United Kingdom (89), Australia (79) (Commonwealth Fund Commission 2008:31–35). Isabella's (Case 6.2) health care experience at County General was inefficient in that she was hospitalized seven extra days due to avoidable medical mistakes all resulting in higher medical costs. Her story also reveals the frustration of not having EMRs available to all American health providers for patients regardless of where they are being treated. Going back a bit further in Isabella's case, however, the inefficiency began with inadequate health care coverage, an overscheduled and poorly supported PCP who was not able to do vital patient–physician consultation and follow-up care along with a health system that did not provide timely patient-friendly same-day appointment or after-hour care. Such an ailing health care delivery system harms the health and economic well-being at individual, family, local, state, and national levels. Efforts to improve health system performance demands not only a reforming policy, but also redesigning the delivery of health care.

Health Care Reform and Redesign

Health care plays a vital interactive role in the complex web of family health as revealed in Figure 1.1, Family Health Determinants Model. Early reform proposals addressing this ailing system often focused on controlling spiraling medical costs and/or increasing access. While these elements are necessary, scholars (Schoen et al. 2007b; Paulus, Davis, and Steele 2008; Shih et al. 2008) argue for a more comprehensive approach that includes enhanced value in delivering health care. David Mechanic (2006) reminds the public that the health system is indeed a business and that in order for true health care change to occur the majority of American families need to be dissatisfied with it. The United States may have reached that point. In 2008, a study of 1,004 adults over age 18 found that 80 percent stated that, based on their health care experiences, the health system requires either fundamental change or complete rebuilding (How et al. 2008:1). Families want a health system that provides (1) affordable and equitable access to all; (2) higher quality and efficiency in delivery performance; and (3) accountability, leadership, and re-organization, *three primary goals* of reform and redesign.

Affordable and Equitable Access

It was widely agreed that providing health care coverage to all Americans is ethically and economically the right action to take, and turning this position into action still remains a challenge. While, the federal government failed to provide leadership in the area of health system reform, individual states attempted some plans to increase access to health care for their citizens. By 2008, universal coverage was enacted in three states (Maine, Vermont, and Massachusetts) and was proposed by 12 more states. The "Massachusetts Health Insurance" plan, which began in late 2006, was largely successful in extending coverage to the uninsured. This reform mandated all state residents purchase health insurance coverage and that employers of 11 or more employees had to "play or pay" in offering affordable health insurance (Kaiser Family Foundation 2008f:1). The state provided aid to low-income families thereby creating more affordable premiums. This reform model also included attempts to raise quality and control costs, such as the "Health Care Quality and Cost Council programs," but the higher than expected costs and concerns over ever-rising health care expenses, along with significant downturns in the national economy during the second half of 2008 were troubling. While the Massachusetts plan may serve as a possible model, reform and redesign of the American health system must be on a national level. Cathy Schoen, Karen Davis, and Sara Collins proposed a national "Building Blocks" framework[11] that provides near universal coverage through a mix of private and public health insurance, which they argue would result in "minimal disruption or increase in national health spending" (2008:646). As seen in the Massachusetts Health Insurance plan, the Building Blocks proposal mandates that all individuals provide evidence of health insurance

[11] For a complete description of the Building Blocks proposal, see Schoen, Cathy, Karen Davis, and Sara Collins. 2008b. "Building Blocks for Reform: Achieving Universal Coverage with Private and Public Group Health Insurance." *Health Affairs* 27(3):646–657.

when filing their taxes. This proposal keeps Medicaid, SCHIP, plus large-employer coverage, but adds additional options for self-employed, uninsured, and small businesses currently not enjoying full health care benefits by offering a national "connector" that offers those under age 65 years a choice of a Medicare-like option with enhanced benefits (e.g., Medicare Extra) or private plans. Financing this proposal includes that all employers must "play or pay" with providing affordable comprehensive coverage and a promise of cost containment measures, such as reduced insurance administration costs and reduction of waste and duplication that would reduce financial strain on employers. Likewise, employers recognize the financial benefits of a healthy workforce. In 2008, 53 percent of small firms (3 to 199 employees) and 88 percent of larger firms (200 or more employees) offered wellness programs, such as smoking cessation, weight loss, fitness/gym membership discounts, nutrition or healthful living classes, Web site resources, and/or company wellness newsletter (Kaiser Family Foundation 2008f:6). Providing national incentives to employers to enhance and expand such programs would be in everyone's financial and health interests. All low-income families (below 150 percent of federal poverty level) would be eligible for Medicaid and SCHIP. Middle- and higher-income families would also experience financial relief through tax credits and lower health care costs as the majority of people would be able to seek medical care before conditions become serious (contrary to what often occurs with the uninsured and underinsured). This proposal claims that near-universal coverage would be reached in the first year, thus dropping the number of uninsured to fewer than 3.6 million (Schoen et al. 2008a:651). In terms of impacts on health care spending, the Building Blocks plan is estimated to increase health spending by only $15 billion or less than 1 percent of the total health spending due to the offsetting savings from lowered administrative and reimbursement costs (2008:653).

Yet, health care reform must be comprehensive and not piecemeal. Ezekiel Emanuel (2008:81-115) explains that authentic healthcare reform must move beyond incremental repairs, mandates, and even single payer plans. He notes that authentic healthcare reform needs to meet ten criteria including: (1) 100 percent guaranteed coverage for all Americans, (2) standard benefits as what members of congress currently receive, (3) freedom of choice from several health care plans that must accept everyone regardless of preexisting conditions, (4) freedom to purchase more health care coverage, (5) eliminate employer-based, group insurance, (6) phase out Medicare, Medicaid, and SCHIP, (7) independent oversight by National Board and 12 regional health boards, (8) patient safety and dispute resolution program handled through National and 12 regional boards, (9) cost and quality control oversight by a new organization, "Institute of Technology and Outcomes Assessment," and (10) dedicated funding so that healthcare has public funding, but delivered through the private sector. His proposal, "Guaranteed Healthcare Access Plan," serves as one element in the dramatic debate over the reform and redesign of the American healthcare system.

While these proposals are just that, they do beg for a pragmatic and timely reform of how Americans pay for and receive health care coverage. Certainly, more proposals will emerge as the debate continues, but many recognize that inaction and status quo will only feed the fires of ever-escalating health spending as more families fall into the ranks of the uninsured and underinsured. President Barack Obama (2009:1) reminds Americans that ". . . health care reform cannot wait, it must not wait, and it will not wait another year." As the health care reform debate gains greater traction, demands for higher quality and efficiency in health care delivery of services rages.

Higher Quality and Efficiency in Delivery Performance

The Commonwealth Fund Commission identified six attributes of a high-quality and efficient health care delivery system including (Shih et al. 2008:ix–x; Audet, Davis, and Schoenbaum 2006):

1. "Patients' clinically relevant information [such as, electronic medical record interoperability, registries, electronic prescribing] is available to all providers at point of care and to patients through universal electronic health record systems.

2. Patient care is coordinated among multiple providers, and transitions across care settings are actively managed [through integrated and comprehensive team-based approaches].

3. Providers (including nurses and other members of care team) both within and across settings have accountability to each other, review each other's work, and collaborate to reliably deliver high-quality, high-value care.

4. Patients have easy access to appropriate care and information after hours; there are multiple points of entry to the system; and providers are culturally competent and responsive to patient's needs [plus engagement of patients and families in ongoing care].

5. There is clear accountability for the total care of patients [and routine gathering of patient feedback data along with publicly reported performance information].

6. The system is continuously innovating and learning in order to improve the quality, value, and patients' experiences of health care delivery."

These six attributes demand an end to the fragmentation of the American health care system that hinders providers' efforts toward higher quality and efficiency while frustrating patients and their families who maneuver unguided through a maze of multiple medical settings in search of needed care, especially true for those with chronic conditions. "[O]ur fragmented system rewards high-cost, intensive medical intervention over higher-value primary care, including preventive medicine and the management of chronic illness" (Shih et al. 2008:ix). This emphasis on primary care emerges since primary care is often the "first contact care [for patient, family, and community]; responsibility for patients over time; comprehensive care that meets or arranges for most of a patient's health care needs and coordination of care across a patient's conditions, care providers, and settings" (Berenson et al. 2008:1223).

Achieving the six attributes, therefore, requires a redesign in health care delivery in which PCPs are not only the first point of contact, but also serve as a main source of essential and preventive care. This critical role of PCP has not been lost on other developed nations where financial incentives, expansion of office hours, and extensive access to health information technology, such as electronic medical records, far exceeds what is available to PCP in the United States (Schoen et al. 2006). Patient-centeredness lies at the core of primary care in providing, monitoring, and integrating high-quality acute, chronic, and preventive care. While all five interactive dimensions (i.e., safety, effectiveness, coordination, patient-centeredness, timeliness) of health care quality are vital to high-performing health systems, redesign efforts hinge on the pivotal role of patient-centered primary care practices. Patient-centered, or biopsychosocial care as discussed in Chapter 1, requires respectful engagement of patients in their care as PCPs and patients collaborate on goals, problems, and decision making. Ideally, primary care practices provide a "patient-centered medical home" (PCMH) that facilitates patient–physician partnerships, and when appropriate, extends this partnership to the patient's family in a culturally and linguistically sensitive manner (National Committee for Quality Assurance 2008; American Academy of Family Physicians et al. 2007).

A well supported PCMH is better able to: (1) deliver timely access when care is needed; (2) engage informed patients in their care; (3) gather and use clinical information in treatment and evidence-based decision making; (4) coordinate care that includes follow-up, support, tracking, and communication among health care providers; (5) integrate comprehensive care that is multidimensional and team-based; (6) provide ongoing, regular patient feedback; and (7) offer publicly available information on performance of practices and health care providers (Gerteis et al. 1993; Davis, Schoenbaum, and Audet 2005:954). The ability of PCMH to generate patient registries, "one of the best practices included in the chronic care model"[12] is of

---

[12] The chronic care model (CCM) serves as a practical model to bring research and practice together in prevention and treatment of chronic conditions, since CCM engages patients as active partners in a proactive, patient-centered longitudinal care team [Glasgow, Russell E., C. Tracy Orleans, Edward H. Wagner, Susan J. Curry, and Leif I. Solberg. 2001. "Does the Chronic Care Model Serve Also as a Template for Improving Prevention?" *Milbank Quarterly* 79(4):579–612].

particular importance based on the looming chronic disease rates (see Chapter 3) and high cost of not preventing or delaying early interventions (Audet et al. 2006:758). PCMH may indeed serve as a transformative model for delivering high-quality and efficient primary care. In Cases 6.1 and 6.2, neither Ed nor Isabella had a PCMH that could closely monitor their health care needs or coordinate required treatments. Isabella's (Case 6.2) situation also revealed a fragmented system of unavailable medical records at the point of care and fractured coordination as she was handed off to multiple providers leading to avoidable medical error, waste of resources, and decreased quality of care. Moving the American health system toward universal coverage with higher quality and efficiency demands greater accountability, leadership, and reorganization from within and without the health system.

Greater Accountability, Leadership, and Reorganization in Health Care

In 2007, the Commonwealth Fund Commission called for a "national entity" to provide accountable, collaborative leadership among government and private sector players. The charge of such a national entity is to achieve universal health coverage while simultaneously redesigning the health care delivery system and significantly containing medical costs. It is agreed that the United States health system struggles under the weight of inefficiencies, waste, and excessive administrative costs. Each year a third of medical expenses are due to excessive administration costs (Woolhandler, Himmelstein, and Wolfe 2003). These avoidable expenses are due in large part to an inefficient manner in which hundreds of insurance plans require different forms, payment rules, and referral networks. While no single plan will "fix" the health system, a comprehensive approach holds promise. Experts on health system delivery agree that the following 12 strategies are necessary in redesigning the American health system (Roper 2008; Shih et al. 2008):

- a national entity that sets priorities, performance goals, and endorses national consensus standards for measuring and publicly reporting performance (e.g., Hospital Quality Alliance[13]);
- primary care PCMHs where all patients receive on-going health monitoring and health coaching[14] and "patient-focused episode" care;

---

[13] Hospital Quality Alliance is a national measure of hospital performance credited with improved quality of care [Shih, Anthony and Stephen C. Schoenbaum. 2007. "Measuring Hospital Performance: The Importance of Process Measures." Retrieved September 10, 2008. (www.commonwealthfund.org/usr_doc/1046_Shih_measuring_hosp_performance_process.pdf?section=4039)].

[14] Health coaches work directly (in person and electronically) with patients and their families in developing and maintaining healthful behaviors, such as wise diet, regular activity, elimination of tobacco products, recommended vaccinations, healthful stress management strategies, seeking early health care, and so on.

- redesigning of organizational models to include universal use of health information technologies, evidence-based best practices, multidisciplinary teams, and routine measuring and improving performance;
- reduction in administrative costs and waste, such as the use of uniform forms;
- provider incentives rewarding primary and preventive care in balance with specialty care, and balance support between cognitive and procedural services;
- payment reform that moves away from fee-for-service toward provider accountability for total care for patients, "pay-for-performance," care coordination across medical settings, and "bundled payments" (i.e., payment for treating patients with chronic conditions using follow-up care over time);
- patient incentives to receive care at high-quality, high-value delivery systems;
- provider incentives to engage in high-quality and efficient performance;
- regulatory changes to streamline clinical integration of knowledge and skills among providers;
- accreditation opportunities using the six attributes of ideal delivery system;
- provider training for effectively working in a more organized, team-based environment using systems-based skills and competencies, such as population health;
- government infrastructure support—need for greater government responsibility in assisting certain geographic locations or populations in the development of high-quality delivery systems. For example, government establishing and supporting infrastructure, such as health information technology, after-hour coverage, and chronic care medicine.

A story often presents a clearer image than a list of criteria. Geisinger Health System, located in Danville, Pennsylvania, serves as an example of a health care system that is making significant strides in meeting the six attributes of an ideal delivery system through the use of many of the 12 redesign changes noted earlier.

Geisinger-Like Health System: Translating Knowledge into Action

The Geisinger Health System is a real physician-led health care system with a vision of "Heal. Teach. Discover. Serve." based on the themes of "quality, value, partnerships (collaboration among providers, businesses, and educational institutions), and advocacy" (Geisinger Health System 2008:1). Frequently appearing in the literature as an example of innovation in health system delivery, the Geisinger Health System strives in meeting the six attributes through many of the 12 redesigning strategies to better engage and educate patients and their families, improve care coordination and transitions, expand illness preventive care, foster effective chronic care, and restructure acute episodic care in a more patient-centered preventive care approach. The Geisinger Health System uses a "clinical business case" approach to designing improvements in quality and efficiency that demands collaboration, accountability, and evidence-based decision making. A new redesign improvement strategy must include a "payment approach, incentives, and non-financial rewards required to support and reinforce the design . . ." before it is considered. This approach results in a more organized, accountable, and successful redesign strategy (Paulus et al. 2008:1238). To better understand this collaborative environment, let's hear from Kaela Jackson, M.D.[15]

Cases 6.3 Kaela: Creating a Patient-Centered Primary Home

Kaela strived to follow in the career path of her non-Hispanic African American father, Dr. Morse Jackson. So early in her medical career, Kaela decided to be a PCP despite protests from her fiancé who encouraged her to specialize. Her first years as a doctor, however, left her frustrated as she struggled with seeing too many patients in a day and having too little time to discuss their conditions with them and do any follow-up. Dr. Jackson left her first clinic and currently works for Whole Patient Health Systems (WPHS) an innovative doctor-lead organization that she discovered while attending a conference on innovations in using the chronic care model (CCM) with diverse populations. The WPHS working environment is highly collaborative and multidisciplinary team-based. "Working at WPHS allows me to provide an authentic PCMH for my patients" she shared with Adam, a PCP from her former clinic. "I know what a PCMH is, but tell me why you think what is happening at WPHS is so special," Adam ventured. "For one thing, the health information technology at WPHS provides 24/7 access to electronic health records, registries, the most recent research findings, plus direct communication with and referrals to specialists. Patients also have read-only access to their records and are able to schedule appointments, get reminders and follow-ups, refills on prescriptions, culturally and linguistically appropriate educational materials, and even e-mail their primary care physician. For those patients without access to a computer, we have bilingual health coaches who do face-to-face and/or phone contacts," Kaela enthusiastically noted. "Well, that sounds impressive," Adam said adding, "But how about your work environment? I still feel like I am working alone most of the time." "I remember feeling that way back there," Kaela began, "But here at WPHS we work in multidisciplinary teams with the purpose of

---

[15] Dr. Kaela Jackson is a fictional character working in an innovative health care system, WPHS reflects a Geisinger-like health system, but not the Geisinger Health System per se.

providing each patient quality care. Just this week I am working with three bilingual health coaches, a psychologist, an internist, a nutritionist, a yoga–meditation coach, and a cardiologist in a collaborative effort to engage a group of Hispanic middle-aged women, who have been identified during their regular biyearly physical, in a healthy choices program to not only reduce their risks of heart disease and type 2 diabetes, but to prevent these diseases from impacting their children. This is integrative medicine in action, Adam. What is so impressive is how engaged these patients become when we invited them to be part of their health solution." "That sounds wonderful, but expensive. How does WPHS provide such great care and maintain its reputation for efficiency that I read about?" Adam probed. "The key seems to be an incentive program for the medical staff. I mean our payment is based on performance and bundled payments for work with chronic and preventive treatment. I make a good salary at WPHS, but the incentive (financial and ethical) pushes me to provide the highest quality and efficiency in care to my patients," Kaela noted and added, "We are rewarded for finding new ways to provide more value to our patients' care. For example, when a patient has an acute illness, say a urinary tract infection, my team proposed an early intervention design using evidence-based best practices, presented it to the physician board, got it approved and now we identify and aggressively intervene much sooner resulting in reduced illness, sepsis, and costs." "How on earth do you have time to do all that?" Adam signed. "Remember, Adam, at WPHS we are multidisciplinary team-based, so we can collaborate and share care responsibilities since we all are accountable. We actually take lunch breaks—away from our desks—together so we can relax, recharge, and share information." Adam said almost to himself, "I can't remember the last time I had lunch with my colleagues during work hours." Kaela smiled, "I remember. At WPHS there are monthly performance reports based on our patients' evaluation of their health care experience that serve as a way for us to keep improving by learning from what works and what doesn't. These performance reports are publicly offered to the entire WPHS community of patients, providers, and payers." "OK, but I still don't understand how WPHS manages to contain medical costs so well," Adam added as he looked at his watch, he had 10 more patients to see this afternoon. "One of the main ways WPHS has contained and even cut expenses is by slashing administrative costs," Kaela explained. "At WPHS the leadership redesigned the billing system so we use a standard form and follow the same procedure for all medical billing. It is efficient and very economical." "So, sounds like I can't talk you into coming back to our old clinic," Adam chuckled as he stood to leave, then added. "I think we could use some of WPHS's innovations, but I just don't know where to start." Kaela paused then began, "I was told when I was hired that WPHS started as a challenge of *make it the best,*[16] and through system-wide collaboration we continue to strive to meet that challenge. It takes the commitment of providers, payers, and patients to make it work. But once I experienced the difference, I will never go back to the way health care used to be. I guess it starts with wanting something better and working with others to reach it."

Dr. Kaela Jackson is describing a dynamic system that sustains value innovation by: (1) fostering patient engagement in healthful behaviors that mitigate disease and improve purchasing; (2) developing and adopting incentives for safer and more effective drugs, devices, and procedures; (3) encouraging and supporting provider collaborations in delivering appropriate, reliable, and timely care, (4) reducing supply chain costs; and (5) eliminating unnecessary tests (Paulus et al. 2008:1236).

Conclusion

"There is broad consensus that good health and health care are prerequisites for fair life chances and that everyone should have access to appropriate medical resources" (Mechanic 2006:161). The United States is the only developed nation not to have universal health coverage for its citizens, yet it spends more than twice as much as any other nation. In terms of level of health care delivery, national and state level scorecards on American health system performance reveal excessive costs and poor value presenting persuasive arguments for changing the way health care in the United States is organized, delivered, and financed. Since 2000, employers (the primary source of health insurance coverage in the United States) have seen premiums increase over 100 percent and in response continue to shift more of the costs onto workers and their families (Hacker 2006). Rather than reining in rising health care costs, cost-sharing policies (e.g., high deductibles, co-pays, and limitations on needed services) have accelerated rates of families who are underinsured. Underinsured families, similar to the uninsured, often go without needed care (e.g., dental, vaccinations), fail to get follow-up treatments or diagnostic tests, and/or fail to fill prescriptions, which results in treatable illnesses developing into more serious and costly conditions. Another sign of an ailing health system is the growing trend in medical travel or medical tourism where patients (medical refugees) seek quality, affordable care outside of their home nation.

---

[16] Challenge given by the founder of Geisinger Health System, Abigail Geisinger [Paulus, Ronald A., Karen Davis, and Glenn D. Steele 2008. "Continuous Innovations in Health Care: Implications of the Geisinger Experience." *Health Affairs* 27(5):1235–1245].

How well a health system performs on dimensions of healthy lives, access, equity, quality (i.e., effectiveness, coordination, safety, patient-centeredness, and timeliness), and efficiency determines its value on personal, community, national, and international levels. While the United States continues to soar in medical discoveries, it lags in health system delivery. The American health system costs too much and delivers care below its capabilities and requirements. If health system performance was raised to benchmark levels across the nation, there would be fewer amendable deaths, significant savings due to early treatment, reduced insurance administration costs, and 37 million more adults would have regular access to primary care and recommended referrals, plus 70 million more adults would receive all recommended preventative care (i.e., prevention and early intervention) (Commonwealth Fund Commission 2008:40).

"We have reached a vital tipping point—a realization that incremental reforms and continued neglect of our most pressing challenges must end. There is a social and economic imperative to comprehensively rethink and reform America's health care system" (Roper 2008:3). The call is loud and clear, therefore, that reform and redesign must be comprehensive, coordinated, and supported at national, state, community, provider, payer, family, and patient levels. Health care must provide: (1) affordable and equitable access for all Americans; (2) high-quality and efficient delivery performance; and (3) accountability, leadership, and reorganization. Achieving this challengingly complex redesign requires strategies that actively engage patients, providers, payers, businesses, and government. Accountability must be clear, reorganization should be focused on quality and efficiency, and enthusiastic leadership should often remind us that health care is a necessity, not a luxury. Securing comprehensive health care with affordable and equitable access also requires continual striving for high-quality and efficient performance that will result in healthier families, communities, and nation.

Critical Thinking Questions

1. You work in the human resources department for a local computer data company. The supervisor has assigned you the task of coming up with three talking points to help explain why the company needs to be concerned about the rising rate of underinsured employees. Consider issues raised in Case 6.1.

2. Isabella (Case 6.2) teaches in your brother's school. You are outraged over her poor health care experience. If you had to select three of the five quality elements that require greatest attention at County General, which would you name? What is it about each of these three that is so important to health care?

3. You are a new PCP. You have been asked to work on a hospital team in reforming and redesigning how health care is delivered in order to meet new national guidelines and goals as reflected in Case 6.3. For each of the three overlapping goals of health care reform and redesign (affordable and equitable access; higher quality and efficiency of delivery performance; and accountability, leadership, and reorganization), identify two strategies you believe are most important and explain how each would improve family health.

SUMMARY

The goal of this book has been to describe family health in its multiple dimensions (i.e., biopsychosocial model), and primarily explain the interactive influences of its five major determinants (i.e., biology/genetics, behavior patterns, social-cultural circumstances, environmental exposures, and health care policy and services) as presented in Figure 1.1, Family Health Determinants Model. The United States spends more on health care, yet enjoys less access, equity, quality, and efficiency than other developed nations. What is often overlooked during discussions on access to health care, however, is that health care is only one of five determinants. While there is increasing agreement that health care is a right and not a luxury, what may be missed is that *family health* itself is a right and not a privilege. This means that humans have a "social obligation to protect and promote health for all" (Daniels 2008:140). Protecting and promoting family health encompasses all five of the determinants, not just health care. Making family health a right means:

- supporting and wisely using medical advances and genomic research;
- creating healthful behavior options and facilities along with incentives to encourage families to choose to live healthier lives;
- actively addressing health disparities that cross race, ethnicity, sex, age, geographic location, socioeconomic, educational, and sexual orientation lines through better research, education, and health care program delivery and design;
- taking authentic leadership in promoting healthy and eliminating unhealthy environmental exposures, that is, investing in safer air, water, land, food, plus living and working spaces;
- investing in families through affordable, equitable access to higher-quality and efficient health care.

Biology—Genetics

While advances in genomic-related research promise earlier detection, more effective intervention, and prevention, the multifactorial nature of most diseases and illness require comprehensive approaches that recognize the interactions of all health determinants. Twenty-first century families need to recognize the important role of knowing their family health histories and how to access and protect the confidentiality of their genetic information. The purpose of genomic-related advances is to enhance the quality of life while not denying the full cycle of life that includes living and dying well. A valued development springing from genomic-related research fields is a demand for greater collaboration among disciplines, such as in the redesigning of health care delivery systems. All disciplines interested in enhancing health and family health (e.g., medicine, biological sciences, sociology, psychology, social work, family studies, education) must collaborate.

Behavior Patterns

Choosing healthful behavior patterns begins with having accurate and accessible health information, along with guidance, support, and incentives. In order to encourage more healthful behaviors, one has to know the factors driving behaviors, in other words, recognize the impacts of other determinants. For example, more employer-based health insurance programs are moving toward using incentives (e.g., fitness memberships, reduced co-pays) to encourage their employees to engage in more healthful behaviors. Such practices are based on evidence that workers who practice more healthful behaviors are not only less expensive in terms of health care costs, but more productive. This approach of providing opportunities, facilities, and incentives for healthier behavior patterns needs to be applied to families, especially those located in communities of need. Families need to be engaged and supported for they serve as primary role models for healthful behaviors for themselves and others.

Social-Cultural Circumstances

While genetics and behaviors are well accepted as necessary parts of the family health tapestry, the impacts of social-cultural circumstances are less well understood or woven into providing better health and health care opportunities. There is no shame in being ill, but denying respect, care, and/or coverage based on race, ethnicity, sex, age, socioeconomic status, education, geographic location, or type of illness (e.g., mental illness) is disgraceful. Equity of health opportunities demands recognizing that health disparities stem from complex, interrelated factors that need to be corrected in improving health and health care. Families are better able to take greater responsibility for their health and choose more healthful behaviors when their social-cultural circumstances and related disparities are fully addressed. Promoting health and eliminating health disparities are ethical and economic concerns of all Americans as national and primarily as global citizens.

Environmental Exposures

The world population shares a global home. A home in which the air we breathe, water we drink, food we eat, spaces we live, play, and work in are increasingly interconnected. A major family health challenge in the 21st century is securing and allocating resources to meet the escalating prevalence rates of chronic conditions (e.g., heart disease, diabetes, cancers, asthma), while struggling with epidemic and pandemic infectious diseases (e.g., malaria, antibiotic-resistant tuberculosis, HIV/AIDS) that are ravaging developing nations, such as sub-Saharan Africa. Creating healthful environments begins in our homes, work sites (e.g., reducing job strains, work–family conflicts), and communities, but also demands national attention and effort in addressing the health needs of our global community.

Health Care

The United States spends more and gets less for its health care dollars than any other developed nation. The lack of universal health care in the United States has proven to be not only ethically, but fiscally irresponsible. The reality is that providing access to affordable, equitable health care is a hallmark of a truly progressive nation. While access and equity are vital first steps, these must be accompanied by health care reform and redesign that promotes higher quality and efficiency in delivery of health services. Higher-quality health care means raising the level of effectiveness, safety, coordination, patient-centeredness, and timeliness. Overlapping with this drive for higher quality is the need for greater efficiency. Several attributes of a high-quality and efficient health care system include: (1) availability of relevant patient information to all providers and universal use of health information technology; (2) coordinated patient care among providers and settings through integrated, team-based approaches; (3) access to appropriate care when needed to avoid overuse of emergency departments; (4) greater provider accountability within and across settings in pursuit of continuously innovating and learning to improve quality and efficiency of care; (5) patient–physician partnerships and incorporation of patient feedback; and (6) greater efficiency and streamlining of coverage administration. It is argued that a well-supported, patient-centered medical home is better able to meet higher-quality and efficiency demands since it provides the system where health care is less fragmented and more focused on primary care.

Just as the health of each family member impacts the entire family unit, the health of each family influences the well-being of the larger community on local, national, and global levels. The greatness and wisdom of a nation are found in how it cares for its citizens, that is, all of its citizens. As the opening quote to Chapter 1 explains, it has long been recognized that health, in other words, family health, is fundamental to being able to perform well in our home, work, and community. Family health, therefore, is not a privilege for the few, but a personal, national, and global right and responsibility.

REFERENCES

Acevedo-Garcia, Dolores, Mah-J Soobader, and Lisa R. Berkman. 2005. "The Differential Effect of Foreign-Born on Low Birth Weight by Race/Ethnicity and Education." *Pediatrics* 115(1):20–30.

Acevedo-Garcia, Dolores, Theresa L. Osypuk, Nancy McArdle, and David R. Williams. 2008. "Toward a Policy-Relevant Analysis of Geographic and Racial/Ethnic Disparities in Child Health." *Health Affairs* 27(2):321–33.

Ader, Robert. 2000. "On the Development of Psychoneuroimmunology." *European Journal Pharmacology.* 405:167–76.

Ader, Robert and Nicholas Cohen. 1975. "Behaviorally Conditioned Immunosuppression." *Psychosomatic Medicine* 37(4):333–40.

Advocates for Youth. 2008. "Adolescent Sexual Health in Europe and the U.S.—Why the Difference?" Retrieved August 10, 2008 (www.advocatesforyouth.org/PUBLICATIONS/factsheet/fsest.htm).

Agency for Healthcare Research and Quality. 2008. "Never Events." Retrieved August 3, 2008. www.psnet.ahrq.gov/primer.aspx?primerID=3

Akinbami, Lara J. 2006a. "Asthma Prevalence, Health Care Use and Mortality: United States, 2003–2005." Retrieved July 7, 2008 (www.cdc.gov/nchs/products/pubs/pubd/hestats/ashtma03-05/asthma03-05.htm).

———. 2006b. "The State of Childhood Asthma, United States, 1980–2005." Advance Data from Vital and Health Statistics. No. 381, Hyattsville, MD: National Center for Health Statistics. Retrieved July 7, 2008 (www.cdc.gov/nchs/data/ad/ad381.pdf).

AllAfrica. 2008. "Nigeria: Fresh Wave of Measles and CSM Attack." Retrieved April 16, 2008 (http://allafrica.com/stories/200804150688.html).

Allen, F. Moyra and Marguerite Warner. 2002. "A Developmental Model of Health and Nursing." *Journal of Family Nursing* 8(2):96–135.

Alzheimer's Association. 2008. "Caregiver Stress." Retrieved April 12, 2008 (www.alz.org/living_with_alzheimers_caregiver_stress_lwa.asp).

American Academy of Family Physicians. 2008. "Dysthymic Disorder: When Depression Lingers." Retrieved May 3, 2008 (http://familydoctor.org/online/famdocen/home/common/mentalhealth/depression/054.html).

American Academy of Family Physicians, American Academy of Pediatrics, American College of Physicians, and American Osteopathic Association. 2007. "Joint Principles of the Patient-Centered Medical Home." Retrieved August 2, 2008 (www.medicalhomeinfo.org/JointStatement.pdf).

American Cancer Society. 2002. "Breast Cancer Rates on the Rise among Asian Americans: Japanese American Women May Be Hardest Hit." Retrieved March 10, 2008 (www.cancer.org/docroot/NWS/content/NWS_1_1x_Breast_Cancer_Rates_On_The_Rise_Among_Asian_Americans.asp).

———. 2003. "Cancer Facts and Figures 2003." Retrieved May 4, 2008. (www.cancer.org/downloads/STT/CAFF2003PWSecured.pdf).

———. 2008. "What Is Hospice Care?" Retrieved April 7, 2008 (www.cancer.org/docroot/ETO/content/ETO_2_5X_What_Is_Hospice_Care.asp?sitearea=ETO).

American Dental Education Association. 2007. "Oral Health Care: Essential to Health Care Reform." Retrieved August 10, 2008 (www.adea.org/policy_advocacy/federal_legislative_regulatory_resources/Documents/Principles%20and%20Statement.HCR.June.2008.doc).

American Heart Association. 2008a. "Silent Ischemia and Ischemic Heart Disease." Retrieved March 9, 2008 (www.americanheart.org/presenter.jhtml?identifier=4720).

———. 2008b. "Overweight in Children." Retrieved May 2, 2008 (www.americanheart.org/presenter.jhtml?identifier=4670).

American Medical Association. 2004. *American Medical Association Family Medical Guide*. New York: Random House.

American Medical Informatics Association. 2008. "Biomedical and Health Informatics." Retrieved June 12, 2008. www.amia.org/files/shared/What_is_Informatics__Fact_Sheet_03_24_09_0.pdf

American Psychiatric Association. 1994. *Diagnostic and Statistical Manual of Mental Disorders*. 4th ed. Washington DC: American Psychiatric Association.

America's Health Insurance Plans. 2007. "Individual Health Insurance 2006Antonovsky, Aaron. 1979. *Health, Stress, and Coping: New Perspectives on Mental and Physical Well-being*. San Francisco, CA: Jossey-Bass.

———. 1994. "The Sense of Coherence: An Historical and Future Perspective." Pp. 3–20 in *Sense of Coherence and Resiliency: Stress, Coping, and Health*, edited by H. I. McCubbin, E. A. Thompson, A. I. Thompson, and J. E. Fromer. Madison, WI: University of Wisconsin Press.

Appelbaum, Eileen, Annette D. Bernhardt, and Richard J. Murnane, eds. (2003). *Low-wage America: How employers are reshaping opportunity in the workplace*. New York: Russell Sage Foundation.

Armitage, Christopher J. and Mark Conner. 2000. "Social Cognition Models and Health Behavior: A Structured Review." *Psychology and Health* 15(2):173–89.

Armstrong, Katrina, Ellyn Micco, Amy Carney, Jill Stopfer, and Mary Putt. 2005. "Racial Differences in the Use of BRCA1/2 Testing Among Women with a Family History of Breast or Ovarian Cancer." *Journal of the American Medical Association* 293(14):1729–36.

Aronowitz, Robert. 2008. "Framing Disease: An Underappreciated Mechanism for the Social Patterning of Health." *Social Science and Medicine* 67(1):1–9.

Asthma and Allergy Foundation of America. 2008. "Asthma Facts and Figures." Retrieved July 7, 2008 (www.aafa.org/display.cfm?id=8&sub=42).

Audet, Anne-Marie, Karen Davis, and Stephen C. Schoenbaum. 2006. "Adoption of Patient-Centered Care Practices by Physicians." *Archives of Internal Medicine* 166:754–59.

Bearman, Peter S. and Hanah Brückner. 2001. "Promising the Future: Virginity Pledges and the Transition to First Intercourse." *American Journal of Sociology* 106(4):859–912.

Beasley, Richard, Matthew Masoli, Denise Fabian, and Shaun Holt. 2004. "Global Burden of Asthma." Retrieved July 6, 2008 (www.ginasthma.com/download.asp?intId=29).

Belkic, Karen, Paul A. Lansbergis, Peter L. Schnall, and Dean Baker. 2004. "Is Job Strain a Major Source of Cardiovascular Disease Risk?" *Scandinavian Journal of Work Environment Health* 30(2):85–128.

Benard, Bonnie. 1991. "Fostering Resiliency in Kids: Protective Factors in the Family, School, and Community." Western Center for Drug-Free Schools and Communities, Portland, OR.

Bennett, Michael P. and Cecile Lengacher. 2008. "Humor and Laughter May Influence Health: Laughter and Health Outcomes." *Evidence-Based Complementary and Alternative Medicine* 5(1):37–40.

Bennett, Michael P., J. M. Zeller, L. Rosenberg, and J. McCann. 2003. "The Effect of Mirthful Laughter on Stress and Natural Killer Cell Activity." *Alternative Therapies in Health and Medicine* 9(2):38–45.

Berenson, Robert A., Terry Hammons, David N. Gans, Stephan Zuckerman, Katie Merrell, William S. Underwood, and Aimee F. Williams. 2008. "A House Is Not a Home: Keeping Patients at the Center of Practice Redesign." *Health Affairs* 27(5):1219–30.

Bergstrand, Jonas. 2008. "Operating Profit: Why Put Up with Expensive, Run-of-the-Mill Health Care at Home When You Can Be Treated Just as Well Abroad?" *The Economist*, August 14. Retrieved August 20, 2008 (www.economist.com/business/displaystory.cfm?story_id=11919622).

Bhatia, Subhash and Shashi Bhatia. 1999. "Depression in Women: Diagnostic and Treatment Considerations." *American Family Physician* 60(July):225–40. (www.aafp.org/afp/990700ap/225.html).

Bianchi, Suzanne M., Lynne M. Casper, and Rosalind Berkowitz Kind, eds. 2005. *Work, Family, Health, and Well-being*. Mahwah, NJ: Lawrence Erlbaum Associates.

Bird, Thomas D. 2007. "Alzheimer Disease Overview." *Gene Reviews*. Retrieved March 8, 2008 (www.geneclinics.org/profiles/alzheimer/details.html).

Bleakley, Amy, Michael Hennessy, and Marin Fishbein. 2006. "Public Opinion on Sex Education in U.S. Schools." *Archives of Pediatrics and Adolescent Medicine* 160(11):1151–6.

Bloland, Peter B. and Holly A. Williams. 2002. *Malaria Control during Mass Population Movements and Natural Disasters*. Washington, D.C.: The National Academies Press.

Bomar, Perri J. 1996. *Nurses and Family Health Promotion*. Philadelphia, PA: W. B. Saunders.

———. 2004. *Promoting Health in Families: Applying Family Research and Theory to Nursing Practice*. Philadelphia, PA: W. B. Saunders.

Bond, Meg A., Alketa Kalaja, Pia Karkkanen, Dianne Cazeca, Sivan Daniel, Lana Tsurikova, and Laura Punnett. 2008. "Expanding Our Understanding of the Psychosocial Work Environment: A Compendium of Measures of Discrimination, Harassment and Work-Family Issues." Centers for Disease Control and Prevention. Retrieved August 12, 2008 (www.cdc.gov/niosh/docs/2008-104/pdfs/2008-104.pdf).

Borrell-Carrió, Francesc, Anthony L. Suchman, and Ronald M. Epstein. 2004. "The Biopsychosocial Model 25 Years Later: Principles, Practice, and Scientific Inquiry." *Annals of Family Medicine, Inc.* 2(6):576–82.

Boss, Pauline. 1988. *Family Stress Management*. Newbury Park, NJ: Sage.

———. 1999. *Ambiguous Loss: Learning to Live with Unresolved Grief*. Cambridge, MA: Harvard University Press.

———. 2006. *Loss, Trauma, and Resilience: Therapeutic Work with Ambiguous Loss*. New York: W. W. Norton and Company.

———. 2007. "Ambiguous Loss Theory: Challenges for Scholars and Practitioners." *Family Relations* 56(2):105–111.

Bouzigon, Emmanuelle, Eve Corda, Hugues Aschard, Marie-Hélène Dizier, Anne Boland, Jean Bousquet, Nicolas Chateigner, Frédéric Gormand, Jocelyne Just, Nicole Le Moual, Pierre Scheinmann, Valérie Siroux, Daniel Vervloet, Diana Zelenika, Isabelle Pin, Francine Kauffmann, Mark Lathrop, and Florence Demenais. 2008. "Effect of 17q21 Variants and Smoking Exposure in Early-Onset Asthma." *New England Journal of Medicine* 359:1–10. Retrieved October 3, 2008 (http://content.nejm.org/cgi/reprint/NEJMoa0806604v1.pdf).

British Medical Association. 2008. "Child and Adolescent Mental Health—A Guide for Healthcare Professionals." Retrieved June 1, 2008 (www.bma.org.uk/health_promotion_ethics/child_health/Childadolescentmentalhealth.jsp).

Brodie, Mollyann, Elizabeth Hamel, Claudia Deane, and Carolina Gutiérrez. 2008. "Health Security Watch—April 2008 Tracking Poll." Retrieved March 5, 2008 (www.kff.org/healthpollreport/CurrentEdition/security/index.cfm).

Broman, Clifford L. 2001. "Work Stress in the Family Life of African Americans." *Journal of Black Studies* 31(6):835–46.

Broome, Marion E., Kathleen Knafl, Karen Pridham, and Suzanne Feetham, eds. 1998. *Children and Families in Health and Illness*. Thousand Oaks, CA: Sage.

Brown, Theodore M. 2005. "Emotions and Disease in Historical Perspective." Retrieved May 4, 2008 (www.nlm.nih.gov/hmd/emotions/historical.html).

Brückner, Hannah and Peter Bearman. 2005. "After the Promise: The STD Consequences of Adolescent Virginity Pledges." *Journal of Adolescent Health* 36(4):271–8.

Bruss, Mozhden B., Brooks Applegate, Jackie Quitugua, Rosa T. Palacios, and Joseph R. Morris. 2007. "Ethnicity and Diet of Children: Development of Culturally Sensitive Measures." *Health Education and Behavior* 34(5):735–47.

Burdette, Amy M. and Terrence D. Hill. 2008. "An Examination of Processes Linking Perceived Neighborhood Disorder and Obesity." *Social Science and Medicine* 67:38–46.

Burke, Wylie, Muin J. Khoury, Alison Stewart, and Ronald L. Zimmern. 2006. "The Path From Genome-Based Research to Population Health: Development of an International Public Health Genomics Network." *Genetics in Medicine* 8(7):451–8.

Burris, Scott. 2008. "Stigma, Ethics and Policy: A Commentary on Bayer's 'Stigma and the Ethics of Public Health: Not Can We but Should We.'" *Social Science and Medicine* 67(3):473–5.

California Newsreel and the National Minority Consortia of Public Television. 2008. "Unnatural Causes: Is Inequality Making Us Sick?" Retrieved May 14, 2008 (www.unnaturalcauses.org).

Cantor, Joel C., Cathy Schoen, Dina Belloff, Sabrina K. H. How, and Douglas McCarthy. 2007. "Aiming Higher: Results from a State Scorecard on Health System Performance." Retrieved August 3, 2008 (www.commonwealthfund.org/usr_doc/StateScorecard.pdf?section=4039).

Carey, Michelle A., Jeffrey W. Card, James W. Voltz, Samuel J. Arbes, Jr., Dori R. Germolec, Kenneth S. Korach, and Darryl C. Zeldin. 2008. "It's All About Sex: Male-Female Differences in Lung Development and Disease." *Trends in Endocrinology and Metabolism* 18(8):308–313.

Caruso, Claire C., Edward M. Hitchcock, Robert B. Dick, John M. Russo, and Jennifer M. Schmit. 2004. "Overtime and Extended Work Shifts: Recent Findings on Illnesses, Injuries, and Health Behaviors." Retrieved August 3, 2008 (www.cdc.gov/niosh/docs/2004-143/pdfs/2004-143.pdf).

Center for Health and Health Care in Schools. 2008. "Strengthening the Well Being of Children and Youth through Health Programs in Schools." Retrieved May 10, 2008 (www.healthinschools.org).

Center for State and Local Government Excellence. 2007. "Data Report—Security: What Americans Want From a Job." Retrieved May 9, 2008 (www.slge.org/vertical/Sites/{A260E1DF-5AEE-459D-84C4-876EFE1E4032}/uploads/{085268BE-44AB-4123-9070-38C83140C87B}.PDF).

Centers for Disease Control and Prevention. 2005. "Use of Social Networks to Identify Persons with Undiagnosed HIV Infection—Seven U.S. Cities, October 2003–September 2004." *Morbidity and Mortality Weekly Report* 54(24):601–05. Retrieved August 2, 2008 (www.cdc.gov/mmwr/preview/mmwrhtml/mm5424a3.htm).

———. 2007. "Data Table for Figure 15.5. Page 5. "Prevalence of Current Asthma among Persons of all Ages, by Age Group and Sex: United States, 2006." Retrieved July 7, 2008 (www.cdcov/nchs/data/nhis/earlyrelease/200706_15.pdf).

———. 2008a. "Update: Measles Outbreaks Continue in U.S." Retrieved May 1, 2008 (www.cdc.gov/Features/MeaslesUpdate).

———. 2008b. "Overweight and Obesity." Retrieved May 10, 2008 (www.cdc.gov/nccdphp/dnpa/obesity/index.htm).

———. 2008c. "Age-Specific Percentage of Civilian, Noninstitutionalized Population with Diagnosed Diabetes by Race and Sex, United States, 2006." Retrieved July 11, 2009. (www.cdc.gov/diabetes/statistics/prev/national/fig2004.htm).

———. 2008d. "HIV/AIDS in the United States." Retrieved May 20, 2008 (www.cdc.gov/hiv/resources/factsheets/us.htm).

———. 2008e. "Vaccination Coverage among U.S. Adults." *National Immunization Survey—Adult, 2007.* Retrieved May 15, 2008 (www.cdc.gov/vaccines/stats-surv/nis/downloads/nis-adult-summer-2007.pdf).

———. 2008f. "2008 National STD Prevention Conference: Confronting Challenges, Applying Solutions." Retrieved May 20, 2008 (www.cdc.gov/STDConference/2008/media/release-11march2008.htm).

———. 2008g. "Malaria: Topic Home." Retrieved July 20, 2008 (www.cdc.gov/malaria/).

———. 2008h. "Community-Associated MRSA Information for the Public." Retrieved August 1, 2008. (www.cdc.gov/ncidod/dhqp/ar_mrsa_ca_public.html#2).

———. 2008i. "Estimates of New HIV Infections in the United States." CDC HIV/AIDS Facts. Retrieved August 3, 2008 (www.cdc.gov/hiv/topics/surveillance/resources/factsheets/pdf/incidence.pdf).

———. 2008j. "HIV/AIDS and African Americans." Retrieved September 9, 2008 (www.cdc.gov/hiv/topics/aa/index.htm).

———. 2008k. "Chronic Obstructive Pulmonary Disease (COPD)." Retrieved July 2, 2008 (www.cdc.gov/nceh/airpollution/copd/copdfaq.htm).

———. 2008l. "Chronic Disease Overview." Retrieved September 4, 2008 (http://cdc.gov/nccdphp/overview.htm).

———. 2009. "Chronic Disease Prevention and Health Promotion." Retrieved July 10, 2009. www.cdc.gov/nccdphp/publications/aag/ddt.htm

Centers for Medicare and Medicaid Services. 2008. "National Health Expenditure Projections 2007–2017." Retrieved August 1, 2008 (www.cms.hhs.gov/NationalHealthExpendData/Downloads/proj2007.pdf).

Chaiken, Miriam S., Hedwig Deconinck, and Tedbabe Degefie. 2006. "The Promise of a Community-Based Approach to Managing Severe Malnutrition: A Case Study from Ethiopia." *Food and Nutrition Bulletin* 27(2):95–104.

Chen, Tian-hui, Lu Li, and Michael M. Kochen. 2005. "A Systematic Review: How to Choose Appropriate Health-Related Quality of Life (HRQOL) Measures in Routine General Practice?" *Journal of Zhejiang University Science* 6(9):936–40.

Chen, Yu and Martin J. Blaser. 2007. "Inverse Associations of *Helicobacter Pylori* With Asthma and Allergy." *Archives of Internal Medicine* 167(8):821–7.

Children's Defense Fund. 2008. "Health Coverage for All Children Campaign: Reauthorization of the State Children's Health Insurance Program (SCHIP)." Retrieved March 1, 2008 (www.childrensdefense.org/site/PageServer?pagename=healthy_child_SCHIP_update).

Chin, Steve H. and Richard Balon. 2006. "Attitudes and Perceptions toward Depression and Schizophrenia among Residents in Different Medical Specialties." *Academic Psychiatry* 30(3):262–3.

Christakis, Nicholas A. and James H. Fowler. 2008. "The Collective Dynamics of Smoking in a Large Social Network." *New England Journal of Medicine* 358:2249–58.

Christensen, Karl B., Helene Feveile, Merete Labriola, and Thomas Lund. 2007. "The Impact of Psychosocial Work Environment Factors on the Risk of Disability Pension in Denmark." *European Journal of Public Health* 18(3):235–7.

Citrin Toby and Stephen M. Modell. 2004. *Genomics and Public Health: Ethical, Legal, and Social Issues.* Atlanta, GA: Office of Genomics and Disease Prevention, Centers for Disease Control and Prevention.

Claxton, Gary, Jon R. Gabel, Bianca DiJulio, Jeremy Pickreign, Heidi Whitmore, Benjamin Finder, Marian Jarlenski, and Samantha Hawkins. 2008. "Health Benefits In 2008: Premiums Moderately Higher, While Enrollment In Consumer-Directed Plans Rises In Small Firms." *Health Affairs* 27(6):w492–w502. Retrieved September 25, 2008 (http://content.healthaffairs.org/cgi/content/full/hlthaff.27.6.w492/DC1).

Cohen, Bernard I. 1985. *Revolution in Science.* Cambridge, MA: Harvard University Press.

Cohen, Hillel W., Robert M. Gould, and Victor W. Sidel. 2004. "The Pitfalls of Bioterrorism Preparedness: The Anthrax and Smallpox Experiences." *American Journal of Public Health* 94(10):1667–71.

Cohen, Jonathan. 2007. *Sick: The Untold Story of America's Health Care Crisis—and the People Who Pay the Price*. New York: HarperCollins.

Cohen, Robin A., Michael E. Martinez, and Heather L. Free. 2008. "Health Insurance Coverage: Early Release of Estimates from the National Interview Survey, January–September 2007." National Center for Health Statistics, Figure 4, p. 13. Retrieved March 10, 2008 (www.cdc.gov/nchs/data/nhis/earlyrelease/insur200803.htm).

Commission on Social Determinates of Health (CSDH). 2008. "Closing the Gap in a Generation: Health Equity through Action on the Social Determinants of Health." Final Report of the CSDH. Geneva, World Health Organization. Retrieved August 10, 2008 (http://whqlibdoc.who.int/publications/2008/9789241563703_eng.pdf).

Commonwealth Fund Commission. 2007. "A High Performance Health System for the United States: An Ambitious Agenda for the Next President." Retrieved June 6, 2008(www.commonwealthfund.org/usr_doc/Ambitious_Agenda_1075.pdf?section=4039).

———. 2008. "Why Not the Best?: Results from the National Scorecard on U.S. Health System Performance, 2008." Retrieved August 3, 2008 (www.commonwealthfund.org/usr_doc/Why_Not_the_Best_national_scorecard_2008.pdf).

Consumer Reports. 2007. "Are You Really Covered?" Retrieved March 20, 2008 (www.consumerreports.org/cro/health-fitness/health-care/health-insurance-9-07/overview/0709_health_ov.htm).

Corbie-Smith, Giselle, Stephen B. Thomas, Diane Marie M. St. George. 2002. "Distrust, Race, and Research." *Archives of Internal Medicine* 162:2458–63.

Crawford, Barbara, Ellen Beth Levitt, and Gwen Fariss Newman. 2000. "Laughter Is Good for Your Heart, According to a New University of Maryland Medical Center Study." Retrieved July 10, 2008 (www.umm.edu/news/releases/laughter.htm).

Currey, Aaron, Carl Latkin, and Melissa Davey-Rothwell. 2008. "Pathways to Depression: The Impact of Neighborhood Violent Crime on Inner-City Residents in Baltimore, Maryland, USA." *Social Science and Medicine* 67(1):12–30.

Dahlgren, Göran. and Margaret Whitehead. 1991. *Policies and Strategies to Promote Equity and Health*. Stockholm, Sweden: Institute of Future Studies.

Daly, Kerry. 2003. "Family Theory Versus the Theories Families Live By." *Journal of Marriage and Family* 65(4):771–84.

Daniels, Norman. 2008. *Just Health: Meeting Health Needs Fairly*. New York: Cambridge Press.

Davis, Karen, Stephen C. Schoenbaum, and Anne-Marie Audet. 2005. "A 2020 Vision of Patient-Centered Primary Care." *Journal of General Internal Medicine* 20(10):953–7.

Davis, Karen, Cathy Schoen, Stephen C. Schoenbaum, Michelle M. Doty, Alyssa L. Holmgren, Jennifer L. Kriss, and Katherine K. Shea. 2007. "Mirror, Mirror on the Wall: An International Update on the Comparative Performance of American Health Care." The Commonwealth Fund, May 29. Retrieved July 20, 2008 (www.commonwealthfund.org/publications/publications_show.htm?doc_id=482678).

Deapen, Dennis, Lihua Liu, Carin Perkins, Leslie Bernstein, and Ronald K. Ross. 2002. "Rapidly Rising Breast Cancer Incidence Rates Among Asian-American Women." *International Journal of Cancer* 99(5):747–50.

Deloitte Center for Health Solutions. 2008. "Medical Tourism: Consumers in Search of Value." Retrieved August 3, 2008 (www.deloitte.com/dtt/cda/doc/content/us_chs_MedicalTourismStudy(1).pdf).

DeNavas-Walt, Carmen, Bernadette D. Proctor, and Jessica Smith. 2007. "Income, Poverty, and Health Insurance Coverage in the United States: 2006." Current Population Reports: Consumer Income, U.S. Census Bureau, August. Retrieved February 20, 2008 (www.census.gov/prod/2007pubs/p60-233.pdf).

Dey, Sujoya, Marcus D. Flather, Gerard P. Devlin, David Brieger, Enrique P. Gurfinkel, Gabriel Steg, Gordon FitzGerald, Elizabeth A. Jackson, and Kim A. Eagle. 2008. "Sex-related Differences in the Presentation, Treatment and Outcomes among Patients with Acute Coronary Syndromes: The Global Registry of Acute Coronary Events." *Heart*. Retrieved June 4, 2008 (http://heart .bmj.com/cgi/content/abstract/hrt.2007.138537v1).

Doctors without Borders. 2008. "Top Ten Humanitarian Crises of 2008 Retrieved July 11, 2009. (www.doctorswithoutborders.org/publications/topten/story.cfm?id=3232).

Doherty, William J. and Hamilton I. McCubbin, eds. 1985. "Special Issue: The Family and Health Care." *Family Relations: Interdisciplinary Journal of Applied Family Studies* 34(1):5–137.

Doherty William J. and Macaran A. Baird. 1987. *Family-Centered Medical Care: A Clinical Casebook*. New York: Guilford Press.

Doherty, William J. and Thomas L. Campbell. 1988. *Families and Health*. Thousand Oaks, CA: Sage.

Duran, D., J. Beltrami, R. Stein, A. Voetsch, and B. Branson. 2008. "Persons Tested for HIV—United States, 2006." *Morbidity and Mortality Weekly Report* 57(31):845–9. Retrieved August 8, 2008 (www.cdc.gov/mmwr/preview/mmwrhtml/mm5731a1.htm).

Durant, Will. 1966. *The Life of Greece*. New York: Simon and Schuster.

Economos, Christina D., Raymond R. Hyatt, Jeanne P. Goldberg, Aviva Must, Elena N. Naumova, Jessica J. Collins, and Miriam E. Nelson. 2007. "A Community Intervention Reduces BMI Z-Score in Children: Shape Up Somerville First Year Results." *Obesity* 15(5):1325–536.

Ell, Kathleen and Helen Northen. 1990. *Families and Health Care: Psychosocial Practice*. New York: Aldine de Gruyter.

Engel, George. 1977. "The Need for a New Medical Model: A Challenge for Biomedicine," *Science* 196:129–35.

———. 1980. "The Clinical Application of the Biopsychosocial Model." *American Journal of Psychiatry* 137:535–43.

Eysenbach, Gunther. 2000. "Consumer Health Informatics." *British Medical Journal* 320:1713–6.

Ezekial, Emanuel J. 2008. *Healthcare Guaranteed: A Sample, Secure Solution for America*. NY: Public Affairs.

Fabin, Dan. 2008. "China's Children of Smoke: Epidemiologists Find Molecular Clues to Air Pollution's Impact on Youngsters." *Scientific American* (August):72–79.

Families USA. 2009. "Americans at Risk: One in Three Uninsured." Retrieved July 11, 2009. (www .familiesusa.org/resources/publications/reports/americans-at-risk.html.

Feldbaum, Harley, Kelley Lee, and Preeti Patel. 2006 "The National Security Implications of HIV/AIDS." *Public Library of Science—Medicine* 3(6):e171. Retrieved May 4, 2008 (http://medicine.plosjournals.org/perlserv/?request=get-document&doi=10.1371/journal .pmed.0030171).

Ferguson, Tom. 2000. "Online Patient-Helpers and Physicians Working Together: A New Partnership for High Quality Health Care." *British Medical Journal* 321(7269):1129–32.

Fernandez, Don. 2008. "Asthma Health Center—Olympics in Beijing: Air Quality Woes." Retrieved July 30, 2008. (www.webmd.com/asthma/news/20080725/olympics-in-beijing-air-quality-woes).

Ferrie, Jane, ed. 2004. "Work, Stress, and Health: The Whitehall II Study." Retrieved May 27, 2008. (www.ucl.ac.uk/whitehallII/findings/Whitehallbooklet.pdf).

Fine, Michael J., Said A. Ibrahim, and Stephen B. Thomas. 2005. "The Role of Race and Genetics in Health Disparities Research." *American Journal of Public Health* 95(12):2125–28.

Finkelstein, Eric A., Ian C. Fiebelkorn, and Guijing Wang. 2003. "National Medical Spending Attributable to Overweight and Obesity: How Much, and Who's Paying?" *Health Affairs* 22(1):219–26.

Francini, Kristin and Lisa Tumminello. 2008. "Longer Work Days Leave Americans Nodding Off on the Job." National Sleep Foundation. Retrieved July 6, 2008 (www.sleepfoundation.org/article/ press-release/longer-work-days-leave-americans-nodding-the-job.

Frank, Jacquelyn. 2008. "Alzheimer's Study Finds Grief Is the Heaviest Burden for Caregivers." Retrieved April 24, 2008 (www.uindy.edu/news/?p=577).

Friedrich, M. J. 2007. "Researchers Address Childhood Obesity through Community-Based Programs." *Journal of the American Medical Association* 298(23):2728–30.

Galinsky, Ellen, James T. Bond, Kelly Sakai, Stacy S. Kim, and Nicole Giuntoli. 2008. "2008 National Study of Employers." Alfred P. Sloan Foundation. Retrieved August 14, 2008 (http://familiesandwork.org/site/research/reports/2008nse.pdf).

Gallup. 2007. "No Increase in Public Pressure for Healthcare Reform." Retrieved January 3, 2008 (www.gallup.com/poll/102931/Increase-Public-Pressure-Healthcare-Reform.aspx).

Garcia, Cecilia. 2004. "Dealing With Diabetes: A Community-Based Approach." Retrieved April 7, 2008 (www.connectforkids.org/node/627).

Garcia, Julie A. and Jennifer Crocker. 2008. "Reasons for Disclosing Depression Matter: The Consequences of Having Egosystem and Ecosystem Goals." *Social Science and Medicine* 67(3):453–62.

Garmezy, Norman. 1981. "Children under Stress: Perspectives on Adolescents and Correlates of Vulnerability and Resilience to Psychopathology." Pp. 196–269 in *Further Explorations in Personality*, edited by A. I. Rubin, J. Arnoff, A. M. Barclay, and R. A.Zucker. New York: Wiley.

Gehlert, Sarah, Dana Sohmer, Tina Sacks, Charles Mininger, Martha McClintock, and Olufunmilayo Olodade. 2008. "Targeting Health Disparities: A Model Linking Upstream Determinants to Downstream Interventions." *Health Affairs* 27(2):339–49.

Geisinger Health System. Retrieved October 2, 2008. (www.geisinger.org/about).

Genetics Home Reference. 2006. "Alzheimer Disease." Retrieved April 20, 2008 (www.ghr.nlm.nih.gov/condition=alzheimerdisease).

Gennari, John. 2002. "Biomedical Informatics Definition." Retrieved November 9, 2008 (http://faculty.washington.edu/gennari/MedicalInformaticsDef.html).

Genome-Based Research and Population Health. 2005. "Report of an Expert Workshop Held at the Rockefeller Foundation Study and Conference Centre, Bellagio, Italy, 14–20 April 2005." Retrieved March 10, 2008 (http://dceg.cancer.gov/files/genomicscourse/bellagio-011807.pdf).

Gerteis, Margaret, Susan Edgman-Levitan, Jennifer Daley, and Thomas L. Delanco, eds. 1993. *Through the Patient's Eyes: Understanding and Promoting Patient-Centered Care*. San Francisco: Jossey-Bass.

Gibbs, Nancy. 2008. "The Light of Death." *Time*, May, p. 56.

Gilliss, Catherine Lynch 1989. "Why Family Health Care?" Pp. 3–8 in *Toward a Science of Family Nursing*, edited by C. L. Gilliss, B. L. Highley, B. M. Roberts, and I. M. Martinson. Menlo Park, CA: Addison-Wesley.

Glasgow, Russell E., C. Tracy Orleans, Edward H. Wagner, Susan J. Curry, and Leif I. Solberg. 2001. "Does the Chronic Care Model Serve Also as a Template for Improving Prevention?" *Milbank Quarterly* 79(4):579–612.

Goettlich, Paul. 2006. "What Are Endocrine Disruptors?" Retrieved May 3, 2008 (www.mindfully.org/Pesticide/EDs-PWG-16jun01.htm).

Goffman, Erving. 1963. *Stigma: Notes on the Management of Spoiled Identity*. New York: Simon and Schuster.

Gonzalas, Chris J. 2008. "Sarah: What a Depressed Teenage Wished She Could Say." Case 4.2. Interviewed by J. R. Grochowski, August 3, 2008.

Gostick, Adrian and Scott Christopher. 2008. *The Levity Effect: Why It Pays to Lighten Up*. New York: John Wiley and Sons.

Greer, Steven. 2000. "What's in a Name: Neuroimmunomodulation or Psychoneuroimmunology?" *Annals of the New York Academy of Sciences* 917:568–74.

Grieser, Mira, Dianne Neumakr-Sztainer, Brit I. Saksvig, Jung-Sun Lee, Gwen M. Felton, and Martha Y. Kubik. 2008. "Black, Hispanic, and White Girl's Perceptions of Environmental and Social Support and Enjoyment of Physical Activity." *Journal of School Health* 78(6):314–20.

Grochowski, Janet R. 1997. "Strategic Living Context Communities: Families Who Thrive in the Future." Peer reviewed paper presented at the annual meetings of the International World Future Society, July, San Francisco, CA.

———. 2000. "Families as 'Strategic Living Communities.' " Peer reviewed paper presented at the annual meetings of the American Academy of Health Behavior, September, Santa Fe, NM.

———. 2006a. "Resiliency: Families at Their Best." Pp. 61–92 in *Families with Futures: A Survey of Family Studies for the 21st Century,* edited by M. W. Karraker and J. R. Grochowski. Mahweh, NJ: Lawrence Erlbaum Associates.

———. 2006b. "Family Wellness: Beyond Absence of Illness." Pp. 125–58 in *Families with Futures: A Survey of Family Studies for the 21st Century,* edited by M. W. Karraker and J. R. Grochowski. Mahweh, NJ: Lawrence Erlbaum Associates.

Grzywacz, Joseph G. and Brenda L. Bass. 2003. "Work, Family, and Mental Health: Testing Different Models of Work–Family Fit." *Journal of Marriage and Family* 65(1):248–61.

Guerra, Carlos A., Priscilla W. Gikandi, Andrew J. Tatem, Abdisalan M. Noor, Dave L. Smith, Simon I. Hay, Robert W. Snow. 2008. "The Limits and Intensity of *Plasmodium falciparum* Transmission: Implications for Malaria Control and Elimination Worldwide." *Public Library of Science—Medicine* 5(2):e38.doi:10.137/journal.pmed.0050038. Retrieved July 3, 2008 (http://medicine.plosjournals.org/archive/1549-1676/5/2/pdf/10.1371_journal.pmed.0050038-S.pdf).

Guttmacher Institute. 2003. "New Medical Records Privacy Rule: The Interface with Teen Access to Confidential Care." Retrieved March 9, 2008 (www.guttmacher.org/pubs/tgr/06/1/gr060106.html).

Hacker, Jacob. S. 2006. *The Great Risk Shift: The Assault on American Jobs, Families, Health Care, and Retirement and How You Can Fight Back.* New York: Oxford University Press.

Halbert Chanita Hughes, Lisa Jay Kessler, and Edith Mitchell. 2005. "Genetic Testing For Inherited Breast Cancer Risk in African Americans." *Cancer Investigation* 23(4):285–95.

Haley, Jennifer, Genevieve Kenney, and Jennifer Pelletier. 2008. "Access to Affordable Dental Care: Gaps for Low-Income Adults." Kaiser Low-Income Coverage and Access Survey. Retrieved August 20, 2008 (www.kff.org/medicaid/upload/7798.pdf).

Hamilton, Brady E., Joyce A. Martin, and Stephanie J. Ventura. 2007. "Births: Preliminary Data for 2006." Centers for Disease Control and Prevention, National Vital Statistics Reports 56(7). Retrieved May 3, 2008 (www.cdc.gov/nchs/ata/nvsr/nvsr56/nvsr56_07.pdf).

Hammer, Tove Helland, Per Oystein Saksvik, Kjell Nytro, Hans Torvatn, and Mahmut Bayazit. 2004. "Expanding the Psychosocial Work Environment: Workplace Norms and Work–Family Conflict as Correlates of Stress and Health." *Journal of Occupational Health Psychology* 9(1):83–97.

Hannah, Kathryn J., Marion J. Ball, and Margaret J. A. Edwards. 2006. *Introduction to Nursing Informatics.* New York: Springer.

Harmon, Amy. 2008. "Insurance Fears Lead Many to Shun DNA Tests." *New York Times.* Retrieved February, 2008 (www.nytimes.com/2008/02/24/health/24dna.html?pagewanted=1&_r=1&hp).

Harris Poll. 2001. "Attitudes in the American Workplace VII." Retrieved August 3, 2008 (www.stress.org/2001Harris.pdf).

Harvard Medical School. 2004. *Harvard Medical School Family Health Guide.* New York: Free Press.

Harvard School of Public Health. 2008. "The Project on Global Working Families." Retrieved August 7, 2008 (www.hsph.harvard.edu/globalworkingfamilies/US.htm).

Hauser, Debra. 2008. "Five Years of Abstinence-Only-Until-Marriage Education: Assessing the Impact." Retrieved June 20, 2008. (www.advocatesforyouth.org/publications/stateevaluations/index.htm).

Hertzman, Clyde. 1999. "The Biological Embedding of Early Experience and Its Effects on Health in Adulthood." *Annals of the New York Academy of Sciences* 896(1):85–95.

Heymann, Jody, Stephanic Simmons, and Alison Earle. 2005. "Global Transformations." Pp. 507–526 in *Work, Family, Health, and Well-being,* edited by S. Bianchi, L. Casper, and R. B. King. Mahwah, NJ: Lawrence Erlbaum Associates.

Hill, Rubin. 1949. *Families under Stress.* West, CT: Greenwood.

Hirsh, Jacob B. and Michael Inzlicht. 2008. "The Devil You Know: Neuroticism Predicts Neural Response to Uncertainty." *Psychological Science* 19:962–7.

How, Sabrina K. H., Anthony Shih, Jennifer Lau, and Cathy Schoen. 2008. "Public Views on U.S. Health System Organization: A Call for New Directions." Retrieved September 1, 2008. (www .commonwealthfund.org/~/media/Files/Publications/Data Brief/2008/Aug/Public Views on US Health System Organization A Call for New Directions/How_publicviewsUShltsysorg_1158_db pdf.pdf

Huebner, Angela, Jay A. Mancini, Ryan M. Wilcox, Saralyn R. Grass, and Gabriel A. Grass. 2007. "Parental Deployment and Youth in Military Families: Exploring Uncertainty and Ambiguous Loss." *Family Relations* 56(2):112–22.

Hunter, David J., Muin J. Khoury, and Jeffrey M. Drazen. 2008. "Letting the Genome Out of the Bottle—Will We Get Our Wish?" *New England Journal of Medicine* 358(2):105–07.

Insel, P. M. and W. T. Roth. 2008. *Core Concepts in Health Brief.* Boston, MA: McGraw-Hill.

Institute of Health and Social Policy. 2009. "The Project on Global Working Families." Retrieved July 30, 2009. (www.hsph.harvard.edu/globalworkingfamilies/).

Institute of Medicine. 2001. "Crossing the Quality Chasm: A New Health System for the 21st Century." Retrieved August 5, 2008 (www.iom.edu/?id=12736).

———. 2003. *Unequal Treatment: Confronting Racial and Ethnic Disparities in Health Care.* Washington, DC: National Academy of Sciences.

Institute for Vaccine Safety. 2007. "Vaccine Exemptions." Baltimore, MD: Johns Hopkins Bloomberg School of Public Health. Retrieved May 1, 2008 (www.vaccinesafety.edu/cc-exem.htm).

International HIV/AIDS Alliance. 2008. "Children Living with HIV/AIDS." Retrieved August 2, 2008 (www.ovcsupport.net/sw3699.asp).

International Labour Office. 2007. "Global Employment Trends for Women—2007." Retrieved August 10, 2008 (www.ilo.org/public/english/employment/strat/download/getw07.pdf).

———. 2008. "Global Employment Trends for Women—March 2008." Retrieved August 10, 2008 (www.ilo.org/wcmsp5/groups/public/—dgreports/—dcomm/documents/publication/wcms_091225.pdf).

International Society for NeuroImmunoModulation. 2008. "What Is the International Society for NeuroImmunoModulation (ISNIM)?" Retrieved July 2, 2007 (www.isnim.org).

Jacobs, Jerry and Kathleen Gerson. 2004. *The Time Divide: Work, Family and Gender Inequality.* Boston, MA: Harvard University Press.

Jacobs, Paul. 2008. "Wages and Benefits: A Long-Term View." Kaiser Family Foundation, Health Security Watch, June. Retrieved January 30, 2008. (www.kff.org/insurance/snapshot/chcm012808oth.cfm

Jacobs, Paul and Gary Claxton. 2008. "How Non-Group Health Care Coverage Varies with Income." Kaiser Family Foundation. Retrieved March 20, 2008 (www.kff.org/insurance/upload/7737.pdf).

Jamison, Kay Redfield. 2006. "The Many Stigmas of Mental Illness." *Lancet* 367(February):533–4.

Jayadev, Suman, Ellen J. Steinbart, Yueh-Yun Chi, Walter A. Kukull, Gerard D. Schellenberg, and Thomas D. Bird. 2008. "Conjugal Alzheimer Disease: Risk in Children when Both Parents Have Alzheimer Disease." *Archives of Neurology* 65(3):373–8.

Jiang, J., X. Xia, T. Greiner, G. Wu, G. Lian, and U. Rosenqvist. 2007. "The Effects of a 3-Year Obesity Intervention in Schoolchildren in Beijing." *Child: Care, Health and Development* 33(5):641–6.

Johns Hopkins. 1999. *Johns Hopkins Family Health Book: The Essential Home Medical Reference to Help You and Your Family Promote Good Health and Manage Illness.* New York: HarperCollins.

———. 2007. "Alzheimer's Disease to Quadruple Worldwide by 2050." Retrieved May 10, 2008 (www.jhsph.edu/publichealthnews/press_releases/2007/brookmeyer_alzheimers_2050.html).

Kaiser Family Foundation. 2002. "Uninsured in America: Is Health Coverage Adequate?" Retrieved January 4, 2008 (www.kff.org/uninsured/loader.cfm?url=/commonspot/security/getfile.cfm& PageID=14136.

———. 2007. "Health Insurance Premiums Rise 6.1 Percent in 2007, Less Rapidly than in Recent Years, but Still Faster than Wages and Inflation." Retrieved August 2, 2008 (www.kff.org/insurance/ehbs091107nr.cfm).

———. 2008a. "Black Americans and HIV/AIDS." HIV/AIDS Policy Fact Sheet. Retrieved June 22, 2008 (www.kff.org/hivaids/upload/6089_05.pdf).

———. 2008b. "Women and HIV/AIDS in the United States." HIV/AIDS Policy Fact Sheet. Retrieved August 1, 2008 (www.kff.org/hivaids/upload/6092_05.pdf).

———. 2008c. "The HIV/AIDS Epidemic in the United States." HIV/AIDS Policy Fact Sheet. Retrieved August 1, 2008 (www.kff.org/hivaids/upload/3029-08.pdf).

———. 2008d. "The Global HIV/AIDS Epidemic." Retrieved July 8, 2008 (www.kff.org/hivaids/upload/3030-11.pdf).

———. 2008e. "Employer Health Benefits: 2008 Summary of Findings." Retrieved August 8, 2008 (http://ehbs.kff.org/images/abstract/7791.pdf).

———. 2008f. "Massachusetts Health Care Reform: Two Years Later." Retrieved June 8, 2008 (www.kff.org/uninsured/upload/7777.pdf).

Kam, Katherine. 2007. "What is Integrative Medicine?" *WebMD.* Retrieved May 8, 2008 (www.webmd.com/a-to-z-guides/features/alternative-medecine-therapy).

Karasek Robert. 1979. "Job Decision Latitude, Job Demands, and Mental Strain: Implications for Job Redesign." *Administrative Science Quarterly* 24:285–308.

Karasek, Robert and Töres Theorell. 1990. *Healthy Work: Stress, Productivity, and the Reconstruction of Working Life.* New York: Basic Books.

Karraker, Meg Wilkes. 2008. *Global Families.* Boston: Allyn and Bacon.

Kaufman, Leslie and Adam Karpati. 2007. "Understanding the Sociocultural Roots of Childhood Obesity: Food Practices among Latino Families of Bushwick, Brooklyn." *Social Science and Medicine* 64(11):2177–88.

Kavanaugh, Molly. 2008. "Laugh Your Way to Better Health." *Star Tribune*, Minneapolis, MN. Retrieved August 10, 2008(www.startribune.com/lifestyle/health/19714154.html?page=1&c=y).

Keefe, Janice and Pamela Fancey. 2000. "The Care Continues: Responsibility for Elderly Relatives before and after Admissions to a Long-Term Care Facility." *Family Relations* 49(3):235–44.

Kennedy, Steven, James Ted McDonald, and Nicholas Biddle. 2006. "The Healthy Immigrant Effect and Immigrant Selection: Evidence from Four Countries." SEDAP: A Program for Research on Social and Economic Dimensions of an Aging Population. Retrieved May 24, 2008.(http://socserv2.socsci.mcmaster.ca/~sedap/p/sedap164.pdf).

Keusch, Geraod T., Joan Wilentz, and Arthur Kleinman. 2006. "Stigma and Global Health: Developing a Research Agenda." *The Lancet* 367:525–7.

Kimbro, Rachel Tolbert, Sharon Bzostek, Noreen Goldman, and Germán Rodriquez. 2008. "Race, Ethnicity, and the Education Gradient in Health." *Health Affairs* 27(2):361–72.

Kindig, David A. 2007. "An Expanded Population Health Model." Altarum Policy Roundtable Report—Determinants of U.S. Population Health: Translating Research into Future Policies, Exhibit 2, p. 4, Washington, DC. Retrieved May 1, 2008 (www.altarum.org/files/pub_resources/07_28Nov_Roundtable_Determinants_of_Health-RTR.pdf).

Knickman, James R. and Emily K. Snell. 2002. "The 2030 Problem: Caring for Aging Baby Boomers—Statistical Data Included." Health Services Research. Retrieved April 2, 2008 (www.findarticles.com/p/articles/mi_m4149/is_4_37/ai_91568394).

Kriss, Jennifer L., Sara R. Collins, Bisundev Mahato, Elise Gould, and Cathy Schoen. 2008. "Rite of Passage? Why Young Adults Become Uninsured and How New Policies Can Help, 2008 Update." Retrieved May 25, 2008 (www.commonwealthfund.org/usr_doc/Kriss_riteofpassage2008_1139_ib.pdf).

Kubler-Ross, Elizabeth. 1969. On Death and Dying. New York: Macmillan. Kuttner, Robert. 2008. "Market-Based Failure—A Second Opinion on U.S. Health Care Costs." The New England Journal of Medicine 358(6):549–51.

Landsbergis, Paul A., Susan J. Schurman, Barbara A. Israel, Peter L. Schnall, Margrit K. Hugentobler, Janet Cahill, and Dean Baker. 1993. "Job Stress and Heart Disease: Evidence and Strategies for Prevention." Retrieved November 2, 2008 (www.workhealth.org/prevention/prjscvd.html).

Lear, Julia Graham. 2007. "Health at School: A Hidden Health Care System Emerges from the Shadows." Health Affairs 26(2):409–19.

Lewis, Deborah, Gunther Eysenbach, Rita Kukafka, P. Zoë Stavri, and Holly Jimison, eds. 2005. Consumer Health Informatics. New York: Springer.

Library of Congress. 2008. "Subtitle B: Paul Wellstone and Pete Domenici Mental Health Parity and Addiction Equity Act of 2008." Retrieved October 6, 2008 (http://thomas.loc.gov/cgi-bin/bdquery/z?d110:HR01424:@@@D&summ2=m&).

Lie, Jihong, Kevin J. Bennett, Nusrat Harun, Xia Zheng, Janice C. Probst, and Russell R. Pate. 2007. "Overweight and Physical Inactivity among Rural Children Aged 10–17: A National and State Portrait." Retrieved May 1, 2008 (http://rhr.sph.sc.edu/report/SCRHRC_ObesityChartbook_Exec_Sum_10.15.07.pdf).

Lincoln, Karen D., Linda M. Chatters, Robert Joseph Taylor, and James S. Jackson. 2007. "Profiles of Depressive Symptoms among African Americans and Caribbean Blacks." Social Science and Medicine 65(2):200–13.

Link, Bruce G. and Jo C. Phelan. 2001. "Conceptualizing Stigma." Annual Review of Sociology 27:363–85.

Link, Bruce G., Dorothy M. Castille, and Jennifer Stuber. 2008. "Stigma and Coercion in the Context of Outpatient Treatment for People with Mental Illness." Social Science and Medicine 67:409–19.

Link, Michael W., Indu B. Ahluwalia, Mary L. Euler, Carolyn B. Bridges, Susan Y. Chu, and Pascale M. Wortley. 2006. "Racial and Ethnic Disparities in Influenza Vaccination Coverage among Adults during the 2004–2005 Season." American Journal of Epidemiology 163(6):571–78.

Litman. T. J. 1974. "The Family as a Basic Unit in Health and Medical Care: A Sociobehavioral Overview." Social Science and Medicine 8:495–519.

Mahajan, A., V. R. Tandon, S. Verma, J. B. Singh, and M. Sharma. 2008. "Prevalence of Tuberculosis, Hepatitis C and Syphilis Co-infections among HIV/AIDS Patients." Indian Journal of Medical Microbiology 26(2):196–7.

Marcotty, Josephine. 2008. "Moving Beyond 'More Is Better.'" Star Tribune, March 16, pp. A1, A18.

Matarazzo, Joseph D. 1982. "Behavioral Health's Challenge to Academic, Scientific, and Professional Psychology." American Psychologist 35:807–17.

Mathers, Colin D. and Dejan Loncar. 2006. "Projections of Global Mortality and Burden of Disease from 2002 to 2030." Public Library of Science—Medicine 3(11):e442.doi:10.1371/journal.pmed.0030442. Retrieved July 2, 2008 (www.plosmedicine.org).

Mayo Clinic. 2003. Mayo Clinic Family Health Book. New York: William Morrow.

———. 2007. "Sepsis." Retrieved July 7, 2008 (www.mayoclinic.com/health/sepsis/DS01004).

———. 2008a. "Depression in Women: Understanding the Gender Gap." Retrieved June 22, 2008 (www.mayoclinic.com/health/depression/MH00035).

———. 2008b. "Mayo Clinic Study Reveals Rural, Unmarried Women at Higher Risk for Depression." Retrieved June 22, 2008 (www.eurekalert.org/pub_releases/2008-06/mc-mcs061108.php).

———. 2008c. "Mental Health: Overcoming the Stigma of Mental Illness." Retrieved June 22, 2008 (www.mayoclinic.com/health/mental-health/MH00076).

McBride, J. LeBron. 2006. *Family Behavioral Issues in Health and Wellness*. New York: The Haworth Press.

McConnell, Kathy. 2002. "Be Active, Eat Well: A Community Building Approach." Retrieved May 2, 2008 (http://www.goforyourlife.vic.gov.au/hav/admin.nsf/Images/BAEW_Project_Brief.pdf/$File/BAEW_Project_Brief.pdf).

McCubbin, Hamilton I. and Joan M. Patterson. 1983. "The Family Stress Process: The Double ABCX Model of Adjustment and Adaptation." *Marriage and Family Review* 6:7–37.

McCubbin, Marilyn A. 1989. "Family Stress, Resources, and Family Types: Chronic Illness in Children." *Family Relations* 37:203–10.

McCulloch, Adam. 2008. "Medical Tourism 2008." Retrieved August 19, 2008 (www.forbestraveler.com/beneficial-travel/medical-tourism-2008-story-1.html).

McGinnis, J. Michael, Pamela Williams-Russo, and James R. Knickman. 2002. "A Case for More Active Policy Attention to Health Promotion." *Health Affairs* 21(2):78–93.

Mead, Holly, Lara Cartwright-Smith, Karen Jones, Christal Ramos, Kristy Woods, and Bruce Siegel. 2008. *Racial and Ethnic Disparities in U.S. Health Care: A Chartbook*. New York: The Commonwealth Fund.

Meara, Ellen R., Seth Richards, and David M. Cutler. 2008. "The Gap Gets Bigger: Changes in Mortality and Life Expectancy, by Education, 1981–2000." *Health Affairs* 27(2):350–60.

Mechanic, David. 2006. *The Truth about Health Care: Why Reform Is Not Working in America*. New Brunswick, NJ: Rutgers University Press.

Mechanic, David and Jennifer Tanner. 2007. "Vulnerable People, Groups, and Populations Societal View." *Health Affairs* 26(5):1220–30.

Medical News Today. 2007 "Los Angeles Times Examines High-Deductible Health Plans." Retrieved January 3, 2008 (www.medicalnewstoday.com/articles/73091.php).

Medical Research Council. 2007. "Concerted Effort from Leading Health Experts Offers Global Prescription to Tackle the Most Fatal Diseases." Retrieved June 5, 2008 (www.mrc.ac.uk/Newspublications/News/MRC004224.

MedicineNet. 2008a. "Definition of Ambulatory Care." Retrieved July 8 2008 (www.medterms.com/script/main/art.asp?articlekey=2218).

———. 2008b. "Gum Disease." Retrieved September 8, 2008 (www.medicinenet.com/gum_disease/page4.htm#tocg).

Medline Plus. 2008a. "Genetic Testing." U.S. National Library of Medicine and the National Institutes of Health. Retrieved April 10, 2008 (www.nlm.nih.gov/medlineplus/genetictesting.html).

———. 2008b. "Pediatric Asthma." Retrieved July 9, 2008 (www.nlm.nih.gov/medlineplus/ency/article/000990.htm).

Meersman, Tom. 2008. "Too Dirty to Breathe." *Minneapolis Star Tribune*, March 13, p. A7.

Mehrotra, Ateev, Margaret C. Wang, Judith R. Lave, John L. Adams, and Elizabeth A. McGlynn. 2008. "Retail Clinics, Primary Care Physicians, and Emergency Departments: A Comparison of Patients' Visits." *Health Affairs* 27(5):1272–82.

Melgert, Barbro N., Anuradha Ray, Machteld N. Hylkema, Wim Timens, and Dirje S. Postma. 2007. "Are There Reasons Why Adult Asthma Is More Common in Females?" *Current Allergy and Asthma Reports* 7(2):143–50.

MetLife Foundation. 2006. "MetLife Foundation Alzheimer's Survey: What America Thinks." Retrieved February 3, 2008 (www.metlife.com/WPSAssets/20538296421147208330V1FAlzheimersSurvey .pdf).

Meyer, Ilan. 2003. "Prejudice, Social Stress, and Mental Health in Lesbian, Gay, and Bisexual Populations: Conceptual Issues and Research Evidence." National Institutes of Health. Retrieved April 7, 2008 (www.pubmedcentral.nih.gov/articlerender.fcgi?artid=2072932).

Meyer, Ilan, Sharon Schwartz, and David M. Frost. 2008. "Social Patterning of Stress and Coping: Does Disadvantaged Social Statuses Confer More Stress and Fewer Coping Resources?" *Social Science and Medicine* 67:368–79.

Minnesota Department of Health. 2008. "Causes and Symptoms of Cholera." p. 1. Retrieved July 20, 2008 (www.health.state.mn.us/divs/idepc/diseases/cholera/basics.html).

Moen, Phyllis and Kelly Chermack. 2005. "Gender Disparities in Health: Strategic Selection, Careers, and Cycles of Control." *The Journals of Gerontology Series B: Psychological Sciences and Social Sciences* 60(2):99–108.

Morbidity and Mortality Weekly Report. 2003. "Measles Epidemic Attributed to Inadequate Vaccination Coverage—Campania, Italy, 2002." Retrieved May 1, 2008 (www.cdc.gov/mmwR/ preview/mmwrhtml/mm5243a4.htm).

———. 2008. "Measles—United States, January 1–April 25, 2008." Retrieved May 1, 2008 (www.cdc.gov/mmwr/preview/mmwrhtml/mm57e501a1.htm?s_cid=mm57e501a1_e).

Moriarty, David G., Mathew M. Zack, and Rosemarie Kobau. 2003. "The Centers for Disease Control and Prevention's Healthy Days Measure—Population Tracking of Perceived Physical and Mental Health over Time." *Health and Quality of Life Outcomes* 1:37. Retrieved February 21, 2008 (www.pubmedcentral.nih.gov/articlerender.fcgi?artid=201011).

National Cancer Institute. 2005. *Theory at a Glance: A Guide for Health Promotion Practice.* Washington, DC: National Institutes of Health. Retrieved January 6, 2008 (www.cancer.gov/ PDF/481f5d53-63df-41bc-bfaf-5aa48ee1da4d/TAAG3.pdf).

National Center for Health Statistics. 2007. *Health, United States, 2007 with Chartbook on Trends in the Health of Americans.* Hyattsville, MD. Retrieved February 27, 2008 (www.cdc.gov/nchs/ data/hus/hus07.pdf).

———. 2008a. "U.S. Deaths Down Sharply in 2006." Retrieved June 12, 2008 (www.cdc.gov/media/ pressrel/2008/r080611.htm).

———. 2008b. "Prevalence of Overweight among Children and Adolescents: United States, 1999–2002." Retrieved May 3, 2008 (www.cdc.gov/nchs/products/pubs/pubd/hestats/ over-wght99.htm).

———. 2008c. "Prevalence of Overweight among Children and Adolescents: United States, 2003–2004." Retrieved April 8, 2008 (www.cdc.gov/nchs/products/pubs/pubd/hestats/ overweight/overwght_child_03.htm).

National Coalition on Health Care. 2007. "Health Insurance Coverage." Retrieved February 9, 2008 (www.nchc.org/facts/coverage.shtml).

National Committee for Quality Assurance. 2008. "Physician Practice Connections: Patient-Centered Medical Home™." Retrieved September 20, 2008 (www.ncqa.org/tabid/631/Default.aspx).

National Conference for State Legislatures. 2008. "Covering Young Adults through Their Parent's or Guardian's Health Policy." Retrieved February 20, 2008 (www.ncsl.org/programs/health/ dependentstatus.htm).

National Heart, Lung, and Blood Institute. 2008. "About the Heart Truth" Retrieved May 1, 2008 (www.nhlbi.nih.gov/health/hearttruth/whatis/index.htm).

National Human Genome Research Institute. 2008. "Frequently Asked Questions about Genetic Disorders." Retrieved April 12, 2008 (www.genome.gov/19016930).

National Institute of Allergy and Infectious Diseases. 2008. "Air Pollution Affects Respiratory Health in Children with Asthma, Study Shows." *ScienceDaily*. Retrieved July 9, 2008 (www.sciencedaily.com/releases/2008/04/080415019.htm).

National Institute of Drug Abuse and Addiction. 2008. "NIDA Researchers Identify Genetic Variant Linked to Nicotine Addiction and Lung Cancer." Retrieved May 20, 2008 (www.nida.nih.gov/newsroom/08/NR4-02a.html).

National Institute of Mental Health. 2008. "The Numbers Count: Mental Disorders in America." Retrieved June 1, 2008 (www.nimh.nih.gov/health/publications/the-numbers-count-mental-disorders-in-america.shtml#Intro).

National Institute on Aging, and National Institutes of Health, U.S. Department of Health and Human Services. 2007. "Why Population Aging Matters: A Global Perspective." Retrieved April 2, 2008 (www.nia.nih.gov/NR/rdonlyres/9E91407E-CFE8-4903-9875-D5AA75BD1D50/0/WPAM_finalpdftorose3_9.pdf).

National Institutes of Health. 2006. "Two NIH Initiatives Launch Intensive Efforts to Determine Genetic and Environmental Roots of Common Diseases." Retrieved July 3, 2008 (www.nih.gov/news/pr/feb2006/nhgri-08.htm).

———. 2008. "Theme: New Pathways to Discovery." Retrieved March 4, 2008 (http://nihroadmap.nih.gov/initiatives.asp).

National Network for Immunization Information. 2008. "Vaccine Safety." Retrieved March 9, 2008 (www.immunizationinfo.org/vaccine_safety_detail.cfv?id=132).

National Public Radio, Kaiser Family Foundation, and Harvard University's-Kennedy School of Government. 2004. "Sex Education in America: General Public/Parents Survey." Retrieved June 1, 2008 (www.npr.org/templates/story/story.php?storyId=1622610).

National Quality Forum. 2007. "National Quality Forum: Serious Reportable Events in Healthcare—2006 Update." Retrieved August 3, 2008 (www.qualityforum.org/pdf/reports/sre/txsreexecsummarypublic.pdf).

National Research Council and Institute of Medicine. 2004. *Children's Health, the Nation's Wealth*. Washington, DC: The National Academies Press.

National Stroke Association. 2008. "African Americans and Stroke." Retrieved March 10, 2008 (www.stroke.org/site/PageServer?pagename=AAMER).

Neal, Margaret B. and Leslie B. Hammer. 2006. *Working Couples Caring for Children and Aging Parents*. Mahwah, NJ: Lawrence Erlbaum Associates.

Nolte, Ellen, and C. Martin McKee. 2008. "Measuring the Health of Nations: Updating an Earlier Analysis." *Health Affairs* 27(1):58–71.

Norrie, Justin. 2007. "Japanese Measles Epidemic Brings Campuses to Standstill." May 27, p. 1. Retrieved May 5, 2008 (www.smh.com.au/news/world/japanese-measles-epidemic-brings-campuses-to-standstill/2007/05/27/1180205052602.html).

Obama, Barack. 2009. "Health Care." Retrieved July 9, 2009. www.whitehouse.gov/issues/health_care/

Office of Minority Health and Health Disparities. 2007a. "Health Status of Asian American and Pacific Islander Women." Retrieved April 9, 2008 (www.omhrc.gov/templates/content.aspx?ID=3721).

———. 2007b. "Eliminating Racial and Ethnic Health Disparities." Retrieved May 1, 2008 (http://cdc.gov/omhd/About/disparities.htm).

———. 2007c. "Eliminate Disparities in Cardiovascular Disease (CVD)." Retrieved May 1, 2008 (http://cdc.gov/omhd/AMH/factsheets/cardio.htm).

———. 2008. "American Indian—Alaska Native Profile." Retrieved May 20, 2008 (www.omhrc.gov/templates/browse.aspx?lvl=2&lvlID=52).

Oglethorpe, Judy and Nancy Gelman. 2007. "HIV/AIDS and the Environment: Impacts of AIDS and Ways to Reduce Them." Retrieved May 1, 2008. www.worldwildlife.org/what/whowehelp/community/phe/WWFBinaryitem7051.pdf.

Organization for Economic Co-Operation and Development. 2007. "Life Expectancy at Birth." Retrieved July 8, 2008. (http://puck.sourceoecd.org/vl=5307859/cl=14/nw=1/rpsv/factbook/110101.htm).

————. 2008. "OECD Health Data 2008: How Does the United States Compare." Retrieved July 9, 2008:2 (www.oecd.org/dataoecd/46/2/38980580.pdf).

Osseiran, Nada and Gregory Hartl. 2006. "Almost a Quarter of All Disease Caused by Environmental Exposure." World Health Organization. Retrieved July 7, 2008 (www.who.int/mediacentre/news/releases/2006/pr32/en/index.html).

Partnership for Workplace Mental Health. 2006. "A Mentally Healthy Workforce—It's Good for Business." Retrieved May 27, 2008 (www.workplacementalhealth.org/pdf/businesscase12112006.pdf).

Patterson, Joan. 2002. "Integrating Family Resilience and Family Stress Theory." *Journal of Marriage and Family* 62(2):349–60.

Paulus, Ronald A., Karen Davis, and Glenn D. Steele. 2008. "Continuous Innovations in Health Care: Implications of the Geisinger Experience." *Health Affairs* 27(5):1235–45.

Perera, Frederica, Karl Hemminki, Wielaw Jedrychowski, Robin Whyatt, Ulka Campbell, Yanzhi Hsu, Regina Santella, Richard Albertini, and James P. O'Neill. 2002. "In Utero DNA Damage from Environmental Pollution Is Associated with Somatic Gene Mutation in Newborns." *Cancer Epidemiology Biomarkers and Prevention* 11(October):1134–7.

Perlin, David and Ann Cohen. 2002. *The Complete Idiot's Guide to Dangerous Diseases and Epidemics*. Royersford, PA: Alpha.

Perry-Jenkins, Maureen, Abbie E. Goldberg, Courtney P. Piece, and Aline G. Sayer. 2007. "Shift Work, Role Overload, and the Transition to Parenthood." *Journal of Marriage and Family* 69:123–38.

Pescosolido, Bernice A., Jack K. Martin, Annie Lang, and Sigrun Olafsdottir. 2008. "Rethinking Approaches to Stigma: A Framework Integrating Normative Influences on Stigma (FINIS)." *Social Science and Medicine* 67(3):431–40.

Phelan, Jo C., Bruce G. Link, and John F. Dovidio. 2008. "Stigma and Prejudice: One Animal or Two?" *Social Science and Medicine* 67(3):358–67.

Pichichero, M. E., A. Gentile, N. Giglio, V. Umido, T. Clarkson, E. Cernichiari, G. Zareba, C. Gotelli, M. Gotelli, L. Yan, and J. Treanor. 2008. "Mercury Levels in Newborns and Infants after Receipt of Thimerosal-Containing Vaccines." *Pediatrics* 121(2):208–214.

Ping Tsao, Carol I., Aruna Tummala, and Laura Weiss Roberts. 2008. "Stigma in Mental Health Care." *Academic Psychiatry* 32(2):70–72.

Pinquart, Martin and Silvia Sörensen. 2005. "Caregiving Distress and Psychological Health of Caregivers." Pp.165–206 in *Psychology of Stress*, edited by K. V. Oxington. New York: Nova Biomedical Books.

Pipher, Mary. 2000. *Another Country: Navigating the Emotional Terrain of Our Elders*. New York: Penquin Group.

Population Reference Bureau. 2007. "World Population Highlights: Key Findings from PRM's 2007 World Population Data Sheet." 62(3). Retrieved August 1, 2008 (www.prb.org/pdf07/62.3Highlights.pdf).

Pratt, Lois. 1976. *Family Structure and Effective Health Behavior: The Energized Family*. Boston, MA: Houghton Mifflin.

Procter, Kimberley L., Mary C. Rudolf, Richard G. Feltbower, Ronnie Levine, Anne Connor, Michael Robinson, and Graham P. Clarke. 2008. "Measuring the School Impact on Child Obesity." *Social Science and Medicine* 67:341–9.

Pupillo, Jessica. 2008. "Residency Programs Pinpoint Best Practices for Increasing Immunizations." Retrieved May 2, 2008 (www.aafp.org/online/en/home/publications/news/news-now/resident-student-focus/20080130aafpfwyethawards.html).

Rankin, William W., Sean Brennan, Ellen Schell, Jones Laviwa, and Sally H. Rankin. 2005. "The Stigma of Being HIV-Positive in Africa." *Public Library of Science—Medicine* 2(8):e247–e250. Retrieved July 9, 2008 (http://medicine.plosjournals.org/perlserv/?request=get-document& doi=10.1371%2Fjournal.pmed.0020247).

Raphael, Dennis. 2006. "Social Determinants of Health: An Overview of Concepts and Issues." Pp. 115–38 in *Staying Alive: Critical Perspectives on Health, Illness, and Health Care,* edited by D. Raphael, T. Bryant, and M. Rioux. Toronto: Canadian Scholars' Press.

Reinberg, Steven. 2008. "25 Million Americans Are Underinsured." *BusinessWeek,* HealthDay News. Retrieved August 2, 2008 (www.businessweek.com/print/lifestyle/content/healthday/616350.html).

Rhea, Shawn. 2008. "Medical Migration." *Modern Healthcare* (May 5). Retrieved August 10, 2008 (www.deloitte.com/dtt/cda/doc/content/us_chs_Modern%20Healthcare%20Med%20Tourism%20PDF.pdf).

Rhodes, Erinn T. and David S. Ludwig. 2007. "Childhood Obesity as a Chronic Disease—Keeping the Weight Off." *Journal of the American Medical Association* 298: 1695–6.

Riolo, Stephanie A., Tuan Nguyen, John F. Greden, and Cheryl A. King. 2005. "Prevalence of Depression by Race/Ethnicity: Findings from the National Health and Nutrition Survey III." *American Journal of Public Health* 95(6):998–1000.

Roberto, Karen A. and Shannon E. Jarrott. 2008. "Family Caregivers of Older Adults: A Life Span Perspective." *Family Relations* 57(1):100–111.

Robertson, Suzanne M., Steven H. Zarit, Larissa G. Duncan, Michael J. Rovine, and Elia E. Femia. 2007. "Family Caregivers' Patterns of Positive and Negative Affect." *Family Relations* 56(1):12–23.

Rock, V. J., A. Malarcher, J. W. Kahende, K. Asman, C. Husten, and R. Caraballo. 2007. "Cigarette Smoking Among Adults—United States, 2006." *Morbidity and Mortality Weekly Report* 56(44):1157–1161. Retrieved April 6, 2008 (www.cdc.gov/mmwr/preview/mmwrhtml/m5644a2.htm).

Rolland, John S. 2003. "Mastering Family Challenges in Illness and Disability." Pp. 460–92 in *Normal Family Processes,* edited by F. Walsh. New York: Guilford.

———. 2004. "Families and Chronic Illness: An Integrative Model." Pp. 89–116 in *Handbook of the Family, Stress and Trauma,* edited by R.Catherall. Washington, DC: American Psychological Association Press.

———. 2005. "Cancer and the Family: An Integrative Model." *Cancer* 104(11):2584–95.

Rolland, John S. and Janet K. Williams. 2005. "Toward a Biopsychosocial Model for 21st Century Genetics. *Family Process* 44(1):3–24.

Roll Back Malaria. 2005. "Somalia Malaria Strategy 2005–2010." Retrieved July 20, 2008 (www.rollbackmalaria.org/countryaction/nsp/somalia2005-2010.pdf).

Roper, William. 2008. "Statement of William Roper, Chairman of the Board of Directors National Quality Forum Before the Senate Finance Committee, September 9." Retrieved September 10, 2008 (www.finance.senate.gov/hearings/testimony/2008test/090908wrtest.pdf).

Rose, Abigail L., Nikki Peters, Judy A. Shea, and Katrina Armstrong. 2005. "Attitudes and Misconceptions about Predictive Genetic Testing for Cancer Risk." *Community Genetics* 8(3):145–51.

Rowland, Ingrid D. 2008. *Giordano Bruno: Philosopher/Heretic.* Rome: Farrar, Straus and Giroux.

Rugulies, Reiner, Ute Bultmann, Birgit Aust, and Hermann Burr. 2006. "Psychosocial Work Environment and Incidence of Severe Depressive Symptoms: Prospective Findings from a 5-Year Follow-up of the Danish Work Environment Cohort Study." *American Journal of Epidemiology* 163(10):877–87.

Rutter, Michael. 1987. "Psychosocial Resilience and Protective Mechanisms." *American Journal of Orthopsychiatry* 57(3):316–31.

Sankar, Pamela, Mildred K. Cho, Celeste M. Condit, Linda M. Hunt, Barbara Koenig, Patricia Marshall, Sandra Soo-Jin Lee, and Paul Spicer. 2004. "Genetic Research and Health Disabilities." *Journal of the American Medical Association* 291:2985–9.

Santavira, Nina, Camilla Kovero, and Svetlana Solovieva. 2005. "Psychosocial Work Environment, Well-being, and Emotional Exhaustion: A Study Comparing Five Age Groups of Female Workers within the Human Sector." *International Congress Series* 1280(June):130–35.

Santelli, John. 2008. "Committee on Oversight and Government Reform Hearing on Abstinence-Only Programs." April. Retrieved May 10, 2008 (http://oversight.house.gov/documents/20080423113314.pdf).

Sauter, Steven, Lawrence Murphy, Michael Colligan, Naomi Swanson, Joseph Hurrell, Jr., Fredrick Scharf, Jr., Raymond Sinclair, Paula Grubb, Linda Goldenbar, Toni Alterman, Janet Johnston, Anne Hamilton, and Julie Tisdale. 2008. "Stress ... at Work." National Institute for Occupational Safety and Health. Publication No. 99-101. Retrieved August 2, 2008 (www.cdc.gov/Niosh/stresswk.html).

Save the Children. 2008. "CHANGE for Children in Rural America: Toward a Healthier Future." Retrieved April 20, 2008 (http://www.savethechildren.org/programs/us-literacy-and-nutrition/physical.html).

Scharlach, Andew, Wei Li, and Tapashi B. Dalvi. 2006. "Family Conflict as a Mediator of Caregiver Strain." *Family Relations* 55(5):625–35.

Schechter, Robert and Judith K. Grether. 2008. "Continuing Increases in Autism Reported in California's Developmental Services System: Mercury in Retrograde." *Archives of General Psychiatry* 65(1):19–24.

Schoen, Cathy, Karen Davis, and Sara Collins. 2008b. "Building Blocks for Reform: Achieving Universal Coverage with Private and Public Group Health Insurance." *Health Affairs* 27(3):646–57.

Schoen, Cathy, Robin Osborn, Michelle M. Doty, Megan Bishop, Jordon Peugh, and Nandita Murukutla. 2007b. "Toward Higher-Performance Health Systems: Adults' Health Care Experiences in Seven Countries, 2007." *Health Affairs* Web Exclusive 26(6):w717-w734. Retrieved May 20, 2008 (www.commonwealthfund.org/usr_doc/Schoen_towardhigher-performinghltsys2007survey_1069_itl.pdf?section=4039).

Schoen, Cathy, Robin Osborn, Phuong Trang Huynh, Michelle Doty, Jordon Peugh, and Kinga Zapert. 2006. "On the Front Lines of Care: Primary Care Doctors' Office Systems, Experiences, and Views in Seven Countries." *Health Affairs* 25(6):w555–w571. Retrieved September 4, 2008 (http://content.healthaffairs.org/cgi/reprint/25/6/w555?ijkey=3YyH7yDwrJSoc&keytype=ref&siteid=healthaff).

Schoen, Cathy, Sara R. Collins, Jennifer L. Kriss, and Michelle M. Doty. 2008a. "How Many Are Underinsured? Trends among U.S. Adults, 2003 and 2007." *Health Affairs* Web Exclusive 27(4):w298–w309. Retrieved August 18, 2008 (http://content.healthaffairs.org/cgi/content/abstract/26/6/w717?ijkey=btmwgHzAr9YPo&keytype=ref&siteid=healthaff).

Schoen, Cathy, Stuart Guterman, Anthony Shih, Jennifer Lau, Sophie Kasimow, Anne Gauthier, and Karen Davis. 2007a. "Bending the Curve: Options for Achieving Savings and Improving Value in U.S. Health Spending". The Commonwealth Fund Commission on a High Performance Health System. Retrieved June 1, 2008 (www.commonwealthfund.org/usr_doc/Schoen_bendingthecurve_1080.pdf).

Schroeder, Steven A. 2007. "We Can Do Better—Improving the Health of the American People." *New England Journal of Medicine* 357(12):1221–8.

Science Daily. 2007. "Allergy-related Asthma More Common in Children Living in Affluent Countries." Retrieved July 8, 2008 (www.sciencedaily.com/releases/2007/09/070914085223.htm).

————. 2008a. "New Compound Identifies Alzheimer's Disease Brain Toxins, Study Shows." Retrieved May 20, 2008 (www.sciencedaily.com/releases/2008/03/080326114855.htm).

————. 2008b. "Stomach Bug Appears to Protect Kids from Asthma." Retrieved July 15, 2008 (www.sciencedaily.com/releases/2008/07/080715071419.htm).

Seccombe, Karen. 2007. *Families in Poverty*. Boston: Allyn and Bacon.

Seccombe, Karen and Kim Hoffman. 2007. *Just Don't Get Sick: Access to Health Care in the Aftermath of Welfare Reform*. Piscataway, NJ: Rutgers University Press.

Seiler, Bill and Ellen Beth Levitt. 2005. "University of Maryland School of Medicine Study Shows Laughter Helps Blood Vessels Function Better." Retrieved July 12, 2008 (www.umm.edu/news/releases/laughter2.htm).

Shannon, Kate, Thomas Kerr, Shari Allinott, Jill Chettiar, Jean Shoveller, and Mark W. Tyndall. 2007. "Social and Structural Violence and Power Relations in Mitigating HIV Risk of Drug-Using Women in Survival Sex Work." *Social Science and Medicine* 66:911–21.

Shih, Anthony, Karen Davis, Stephen C. Schoenbaum, Anne Gauthier, Rachel Nuzum, and Douglas McCarthy. 2008. "Organizing the U.S. Health Care Delivery System for High Performance." The Commonwealth Fund. Retrieved September 1, 2008 (www.commonwealthfund.org/usr_doc/Shih_organizingushltcaredeliverysys_1155.pdf?section=4039).

Shih, Anthony and Stephen C. Schoenbaum. 2007. "Measuring Hospital Performance: The Importance of Process Measures." Retrieved September 10, 2008. (www.commonwealthfund.org/usr_doc/1046_Shih_measuring_hosp_performance_process.pdf?section=4039)].

Sidel, Ruth. 2006. *Unsung Heroines: Single Mothers and the American Dream*. Berkeley, CA: University of California Press.

SIECUS. 2007. "Sexuality Education and Abstinence-Only-Until-Marriage Programs in the States: An Overview." (http://www.siecus.org/policy/states/2005/analysis.html).

Siegrist, Johannes. 2004. "Psychosocial Work Environment and Health: New Evidence." *Journal of Epidemiology and Community Health* 58:888.

Silver, Jonathan M. 2006. "Behavioral Neurology and Neuropychiatry Is a Subspecialty." *Journal of Neuropsychiatry and Clinical Neurosciences* 18:146–8.

Silverberg Koerner, Susan, DenYelle Baete Kenyon. 2007. "Understanding 'Good Days' and "Bad Days': Emotional and Physical Reactivity among Caregivers for Elderly Relatives." *Family Relations* 56(1):1–11.

Singh, Gopal K. and Mohammond Siahpush. 2006. "Widening Socioeconomic Inequalities in US Life Expectancy, 1980–2000." *International of Epidemiology* 35:969–75.

Smeeth, L., C. Cook, E. Fombonne, L. Heavey, L. C. Rodrigues, P. G. Smith, and A. J. Hall. 2008. "MMR Vaccination and Pervasive Development Disorders: A Case-Control Study." *The Lancet* 364(9438):963–69.

Smith, Michael. 2008. "Expand TB Prevention and Care, U.N. Forum Urges." Retrieved August 2, 2008 (www.medpagetoday.com/HIVAIDS/HIVAIDS/tb/9763).

Smith, Philip J. and John Stevenson. 2008. "Racial/Ethnic Disparities in Vaccination Coverage by 19 months of Age: An Evaluation of the Impact of Missing Data Resulting form Record Scattering." National Center for Biotechnology Information. Retrieved June 22, 2008 (http://www.ncbi.nlm.nih.gov/sites/entrez).

Smith, Philip J., Susan Y. Chu, and Lawrence E. Barker. 2004. "Children Who Have Received No Vaccines: Who Are They and Where Do They Live?" *Pediatrics* 114(1):187–95.

Steinhauer, Jennifer and Gardiner Harris. 2008. "Rising Public Health Risk Seen as More Parents Reject Vaccines." *The New York Times*, March 21. Retrieved March 22, 2008 (www.nytimes.com/2008/03/21/us/21vaccine.html).

Strazdins, Lyndall, Mark S. Clements, Rosemary J. Korda, Dorothy H. Brown, and Rennie M. D'Souza. 2006. "Unsociable Work" Nonstandard Work Schedules, Family Relationships and Children's Well-being." *Journal of Marriage and Family* 68(2):394–410.

Stuber, Jennifer, Ilan Meyer, and Bruce Link. 2008. "Stigma, Prejudice, Discrimination and Health." *Social Science and Medicine* 67(3):351–7.

Surgeon General. 2008. "The Surgeon General's Call to Action to Prevent and Decrease Overweight and Obesity: Overweight in Children and Adolescents." Retrieved April 10, 2008 (www.surgeongeneral.gov/topics/obesity/calltoaction/fact_adolescents.htm).

Sussman, M. 1976. "The Family Life of Older People." Pp. 218–43 in *Handbook of Aging and The Social Sciences*, edited by R. H. Binstock and E. Shanas. New York: Van Nostrand Reinhold.

Szeftel, Alan. 2007. "Asthma Risk—Who & Why?" Retrieved June 10, 2008 (www.medicinenet.com/script/main/art.asp?articlekey=19453).

Thakkinstian, Ammarin, Mark McEvoy, Cosetta Minelli, Peter Gibson, Bob Hancox, David Duffy, John Thompson, Ian Hall, Joel Kaufman, Ting-fan Leung, Peter Joseph Helms, Hakon Hakonarson, Eva Halpi, Ruth Navon, and John Attia. 2005. "Systematic Review and Meta-Analysis of the Association between ß$_2$-Adrenoceptor Polymorphisms and Asthma." *American Journal of Epidemiology* 163(3):201–11.

The Center for Health and Health Care in Schools. 2000. "Minors and the Right to Consent to Health Care." Retrieved March 9, 2008 (www.healthinschools.org/static/papers/guttmacher.aspx).

———. 2007. "Pediatric Oral Health—New Attention to an Old Problem." Retrieved June 7, 2008 (www.healthinschools.org/News-Room/EJournals/Volume-8/Number-2/Pediatric-Oral-Health.aspx).

The Economist. 2008. "DARC Continent." *The Economist* (July 19):88–9.

The Joint Commission. 2008. "Facts about the Joint Commission International." Retrieved July 9, 2008 (www.jointcommission.org/AboutUs/Fact_Sheets/jci_facts.htm).

Thomas, Richard K. 2003. *Society and Health: Sociology for Health Professionals*. New York: Kluwer Academic/Plenum.

Thompson, William W., Cristofer Price, Barbara Goodson, David K. Shay, Patti Benson, Virginia L. Hinrichsen, Edwin Lewis, Eileen Eriksen, Paula Ray, S. Michael Marcy, Jon Dunn, Lisa A. Jackson, Tracy A. Lieu, Steve Black, Gerrie Stewart, Eric S. Weintraub, Robert L. Davis, and Frank DeStefano. 2007. "Early Thimerosal Exposure and Neuropsychological Outcomes at 7 to 10 Years." *The New England Journal of Medicine* 357(13):1281–92.

Thorpe, Kenneth E., David H. Howard, and Katya Galactionova. 2007. "Differences in Disease Prevalence as a Source of the U.S.–European Health Care Spending Gap." *Health Affairs* 26(6):w678–w686. Retrieved September 4, 2008. (http://content.healthaffairs.org/cgi/content/abstract/hlthaff.26.6.w678).

Toossi, Miltra. 2002. "A Century of Change: The U.S. Labor Force, 1950-2050." *Monthly Labor Review*, May:15-28. Retrieved July 11, 2009. http://www.bls.gov/opub/mlr/2002/05/art2full.pdf

Trenholm, Christopher, Barbara Devaney, Ken Fortson, Lisa Quay, Justin Wheeler, and Melissa Clark. 2007. "Impacts of Four Title V, Section 510 Abstinence Education Programs." Retrieved June 1, 2008 (www.mathematica-mpr.com/publications/pdfs/impactabstinence.pdf).

Trenholm, Christopher, Barbara Devaney, Ken Fortson, Melissa Clark, Lisa Quay, and Justin Wheeler. 2008. *Journal of Policy Analysis and Management* 27(2):255–76.

Turnbull, Andrew and Mark Serwotka. 2008. *Work, Stress and Health: The Whitehall II Study*. Retrieved May 28, 2008. (www.ucl.ac.uk/whitehallII/findings/Whitehallbooklet.pdf).

Twyman, Richard. 2003. "Polygenic and Multifactorial Diseases." Retrieved February 10, 2008 (http://genome.wellcome.ac.uk/doc_WTD020852.html).

UNAIDS. 2008a. "2008 Report on the Global AIDS Epidemic, Executive Summary." Retrieved July 30, 2008. (www.unaids.org/en/KnowledgeCentre/HIVData/GlobalReport/2008/2008_Global_report.asp).

————. 2008b. "Core Slides." Retrieved August 1, 2008 (http://data.unaids.org/pub/GlobalReport/2008/2008_globalreport_core_en.ppt).

Underhill, Kristin, Paul Montgomery, and Don Operario. 2007. "Sexual Abstinence Only Programs to Prevent HIV Infection in High Income Countries: Systematic Review." *British Medical Journal*. Retrieved June 1, 2008 (http://bmj.com/cgi/content/full/335/7613/248).

United Health Foundation. 2007. "America's Health Rankings: A Call to Action for People and Their Communities." Retrieved February 29, 2008 (www.unitedhealthfoundation.org/ahr2007/changes.html).

United Nations. 2008. "The International Decade for Action—Water for Life, 2005-2015." Retrieved May 9, 2008 (www.un.org/waterforlifedecade/issues.html#scarcity).

USA Today. 2001. "Gene Map Creates New Frontier for Discrimination." Retrieved March 4, 2008 (www.usatoday.com/news/health/2001-02-11-genome-discrimination.htm).

U.S. Census Bureau. 2004. "U.S. Interim Projections by Age, Sex, Race and Hispanic Origin." Retrieved May 20, 2008 (www.census.gov/ipc/www/usinterimproj/natprojtab01a.pdf).

————. 2007a. "Health Insurance Coverage—2006." Retrieved January 29, 2008 (www.census.gov/hhes/www/hlthins/hlthin06/hlth06asc.html).

————. 2007b. "Older Americans Month: May 2007." Retrieved April 4, 2008 (www.census.gov/PressRelease/www/releases/archives/facts_for_features_special_editions/009715.html).

U.S. Census Bureau—International Data Base (IDB). 2009. Retrieved July 11, 2009. (www.census.gov/ipc/www/idb/informationGateway.php.

U.S. Department of Health and Human Services. 1999. *Mental Health: A Report of the Surgeon General—Executive Summary*. Rockville, MD: U.S. Department of Health and Human Services. Substance Abuse and Mental Health Services Administration. Center for the Mental Health Services. National Institutes of Health. National Institute of Mental Health. Retrieved March 1, 2008 (www.surgeongeneral.gov/library/mentalhealth/summary.html).

————. 2000. "Determinants of Health." *Healthy People 2010 Report*. Retrieved May 3, 2008 (www.healthypeople.gov/Document/html/uih/uih_bw/uih_2.htm).

————. 2003. *New Freedom Commission on Mental Health: Achieving the Promise—Transforming Mental Health Care in America*. Rockville, MD: Department of Health and Human Services No. SMA-03-0832.

————. 2007. "Health, United States, 2007: 292, Table 75. Retrieved March 13, 2008 (www.cdc.gov/nchs/data/hus/hus07.pdf).

————. 2008a. "The 2008 HHS Poverty Guidelines." Retrieved August 3, 2008 (http://aspe.hhs.gov/poverty/08Poverty.shtml).

————. 2008b. *Healthy People 2010*. Retrieved January 7, 2008. (www.healthypeople.gov/About/goals.htm).

U.S. Department of Labor, Bureau of Labor Statistics. 2008. "Employment Characteristics of Families in 2007." USDL 08-0731. Retrieved August 10, 2008 (www.bls.gov/news.release/pdf/famee.pdf).

U.S. Food and Drug Administration. 2006. "My Family Health Portrait." Retrieved March 4, 2008. (www.fda.gov/fdac/features/2006/306_portrait.html).

U.S. National Library of Medicine. 2008a. "Alpha-1 Antitrypsin Deficiency." Retrieved April 20, 2008 (http://ghr.nlm.nih.gov/condition=alpha1antitrypsindeficiency).

————. 2008b. "Sickle Cell Anemia." Retrieved March 3, 2008 (www.nlm.nih.gov/medlineplus/ency/article/000527.htm).

————. 2008c. "Measles." Retrieved March 3, 2008 (www.nlm.nih.gov/medlineplus/ency/article/001569.htm).

————. 2008d. "Pediatric Asthma." Retrieved July 8, 2008 (www.nlm.nih.gov/medlineplus/ency/article/000990.htm).

Valent, Francesca, D'Anna Little, Giorgio Tamburlini, and Fabio Barbone. 2004. "Burden of Disease Attributable to Selected Environmental Factors and Injuries among Europe's Children and Adolescents." Geneva, World Health Organization (WHO Environmental Burden of Disease Series, No. 8). Retrieved July 5, 2008 (www.who.int/quantifying_ehimpacts/publications/9241591900/en/index.html).

Vanagas, Giedrius, Susanna Bihari-Axelsson, and Vitalija Vanagiene. 2004. "Do Age, Gender and Marital Status Influence Job Strain Development for General Practitioner?" *Medicina (Kaunas)* 40(10):1014–8.

Veugelers, Paul J. and Angela L. Fitzgerland. 2005. "Effectiveness of School Programs in Preventing Childhood Obesity: A Multilevel Comparison." *American Journal of Public Health* 95(3):432–5.

Volkow, Nora. 2007. "Genes and Smoking." National Institute of Drug Abuse and Addiction Notes, 21(3). Retrieved May 3, 2008 (www.nida.nih.gov/NIDA_notes/NNvol21N3/DirRepVol21N3.html).

von Bertalanffy, Ludwig. 1968. *General System Theory: Foundations, Developments, Applications.* New York: Braziller.

von Hippel, Paul T., Brian Powell, Douglas B. Downey, and Nicholas J. Rowland. 2007. "The Effect of School on Overweight in Childhood: Gain in Body Mass Index during the School Year and During Summer Vacation." *American Journal of Public Health* 97(4): 696–702.

Walsh, Bryn. 2008. "It's Not Just Genetics." *Time*, June 23, pp. 70–77.

Wang, Philip S., Olga Demler, and Ronald C. Kessler. 2002. "Adequacy of Treatment for Serious Mental Illness in the United States." *American Journal of Public Health* 92(1):92–8.

Wardle, J. S. Carnell, C. M. Haworth, and R. Plomin. 2008. "Evidence for a Strong Genetic Influence on Childhood Adiposity Despite the Force of the Obesogenic Environment." *American Journal of Clinical Nutrition* 87(2):398–404.

Warren, Charles, Nathan R. Jones, Armando Peruga, James Chauvin, Jean-Pierre Baptiste, Vera Costa de Silva, Fatimah el Awa, Agis Tsouros, Khalil Rahman, Berke Fishburn, Douglas W. Bettcher, and Samira Asma. 2008. "Global Youth Tobacco Surveillance, 2000–2007." *Morbidity and Mortality Weekly Report* 57(SS01):1–21. Retrieved May 8, 2008 (www.cdc.gov/mmwr/preview/mmwrhtml/ss5701a1.htm).

Watson, John T., Michelle Gayer, and Maire A. Connolly. 2007. "Epidemics after National Disasters." Centers for Disease Control and Prevention, Emerging Infectious Diseases 13(1). Retrieved July 7, 2008 (www.cdc.gov/Ncidod/eid/13/1/1.htm).

Webster's. 1984. *Webster's II New Riverside University Dictionary.* Boston, MA: Houghton Mifflin.
———. 2003. *Webster's New World Medical Dictionary.* New York: John Wiley and Sons.

Weijing, He, Stuart Neil, Hemant Kulkarni, Edward Wright, Brian K. Agan, Vincent C. Marconi, Mattre J. Dolan, Robin A. Weiss, and Sunil K. Ahuja. 2008. "Duffy Antigen Receptor for Chemokines Mediates Trans-Infection of HIV-1 from Red Blood Cells to Target Cells and Affects HIV-AIDS Susceptibility." *Cell, Host and Microbe* 4(July):52–62.

Wenzel, Richard P. 2002. "Treating Sepsis." *New England Journal of Medicine* 347(13):966–7.

Williams, David R., Hector M. Gonzalez, Stacey Williams, Selina A. Mohammed, Hashim Moomal, and Dan J. Stein. 2008. "Perceived Discrimination, Race and Health in South Africa." *Social Science and Medicine* 67(3):441–52.

Williams, Simon, Ellen Annandale, and Jonathan Tritter. 1998. "The Sociology of Health and Illness at the Turn of the Century: Back to the Future?" *Sociological Research Online* 3(4). Retrieved June 3, 2008 (www.socresonline.org.uk/3/4/1.html).

Wilper, Andrew P., Steffie Woolhandler, Karen Lasser, Danny McCormck, Sarah L. Cutrona, David H. Bor, and David H. Himmelstein. 2008. "Waits to See an Emergency Department Physician: U.S. Trends and Predictors, 1997–2004." *Health Affairs* 27(1/2):w84–w95. Retrieved August 5, 2008 (http://pnhp.org/PDF_files/WaitsEmergencyDepartment-HealthAffairs.pdf).

Wilson, Andrea E., Kim M. Shuey, and Glen H. Elder, Jr. 2003. "Ambivalence in the Relationship of Adult Children to Aging Parents and In-Laws." *Journal of Marriage and Family* 65(4): 1055–72.

Wilson, Kumanan, E. Mills, C. Ross, J. McGowan, and A. Jadad. 2003. "Association of Autistic Spectrum Disorder and the Measles, Mumps, and Rubella Vaccine: A Systematic Review of Current Epidemiological Evidence." *Archives of Pediatric and Adolescent Medicine* 157:628–34.

Wind, Rebecca. 2008. "Perception that Teens Frequently Substitute Oral Sex for Intercourse a Myth." Guttmacher Institute. Retrieved May 3, 2008 (www.guttmacher.org/media/nr/2008/05/20/index.html).

Woodman, Josef. 2008. *Patients beyond Borders*. Chapel Hill, NC: Healthy Travel Media. Retrieved August 10, 2008 (www.patientsbeyondborders.com/about-the-book/introduction.php).

Woolhandler, Steffie, David U. Himmelstein, and Sidney M. Wolfe. 2003. "Administrative Costs in Market-Driven U.S. Health Care System Far Higher than in Canada's Single-Payer System." *New England Journal of Medicine* 349:768–71.

Women's Health, U.S. Department of Health and Human Services. 2003. "The Health of Minority Women." Retrieved June 22, 2008 (www.womenshealth.gov/owh/pub/minority/concerns.htm).

World Health Organization. 2002. "Global Results of the Analysis—Environmental Health Impacts." Retrieved July 20, 2008 (www.who.int/quantifying_ehimpacts/publications/preventingdisease6.pdf).

———. 2007. "A Safer Future: Global Public Health Security in the 21st Century." *The World Health Report 2007*. Retrieved July 6, 2008. (www.who.int/whr/2007/en/index.html).

———. 2008a. "Gender and Women's Mental Health." Retrieved May 5, 2008 (www.who.int/mental_health/prevention/genderwomen/en/).

———. 2008b. "WHO Report on the Global Tobacco Epidemic, 2008: The MPOWER Package." Retrieved July 20, 2008 (www.who.int/tobacco/mpower/mpower_report_full_2008.pdf).

World Wildlife Fund. 2008. "HIV/AIDS and the Environment: Impacts of AIDS and Ways to Reduce Them." Retrieved May 1, 2008 (www.worldwildlife.org/what/whowehelp/community/phe/WWFBinaryitem7051.pdf).

Wozniak, Robert H. 1992. "Mind and Body: René Descartes to William James." Retrieved March 6, 2008. (http://serendip.brynmawr.edu/Mind/).

Yancy, Clyde W. 2008. "Race-Based Therapeutics." *Current Hypertension Reports* 10:276–85.

Zallen, Doris Teichler. 2000. "Is Genetic Information Different?" Genetic Health. Retrieved March 2, 2008 (www.genetichealth.com/ELSI_Is_Genetic_Information_Different.shtml).

Zernike, Kate. 2007. "Love in the Time of Dementia." *New York Times*, November 18, 2007. Retrieved March 2, 2008 (www.nytimes.com/2007/11/18/weekinreview/18zernike.html).

Zick, Cathleen D., Charles J. Mathews, J. Scott Roberts, Robert Cook-Deegan, Robert J. Pokorski, and Robert C. Green. 2005. "Genetic Testing for Alzheimer's Disease and Its Impact on Insurance Purchasing Behavior." *Health Affairs* 24(2):483–90.

INDEX